ADVANCED MANUFACTURING DESIGN & TECHNOLOGY

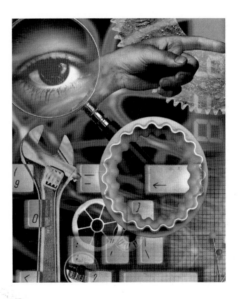

POST-16

Hodder & Stoughton

A MEMBER OF THE HODDER HEADLINE GROUP

The Royal College of Art Schools Technology Project

The project team: David Perry (Project Director), Louise T Davies (Assistant Project Director), Anthony R Booth (Assistant Project Director), Jim Sage (Assistant Project Director), Doris Massiah (Project Assistant), Imelda Rafter-Philips (Admin Support).

Main writers:
Alan Booth, Anthony R Booth, Anne Constable, Lesley Cresswell, Terry Fiehn, Mark Hudson, David Perry, Robin Pellat, Jim Sage, Kalvin Turner.

With contributions from:
Phil Baxendale, Steve Cushing, Alan Goodyer, Pat Hutchinson, Steve Kyffin, Jo Morrison, Glenda Prime, Jane Steenstra, Richard Sydenham, Ruth Wright.

Teacher fellows:
Alan Booth, Claire Buxton, Anne Constable, Corrine Harper, Mark Hudson, Dai James, Mary Moran, Barbara Mottershead, Robin Pellat, Rob Petrie, Brian Russell, Kalvin Turner.

Our special thanks to all contributing authors, including teacher fellows and their schools, and particularly their colleagues, partners, friends and children who have supported them while they were writing to meet deadlines.

The Royal College of Art Schools Technology Project wishes to extend its thanks to the following for their help and support in the writing of this book: Kathleen Lund (Chief Executive), and her colleagues at the TC Trust, the Department for Education and Employment, Offices for Standards in Education (OfSTED), The Royal College of Art and their representatives on the Project Management Group.

Our thanks go to the companies and individuals without whom this book could not have had the insights into the industrial design and manufacturing world which are so necessary to it:
Neil Boyd, Terence Langleys; Michael Dicks at Shima Seiki; Alan Jefferson, Laura Semple & Gavin Southern at British Aerospace; Dalgetty; Dixons Mastercare; The Design Council (Handihaler Case study); Karen France at MBA; Jim Houghton of Network Educational Press; Jonathan Ive at Apple Computers; Michael Kay at the Decorative Tile Works Ltd; MFI; Professor Hal McFie of Reading University; Sandy Moffatt & David Wimpenny of Warwick University Manufacturing Group; Mouchel Engineering; Sony UK; John Stoddard at IDEO; Paul Rigby of Littlewoods Home Shopping; Denfords; Raleigh Industries; Dr Steve Scott at Heinz Foods; The UK Ecolabelling Board; Yoplait.

For the Chapter 5 case studies
Mark Biddle at Home Pac Ltd.; Domida Design; Simon Turner; Frank Walsh; Asda; Derek Waelend at McLaren; Ian Day at Link Plastics (PDSA case study); Paul Clarricoates at SilkJet Ltd (PDSA case study); Leslie Ebbut at the PDSA; Daniel Steenstra at Jaguar; Neil Boyd, Terence Langleys, Michael Dicks at Shima Seiki.

British Library Cataloguing in Publication Data
A catalogue record for this title is available from The British Library

ISBN 0 340 70528 0

First published 1999
Impression number   10 9 8 7 6 5 4 3 2 1
Year   2002   2001   2000   1999

Typeset by Wearset, Boldon, Tyne and Wear.
Printed in Italy for Hodder & Stoughton Educational, a division of Hodder Headline Plc, 338 Euston Road, London NW1 3BH by Printer Trento.

CONTENTS

CONTENTS

Introduction

This book is intended to support your work on all advanced courses in the Design and Technology field including manufacturing and engineering. Think of it as a 'companion' or reader, keep it with you all the time and refer to it as and when you need. It will provide you with a great deal of background understanding and will guide you through your course, and through individual assignments and projects. It will help you prepare for assessment and increase your chances of success.

The book has these components:

- Chapter 1 Taking responsibility for your learning
- Chapter 2 The place of designing and manufacturing in industry
- Chapter 3 Designing
- Chapter 4 Manufacturing
- Chapter 5 Extended case studies

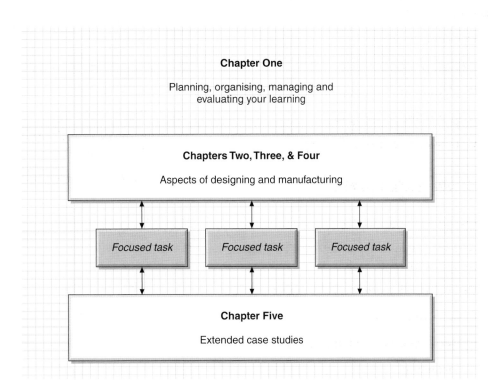

The different parts of this book are meant to work together closely.

Each section has some **focused tasks** to help you make sense of the text, understand the issues and give you practice in aspects of designing and manufacturing. Some of these tasks refer to the extended case studies in chapter 5, for example:

- to identify common features such as similarities in the designing approaches used across a range of different types of product
- to make comparisons across different volumes of production and different types of materials.

Short case studies are included throughout the book to illustrate points in the text.

References to useful information, either in this book, or other STP Design and Technology books, are 'signposted' throughout the text as appropriate.

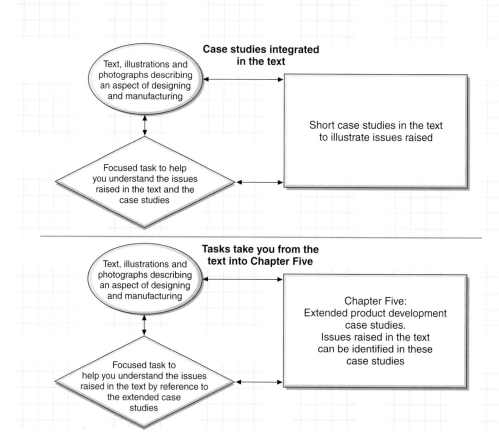

This diagram shows the two ways case studies are used in the book.

Chapter 1 Planning and managing your own learning

Chapter 1 provides you with advice and activities to help you plan, organise, manage and evaluate your work. This is an essential part of all advanced courses.

This chapter can be used in several ways.

1 As a self-contained section used at the beginning of the course to practise basic skills in managing your work.
2 To develop your skills when you are working on assignments throughout your course.
3 As a 'dip in' resource used on a need to know basis, i.e. you refer to it as and when the need arises.

Chapters 2, 3 and 4 Designing and manufacturing

A book of this nature cannot possibly hope to cover every aspect of designing and manufacturing. These chapters provide insights into *key* aspects appropriate for all advanced courses in this field. They include a wide range of examples of products to establish important generic principles. The approach taken is to start with company-wide considerations in chapter 2, relating these to individuals' work – designers, production managers and students – in chapters 3 and 4.

Chapter 5 Extended case studies

Chapter 5 contains extended case studies that tell interesting stories to highlight important features of designing and manufacturing. They are referred to at a number of different points throughout chapters 2, 3 and 4. You can also use these case studies to highlight or illustrate particular points that it is necessary for you to understand on your course.

Everything about this book has been designed to help you become a more independent learner, relying less on your teacher and taking more responsibility for your learning yourself.

CHAPTER ONE Planning and managing your own learning

The purpose of this chapter is to help you take a great deal more responsibility for your own work – increasing the level of autonomy you have, and making you more responsible for your own decisions. This is an essential part of some courses but should be a feature of all your work at advanced level. One of the key aspects of this is to adopt some of the principles of continuous improvement – believing that you can always do better and improve the quality of your work. You will find that this is a recurring feature of this chapter which includes advice on:

- being clear about what you expect from the course and how you can make sure you get what you want and need
- being clear about the requirements and expectations of your course
- how to plan your work
- developing your own action plan, setting targets for yourself and monitoring your progress
- how to manage extended projects and assignments
- how to set quality standards and improve the quality of your work
- how to work with other people outside of the school/college who can help you.

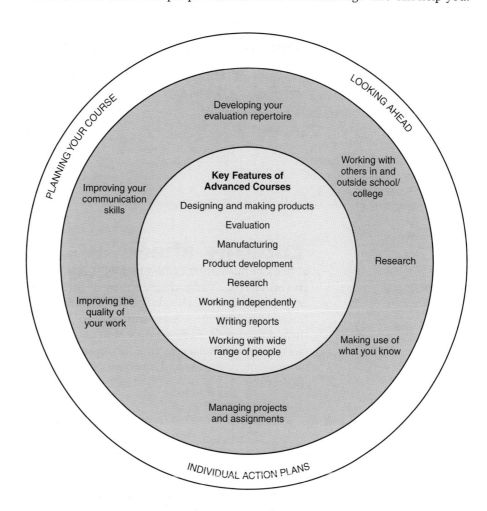

PLANNING YOUR COURSE

LOOKING AHEAD

Developing your evaluation repertoire

Working with others in and outside school/college

Improving your communication skills

Key Features of Advanced Courses

Designing and making products

Evaluation

Manufacturing

Product development

Research

Research

Improving the quality of your work

Working independently

Writing reports

Working with wide range of people

Making use of what you know

Managing projects and assignments

INDIVIDUAL ACTION PLANS

Focused task: Taking responsibility for your own learning

This table describes different ways of organising the learning of a group of students.

Increasing your responsibility and decision making

Content and focus of the activity	Content is predetermined in detail by the tutor and the tutor and texts are seen as the only source of worthwhile knowledge.	The overall aims are made clear to students in general terms and the tutor guides students towards the strategies they wish them to use.	Each area of the task or assignment is discussed with students and a joint plan of action developed; students' ideas for future tasks are given value and are carried out after consultation.
Student role	Students follow the same strategies on a regular basis, are not expected to make any innovative input into the lessons. They move towards the 'right' results through the use of the techniques and procedures prescribed by the tutor. All students follow predetermined activities and routes leading to the same 'correct' results.	Students are encouraged to discuss their ideas for ways of proceeding, but the tutor remains the final decision maker. Students are able to make a choice of tasks/methods/ resources etc. from a selection provided by the tutor. Students make responses based on their work and the tutor determines which is the most valid and guides the students.	Students are enabled to see a direct relationship between their own input, in terms of ideas and application, and their own progress. Students are able to identify key ideas and suitable procedures and ways forward for themselves based on their previous experience and the framework provided by the tutor. Students have the responsibility for deciding the nature of the activities they will undertake and for carrying them out and evaluating the outcomes.

1 Look at the table and decide which method describes what you feel is the best way to learn on an Advanced Manufacturing, Design or Technology course. You might find it easier to do this working with a group of students on the same course.
2 Based on your answer to question 1, think about 2 or 3 initiatives you could take to equip you better to achieve success on your course.
3 Draw up an action plan to help you decide what you need to do and discuss this with your tutor.
4 Use the content list for this chapter to help you find out where to get helpful information.
5 Turn to those sections, read the information and carry out the tasks.

Looking ahead

If you have a clear purpose for following a particular course you are much more likely to get a lot out of it. Your manufacturing, design or technology course may be the vital component in your future career plan or a way of broadening and adding interest to your advanced studies; it may be somewhere in between. In every case you need to be clear about what the course offers to you and how you can make the most of the opportunities it presents.

Focused task: How to get the most from your course

Prepare a table like this to focus the activity (this is probably best done on an A3 sheet). You will find it easier to complete some of this working with a friend or other students from the course.

You may need some information from your tutor to help you.

What do you hope to get from the course? (The list below may help you with this.)	What will naturally come from the course?	What might come from the course but will need you to make the most of the opportunities?	What requires you to take particular options or put a particular focus on your projects?

Some things to think about:

- knowledge and understanding – for example, of materials, systems and control
- technical skills
- improving your designing skills
- greater technological awareness
- improving your IT skills
- problem-solving and decision-making skills
- opportunities to work in teams
- developing your creative thinking
- project and time management skills
- improving your communication skills
- using CAD/CAM
- finding out more about manufacturing in a range of different types and styles of company.

As a result of this activity, make a few notes to help you plan future work. For example, if you are interested in furniture design, you need to make sure that the projects you do allow you to develop this interest as well as meeting the requirements of your manufacturing or design and technology course.

Careers in manufacturing, design or technology

Manufacturing industries take people straight from school, from FE and from Manufacturing degree courses.

If you choose a career in the design field you may need to take a one year Foundation course.

Engineering courses offer many different specialisms.

You have chosen to study a subject that can lead to many different careers when you leave school/college. It always seems as though there is lots of time and you can delay the decision until later, but it is important that you identify a possible career path as soon as possible. It is really important to have a target, otherwise you don't know what you're aiming for! You can always change your mind later, so don't worry if you are not 100% sure. Your course tutor will advise you as to when critical decisions have to be made and will probably encourage you to draw up an action plan.

There are several options available to you:

- enter full time employment and get training on the job. This will lead to accreditation such as NVQs (National Vocational Qualifications)
- take a full time course of study in a vocational course at a College of Further Education. You may be able to continue your study to degree level with some courses
- take an Art Foundation Course at your nearest college and progress to a degree in a design-related subject. It is worth noting that many design-based courses require you to achieve a pass in Art Foundation before you will be accepted for a degree course
- take a full time course of study at University. Do remember that you may need to take a post graduate training course when you have completed your degree to prepare you for your chosen career.

Obtaining careers information

There is a lot of help available to you when you are choosing a career in manufacturing, design or technology.

- A visit to the careers officer will help you to focus on what you would like to do. Do this as early as you can in Year 12 so that you have time to consider the options.
- The manufacturing sectors are keen to encourage young people to work in the manufacturing industry so publish information about careers both on paper and the world wide web.
- Your school library or careers room will contain lots of information about careers and you would be advised to look carefully as there will be information about courses and jobs that you may never have thought of.
- Subject tutors will keep information about careers and courses and will be able to share the experiences of past students who have kept them up to date.
- *Art and Design Courses – on course* is a compendium of all design related courses and contains lots of information about popular and well known areas of study. Published by the Trotman & Co Ltd., this should be available in your careers library.
- Access to information through the World Wide Web and CD ROM is now a feature of most libraries and ECCTIS (www.ectis.co.uk) is a compilation of University courses in Britain. It not only tells you about the courses available at each university but gives you information about the area that you might find yourself living in.

Below are just some of the careers available to students of Art, Design, Technology and Manufacturing. Can you add to the list?

Mechanical Engineer	Fashion Consultant	Food Technologist
Chemical Engineer	Fashion Designer	Naval Architect
Car Designer	Furniture Designer	Product Designer
CNC Operator	Landscape Architect	Production Worker
Civil Engineer	Production Engineer	Graphic Designer
Architect	Quality Controller	Interior Designer

A course in Manufacturing, Design and Technology will equip with you with a wide range of skills and capabilities; this prepares you for careers in many areas that at first sight may not appear obvious. Design education helps you to clarify purposes and tasks, carry out effective research, propose a range of ways of achieving your purposes, make presentations, select the best way forward, take action, and evaluate at all stages of the process. Even accountants and lawyers benefit from a good design education!

Two profiles:

Clare Vetterlein *designer-maker in wood*

Clare studied A level Design and Technology at Islington Sixth Form Centre. On the course her work was of the style of a creative designer-maker who enjoyed the practical approach to her A level projects (but didn't like the theory work!). A very committed student, she was very organised and focused on what she enjoyed.

She followed sixth form with a one year general Art Foundation course at Wimbledon School of Art finding herself moving towards Theatre Design as a specialism, not because of a career aimed in that field, but because it offered the creative and 3-D work which she felt comfortable with. Again, very committed to her work, she was successful.

On leaving Wimbledon she felt she knew where her future direction lay – as a furniture designer and maker but there were very few courses available. She was determined to go to Parnham College (the school for designer-craftworkers set up by John Makepiece in Dorset). However, this course did not qualify for grant aid.

With typical determination she worked for 3 years as a technician back at Islington Sixth Form Centre saving all she could. Combined with loans, this took her through two successful years at Parnham College learning her craft.

In 1995 at the age of 23, Claire set herself up in business as a Designer-Maker in wood. Working mainly to commission and on speculative pieces for exhibitions internationally, her work involves using hardwoods and natural finishes often incorporating carving, colour and gilding.

Jonathan Ive *Director of Design*

Jonathan Ive was appointed Design Director at Apple Computer in 1996 at the age of 29, so should be regarded as one of the most successful young industrial designers in the world. He has produced designs for products which have been put on display in prestigious venues including the Museum of Modern Art in New York City.

His rapid rise in the design world all sprang from a GCE A level in Design and Technology (alongside Chemistry and Art). He followed this with a BA Design for Industry degree course at Newcastle Polytechnic (now Northumbria University) sponsored by a design consultancy and achieved a first class award. This led him into professional design work in a number of product fields.

The iMac, designed by Jonathan Ive.

When he became a partner of Tangerine design studio in London he worked on products as diverse as computers and luxury toilet ceramics. It was work for Apple, when at Tangerine, that opened up his new position.

Planning your course

Research shows us that students often don't work to their maximum potential because they are not clear what the task is! This section will help you to ensure that you are *always* clear about your task.

If you ask someone who cooks a lot how he or she uses a cookery book, you will probably find that the only recipes the person chooses are the ones with illustrations with them. Our brains like to know what the finished product looks like before we start. You can't do a jigsaw if you haven't got the picture on the lid; you can't start a course without knowing all it entails. Well, you could, but you won't perform to your maximum potential. So, to maximise your chances of success, you need to make sure you have the whole picture if you are to do your **absolute best.**

By now you will have realised that all of this chapter is about you taking more responsibility; being able to take responsibility depends on having all of the right information. There are a number of aspects of your course that you need to be clear about from the beginning:

- how you will be assessed during and at the end of the course
- the complete range of coursework and assignments that you need to produce
- individual projects and assignments that will be assessed
- when you need to produce these projects and assignments – what the deadlines are
- written examinations you will take including unit or module tests (interim tests) and terminal (end-of-course) examinations.

Having this information will help you to plan your time and your work more effectively.

Focused task: Producing a course plan

It is useful to produce a plan showing the features of the complete course. Much of this information will be available from your course tutor.

You should also find out if your work will be seen by a standards moderator from the awarding body.

Project/assignment/ interim test	The focus of the project/assignment: • what is the purpose of the task? • what are the main aspects that will be assessed? • what proportion of the final assessment does it account for?	When it needs to be completed/ take place	Any research or other aspects that need to be planned in advance

 Managing projects and assignments   20

What standard of work is expected?

You also need an indication of the standard of work expected from you. The case studies from other students in this book will you give you an idea of what is possible. It is also very useful to talk with other students in higher years taking the same course as you. Your tutor may have a collection of pieces of work from other students and sometimes the examination board provides examples.

You also need to find out at an early stage what you will need to do to meet the requirements of any Higher Education courses that you are interested in. It may well be too late if you leave it until you start to make applications.

Always look for opportunities to show your capability in other ways: *Young Engineer* and other competitions, working on projects with local companies, using people outside the school or college to evaluate and improve your work, commissioning work from 'real' clients, and getting your work publicised in the local paper or an educational journal such as *Designing*, *MODUS* or *Electronics Education* will all help.

You should never be satisfied with meeting the minimum standards; you should always try to exceed expectations – yours, your tutors and the awarding body's. Use the following information on Setting Targets to adopt the attitude 'I can always do better than this'.

Setting targets

A key to success on any course is setting targets and keeping a check on how well you are meeting them. This helps you to plan and monitor your progress through each project/assignment and through the complete course. You will also feel that you are much more in control!

Developing an individual action plan

An **individual action plan** (IAP) is a means of taking responsibility for planning and managing your own learning; it involves setting targets for yourself. The key to developing an IAP is the use of the following questions:

- Where am I now?
- Where do I want to be?
- How am I going to get there?
- What are my next steps?
- How successful was I?

Producing an IAP is about setting targets for your learning; it is not about managing your project – that is dealt with elsewhere in this chapter.

Key questions	Features
Where am I now?	This involves a range of self-assessment techniques to carry out a skills audit appropriate to the task or assignment.
Where do I want to be?	Setting targets for your learning in the context of the task or assignment.
How am I going to get there?	What support is available? How can I make best use of my tutor, other students, other adults? How long have I got – what is the deadline? What resources are available? What skills do I need? Where and when can I work on the assignments? Do I need any special facilities?
What are my next steps?	Planning: • a schedule for the task or assignment • how to use the resources available • how to make best use of people • how to get the information you need • visits • what new skills you need to acquire.
How successful was I?	Assessing your performance against the targets.

Focused task: Developing your own IAP

1 Where am I now? Doing your own skills audit

What skills does the task or assignment require? It might be useful to consider these under the following headings:

- Examining and analysing a situation.
- Undertaking research, collecting data and information about the situation and factors affecting it.
- Analysing the data and information.
- Working with a design brief and preparing a specification which design proposals can be tested against.
- Preparing design proposals and presenting these for evaluation.
- Developing the design proposal into a design for manufacture.
- Skills needed to manufacture the product.
- Working with clients.
- Working with others.

Evaluate your own skills in these areas using a 4 point scale:

Score 4	excellent – more than adequate for the task
Score 3	good – adequate for the task but I need to refresh myself and practise them
Score 2	basic – need to be refined and developed to the level required
Score 1	minimal or non-existent – I need to develop this from scratch

It is a good idea to get a second opinion from your friends or from your tutor.

2 Setting targets

Once you have completed your skills audit you can use this to set some targets.

A target could be raising your score from a 1 or 2 to a level 3 or 4 in particular skills.

You should also plan how you intend to meet these targets using the questions:

- How am I going to get there?
- What are my next steps?

You can also plan how you will evaluate how successful you were.

SMART targets

The acronym SMART is often used to help set targets. It is used to check that the targets are Specific, Measurable, Achievable, Realistic and Time constrained.

Specific	clearly identified; single or small number of related items
Measurable	you need to know when you have achieved the target; how will you evaluate whether you have achieved it?
Achievable	possible for you to achieve given the resources, time available and your own abilities
Realistic	not too optimistic or too challenging given the constraints on you
Time constrained	when will the target be achieved? How long will it take to achieve it? When can you start?

Evaluation

Evaluation is a fundamental part of your course; not only evaluating the products you make but also the processes you use and what you learn as a result. This section helps you to develop and use an extensive evaluation repertoire.

Throughout this book you will make use of a wide range of evaluation strategies; you will develop your own evaluation repertoire. You will use this to:

- evaluate your own work
- make evaluations at key points throughout your project and product development
- evaluate existing products.

Evaluation should be a continuous process, it is not something that is only done at the end of a project or when you have manufactured a product. Every time you have to make a decision you have to make an evaluation.

This could be:

- at a point in the product development process
- looking at evaluation in one of the case studies.

Some examples of evaluation in this book:

- technology assessment – evaluating the potential benefits, costs and impact of available technologies
- risk assessment
- evaluating environmental impact
- understanding products: product analysis and evaluation in designing
- the effects of products on people: design semantics, aesthetics, style, product personality and image
- evaluation for continuous improvement
- evaluation of manufacturing processes.

Each of these will help you to extend or enhance your evaluation repertoire.

Evaluating your learning

Developing the ability to evaluate your own learning is an essential component of any post-16 course and is a particularly important part of the GNVQ grading criteria. This means there will be many marks available and so you will need to think this through carefully.

All advanced courses, for GCE and GNVQ, include self-evaluation in the assessment. You will be concerned with two components:

- evaluating your products
- evaluating the processes you use.

A good evaluation will depend on sound planning and good record keeping. Evaluating your learning involves making a judgement about your performance on a particular project or GNVQ unit. When evaluating you can consider:

- the effectiveness of your planning and management of the project
- use of time
- your research methods and any difficulties encountered
- the quality of information found and how it helped to produce a good project
- the recording of your research findings
- the creativity evident in your work
- the quality of decisions taken
- the degree of design development
- any modifications to the process
- the effectiveness of your manufacturing process.

Using this list will help you to meet course requirements and will focus your attention on the important issues. You may find other aspects of your work worthy of evaluation. If you have been involved with a product or process that is special, you may wish to look critically at this. Don't forget: if you are aiming for the higher grades the degree of originality in your work becomes more important.

It will be easier to evaluate your learning if you lay your responses out in a chart similar to the one shown on page 17.

Complete your evaluation with a clear and concise summary that draws together all your thoughts.

If you are in any doubt about the purpose of the evaluation, consult your course syllabus or unit specification.

What you did well	What you would like to improve	How you changed your course of action

Using others to help with evaluation

Two heads are better than one – and lots of heads are better still! This section shows you how, unashamedly, to use your friends to improve any product you design.

You will have learned at Key Stage 4 just how important teams are in design and technology. You need other people to help you generate ideas, and you need other people to bounce your own ideas off. You should have also learned some useful, techniques from working in groups and teams. But now it's time to explore some more advanced methods of using others to improve your work.

 | **Using teams on projects and assignments** | 29 |

Just so that you're sure that it's not cheating to use other people to help you, here is some fascinating and recent research into what makes learning most effective. As you can see, the last three ways make learning really effective. How can you cash in on this?

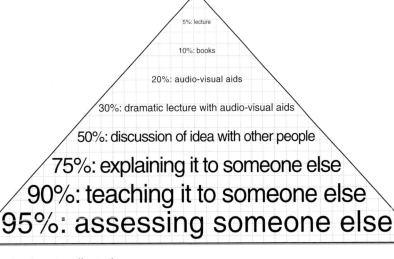

5%: lecture
10%: books
20%: audio-visual aids
30%: dramatic lecture with audio-visual aids
50%: discussion of idea with other people
75%: explaining it to someone else
90%: teaching it to someone else
95%: assessing someone else

What makes learning effective?

Focused task: Using others in evaluation

You are probably already quite used to explaining your ideas or your finished product to a teacher or, even better, to a group. Here is another idea for your class to try in a lesson:

Each person brings along a chosen product they have made, then each:

- runs a seminar for a small group and teaches them the process they need to follow in order to produce the product (this will ensure that the speaker learns the process followed really well)
- lets the group assess his/her work (this will ensure that the assessing group learns the process really well).

 D&T Routes Core Book Chapter 3:
Analysing and evaluating products 25

Here are the rules for the assessing group to follow:

- no assessing group should be larger than 5 or smaller than 3
- one person to speak at a time and say openly what he/she feels
- each to listen very carefully to the speaker
- stick to the task – **to assess the product** – and don't get side-tracked: separate the **person** from the **product**

Product _____

Evaluation of the product

Signed _____

How can I improve

- the product?

- the processes I used?

What else did I learn?

- no-one should put anyone else down – each person's contribution is equally valuable
- be generous with praise and positive comments
- look for ways to improve the product.

At the end of the discussion, the assessing group should present the completed template to the seminar deliverer, who will then complete the bottom part.

Developing key skills

Many people from industry and elsewhere continually reinforce the need for young people to develop a range of key skills. These are the skills needed to make people employable but they are also skills that you can use to improve the quality of your work in school or college.

What is meant by key skills?

These skills are sometimes also referred to as *transferable skills*. In other words, they are not just related to one type of job or career; they are the skills that make people adaptable, flexible and readily re-trainable. Any list of key skills will usually include:

- good communication skills – written, oral, and presentation skills
- numeracy
- ICT skills
- being able to work effectively in teams
- problem-solving, decision-making, analytical and thinking skills
- flexibility and adaptability
- project and time management skills
- creativity
- knowing how to learn – taking responsibility for and managing your own learning.

These key skills should not be considered as 'optional extras' but an important part of your learning to develop your wider capabilities.

- Some of these will be written into your course and may be part of the course assessment.
- You can also be assessed and accredited separately in some of these skill areas.
- You may find that some evidence of your capability in some of these skill areas is required when you apply for employment or a place on a Higher Education course.
- They will be vital for your long term employability and for you to make effective contributions in future employment.

Developing and making use of key skills in your course: the contribution of courses in manufacturing, technology and design

The Design Council is firmly of the belief that

design thinking is transferable thinking and that it could be transferred to the advantage of the learning performance generally. This is because the key attributes which learning must supply are the same key attributes that design thinking has always imparted and which design education has espoused and made its own.

This view is shared by others:

Design is the one thing without which nothing would happen. Design cuts across disciplines and it could be seen as the key discipline.

John Frazer, Professor of Informatics at the University of Ulster

Firms will have to address issues of their culture; people will have to work in integrated teams; people will need to be more outward looking and flexible. People will have to think. This is where design as an approach to thinking plays a significant role. It deals with analysis, interpretation, synthesis and expression.

Dorothy Mackenzie, Director, Dragon International

These quotations illustrate clearly the value of design based courses even to those who are not going to follow a career in the discipline. Your work on Manufacturing, Design and Technology (MDT) courses will play a major role in developing your key skills.

Feature of DTM courses	Link to the development of key skills
Examining and analysing a situation	Analytical skills
Undertaking research, collecting data and information about the situation and factors affecting it	Numeracy ICT
Analysing the data and information	Numeracy ICT Analytical skills
Working with a design brief and preparing a specification which design proposals can be tested against	Numeracy ICT

Feature of DTM courses	Link to the development of key skills
Preparing design proposals and presenting these for evaluation	Creativity Communication skills Numeracy ICT
Developing the design proposal into a design for manufacture	Problem solving and decision making skills Numeracy ICT
Manufacturing the product	Identifying skills needed and developing these as appropriate
Working with clients	Communication skills
Working with others	Teamwork
The complete design and make process	Taking responsibility for your work Project and time management skills

Lifelong learning

Because of the rapidly changing nature of work and the impact of new technologies it is vital to recognise that learning does not stop when you leave formal education. There is a widespread recognition that we all possess a need for lifelong learning. This relates both to learning in the work place and to learning outside of work – for personal pleasure and to improve the quality of life.

Lifelong learning means that we all need to develop the skills to learn and to plan, to organise and to manage our own learning. These skills will be developed in school, college, higher education and through training, but will need to be further developed, refined and applied throughout life. This is supported by the development of the Student's Progress File (previously NRA — National Record of Achievement) which can be used to both support the planning and managing of your learning, and to record key events about your learning.

The Student's Progress File is both a process and a record to be used throughout life, not just for the work you do in school or college.

1 Find out as much as you can about the Student's Progress File.
2 How could you use it to help to take more responsibility for your learning and to keep a record of your achievements in school or college?
3 You will find this useful when you are preparing for jobs or HE applications and interviews.

Managing projects and assignments

A project represents a large time commitment. It is necessary to keep careful control of your project as it progresses. It is easy to spend a disproportionate amount of time on one aspect of your project whilst neglecting other areas. This is easily done: it might be the bit you like the most, or the hardest bit, or the bit that looks most impressive. It will not, however, always lead to success!

When you are planning a project or assignment you need the following information:

- What is the deadline for completion?
- How long do you have – how many weeks and how many hours each week?
- What resources are available for you to use?

OPERATION	MATERIALS/PARTS /COMPONENTS	TOOLS & EQUIPMENT	RISK ASSESSMENT	High Medium Low	TIME EST.	TAKEN ACT.
MAKING THE MOULD						
Prepare base - make it oversized. Part (1)	9mm MDF	Bandsaw & woodglue	Cutting hand or fingers on bandsaw	M	15min	30 mins
Make central block. Part (2)	3 pieces of 9mm MDF	Bandsaw, woodglue & vice grips	" "	M	15min	45 mins
Prepare to correct length and thickness. Part (2)	3 laminated pieces of 9mm MDF & 5mm MDF	Bandsaw & sander	" "	M	10min	10 mins
Add blocks for function buttons and speaker hole. Parts (4-6)	5mm MDF	Sander & slipwax.	" "	M	10min	15 mins
Laminate base to central block. Parts (1) + (2)	Central block 27mm & base 9mm	Woodglue	Gluing fingers together	L	5min	5 mins
Laminate MDF to create external section of mould. Part (3)	3 pieces of 9mm MDF & 5mm MDF	Woodglue, bandsaw & sander	" "	M	15min	15 mins.
Remove waste from external section, file or mill flat, No draft is needed as the block will be split (shown in diagram 3i) Part (3)	Laminated external section of 32mm MDF	Bandsaw & file or mill	" "	M	25-30min	20 mins

This logbook is a detailed account of this student's manufacturing operations.

It is also useful to know how will it be assessed and how it fits into the overall assessment scheme. What proportion of the total assessment is it worth? This will help you work out how important it is against other tasks you have to do and to establish priorities for yourself.

Managing any extended piece of work – a project or assignment – involves the following stages:

- **planning** – breaking the project or assignment down into smaller tasks
- **analysis** – working out how long each task will take, which tasks depend on each other, which can run in parallel and what resources are needed to complete them
- **scheduling** – working out a time and resources plan for the project or assignment
- **monitoring** – making sure that each task is completed on time, noting changes and modifications and preparing a 'lessons learned' report.

Planning

The first task is to prepare a list of activities. This is sometimes known as a **work breakdown structure**. It involves:

1 Listing all the tasks to be done.
2 Putting them into groups of small related tasks if this is appropriate.
3 Putting the tasks into order.
4 Noting those tasks that could be done in parallel.

Sometimes you can use a **flow chart** to help put tasks into order.

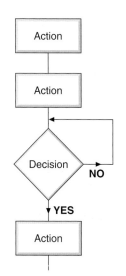

Using a flow chart for planning a project.

Analysis

This involves producing a **Cost**, **Time**, **Resources** (CTR) analysis for each task or group of related tasks. This is usually done using a CTR sheet.

COST TIME RESOURCE (CTR) SHEET	
PROJECT TITLE:	CUSTOMER:
ACTIVITY TITLE AND NUMBER:	
SCOPE (EXPLANATION OF ACTIVITY):	
ASSUMPTIONS (SPECIAL INFORMATION AVAILABLE):	
ACTIVITIES THAT MUST PRECEDE THIS ONE:	DEPENDENT ACTIVITIES: (Activities that cannot start until this one is complete)
DELIVERABLES (OUTPUT OF ACTIVITY):	
PLANNED DURATION: (How long the activity will take)	
RESOURCES (PEOPLE):	HOURS EACH:
OTHER (e.g. computing/equipment/materials):	TOTAL:
PREPARED BY:	DATE:
APPROVED BY:	DATE:

Scheduling

Deciding the order in which aspects of a project are best undertaken ensures efficiency. Usually some must be undertaken ahead of others — producing a **critical path** through the project.

Preparing a scheduling network

The network shows that:
- B and C can both start when A is finished
- D cannot start until both B and C are finished

The figures in each box show the number of weeks each activity takes

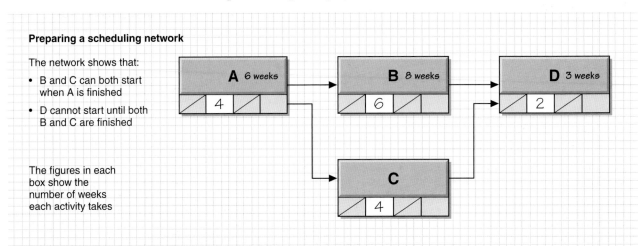

Completing the network

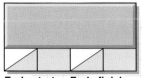

"Forward pass"

Early start | **Early finish**
Week No: | Week No:

This means fitting in the week number for the earliest week each activity can start and finish

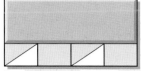

"Reverse pass"

Late start | **Late finish**
Week No: | Week No:

This means working backwards to find the last date each activity can finish. This means that you can work out the Late Start week number

"Float"

This tells you the additional time you have for an activity. It is the difference between the Late and Early week numbers

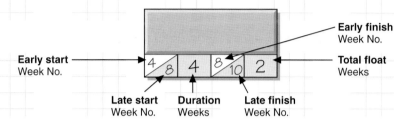

Early start — Week No.

Late start Week No. | Duration Weeks | Late finish Week No.

Early finish Week No.

Total float Weeks

Time Analysis Report

You can now complete a Time Analysis Report

Week No.	Early start	Early finish	Late start	Late finish	Total float
Activity A	1	4	1	4	0
Activity B					
Activity C					
Activity D					

A Time Bar Chart Report

You can use the information you have just worked out to complete a Time Bar Chart Report.
This is a useful way of summarising the activities.

You can add to the Time Bar Chart the resources needed for each activity. This means that it is possible to plan how many people are needed and when.

Resource scheduling

- Add the resources needed for A, B, C and D to your Time Bar Chart.

- Work out the total resources needed for each week.

- This can now be turned into a Resources Schedule.

  Plot the total resources for each week on a histogram.

Use the float to make the best use of your resources.

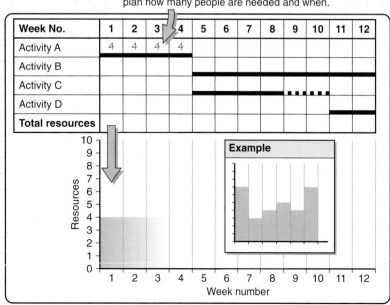

Production schedules

If you are producing a schedule for the manufacture of a product you also need to show:

- the materials and components required;

- the equipment required;

- when these are required.

Identifying the 'critical path'

This is the path with 'least float'. This means finding the path that takes the shortest time.

This needs to be balanced against the best use of your resources. You may find the shortest time means using a lot of people for some weeks and very few in other weeks. This is not good resource management.

Work flow diagrams

Work flow diagrams are used to show the flow of work through the production process. They are useful tools for a production manager and can also help you with the planning and monitoring of your own project.

FLOW PROCESS CHART Product: Bird nest box					Part: side		
Task					Description	Distance	Rate
					Move to cut-off station	2.4 m	
					Cut part to length		50 min/100
					Move to ripping station	2.9 m	
					Rip to width		55 min/100
					Move to sanding		
					Sand sides and edges		95 min/100
					Move to inspection		
					Inspect size and sanding		20 min/100
					Move to storage	10 m	
					Store for assembly		
Operation	Transportation	Inspection	Delay	Storage			

An example of a work flow diagram showing the use of standard symbols.

Focused task: Producing a scheduling network

In this task you will work through the process of producing:

- a network
- a time bar chart
- a resources schedule
- a work flow diagram.

You are the production manager responsible for the manufacture of a new television set. You have been asked to work out the minimum time required to introduce the TV into the market. You will also need to work out how many people need to be allocated to work on the production line.

Your tasks:

1 Arrange the activities in order.
2 Put them onto a network grid.
3 Carry out forward and backward checks.
4 Draw a time bar chart.
5 Produce a resources (people) schedule and histogram.
6 Balance the activities to employ the workforce as efficiently as possible.
7 Work out the critical path and balance this with your resources schedule.
8 Identify where you need to make quality checks – indicate what these checks would be.

The list of activities report for the production of TV.

Activity	Duration (weeks)	Number of people required
Design the TV	26	10
Order packaging material	6	2
Order the electrical components	10	2
Order TV cabinets	6	2
Modify the existing production line	12	10
Receive the packaging material	6	6
Receive electrical components	6	6
Receive the TV cabinets from outside supplier	6	6
Modify the test equipment used in QC	8	10
Assemble the TV sets	4	12
Pack TV sets	2	10
Test TV sets	2	10

Monitoring and control

There are three activities that can be used at this stage:

- a progress report to check if you are keeping to your schedule
- a variation report
- a 'lessons learned' report.

All of these can be used to help you keep a check on your own project or assignment.

An example of a **progress report**.

Activity	Estimated time for activity	Planned start	Planned completion	Actual start	Actual completion	Notes
						For example;
						Reasons for not meeting targets.
						Actions taken to correct or improve the situation.

(Timing spans Planned start, Planned completion, Actual start, Actual completion)

During the project you should prepare a periodic progress report. You should check progress against the plan you prepared earlier. It is best to prepare a chart to do this.

A **variation report** is used if, for any reason, you need to make changes from your original intentions or specification. It would normally include:

- what the variation was, what modifications were made and why
- the impact of the changes (for example, the effects of changing the specification)
- the reasons for the variation and why these were not anticipated.

Special procedures are needed when changing a specification at Avon. A problem area is first highlighted so that alterations can be made. These alterations are termed **non-conformance** and will need to be authorised by a senior person.

A **'lessons learned' report** (part of your evaluation repertoire) could include:

- an overview of the project or assignment and how well it went
- a description of any problems or difficulties you encountered and how you overcame or worked around them
- what you learned as a result of doing the project or assignment – you could match these against the requirements of the course.

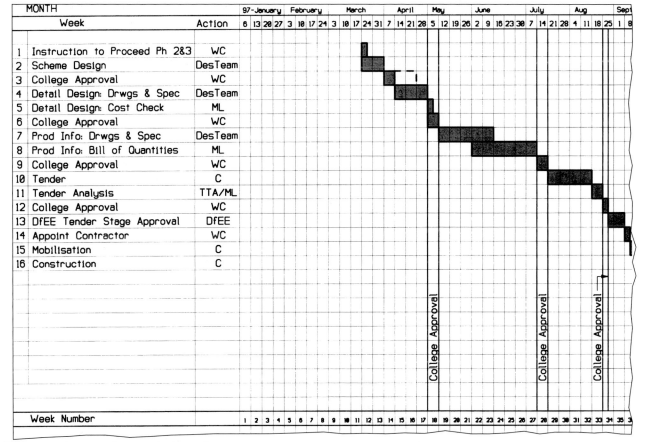

When complex operations require inputs from many sources, GANNT charts enable processes to be carried out on schedule, or components to be delivered on time. These simple charts can help you to map each task against time available and enable you to draw up an order of priority.

			look too big/small for situation.
Surrounding environment.	-Observations -Photographs	Primary Primary	Again so that the design suits it's situation; but this time in terms of different surroundings. (Concrete, wood, grassy areas, etc.)
Public's needs, views and desires.	-Survey public opinion	Primary	To design and manufacture a clock that can, and will, be used by the public, at the same time fulfilling all their needs, views and desires.
Clients need's, views and desires.	-Discussion with the client	Primary	To be able to produce what the client wants, and is sponsoring me to design.
Clock face sizes.	-Manufacturers/suppliers -Experts	Primary Primary	To ensure that the casing is designed to physically accommodate the clock face.
Clock suppliers or manufacturers.	-People in trade -Books/magazines (trade)	Primary Second.	To be able to obtain a clock and general information required on

Research can lead to the gathering of useful information if needs are identified and the activity is planned. Nick has used a simple chart that clearly states what he needs to do.

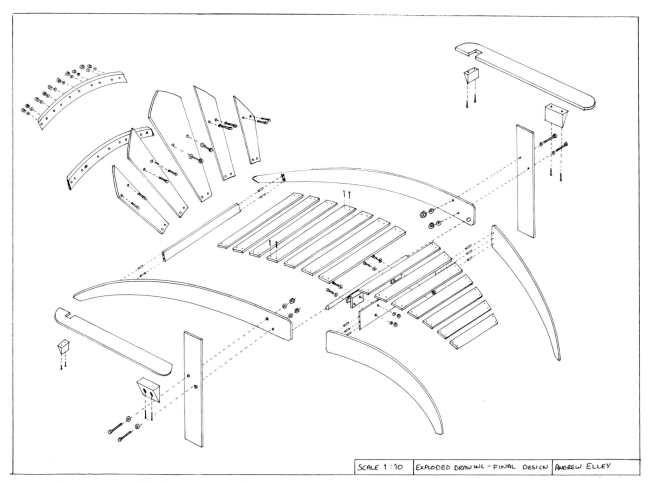

SCALE 1 : 10 | EXPLODED DRAWING - FINAL DESIGN | ANDREW ELLEY

An exploded-drawing view like this ensures that the production of every part is incorporated in an effective manufacturing plan.

Using teams on projects and assignments

In any career associated with design and technology it will be vital that you are able to work well as a member of a team. If you want to be a high flyer, you will need to be able to show your employer that you are a great team player. No problem, you might think. Actually the skills needed to be an effective team worker do not come naturally. They need to learned and then developed to a high enough level to impress a future employer.

Working in groups or teams can be very useful on your course. You can use each other to support the work you are doing. You can use teams to:

- generate ideas for projects
- discuss and solve any problems you might be experiencing
- obtain consumer reactions
- carry out projects
- just offer each other support when you need it.

You can become a great team player by following this **Five Step Plan:**

Step One: Design your team

You are going to become part of a team to solve a problem.

First you need to decide on the problem – this could be anything of your choice. It could be a project you are currently working on or something quite simple such as:

- designing a plan of your building to help visitors find their way round
- a design for a new currency unit (a 99p piece for those irritating £x.99p purchases, for example)
- a series of badges for your teacher to wear to show what mood he/she is in!
- a fold-up book stand for cooks to put their recipe books on with a clear front guard designed to protect the page from splatters.

This is what you do:

1 On your own, write down one or two projects you would like to work on.
2 Join with one other person and, together, agree one or two things you would both like to do.
3 Join another pair and agree the project that your new team of four is to work on.

Step Two – Design your tasks

It is usual in industry that each team member has his or her role in the team defined right from the outset. Depending on what your project is, you might need different people to:

- research; plan; cost; build; evaluate; control quality; progress chase.

Or it might be more appropriate to your project to have:

- a team leader; secretary; treasurer and 'workers'.

At this point, in your team write up a list of the roles and functions your task demands. Do this carefully. Every minute you spend on this process will save you ten minutes later on. In industry, you will be saving your company a lot of money by careful planning in the early stages to avoid hold-ups later.

Step Three – Design your plan

Now you all know the roles and functions of your task, the next step is to organise yourselves. First, the rules:

- the success of this project is dependent on the work of each member
- each is equally responsible for its completion
- each member's contribution is equally valuable
- everyone needs to be completely focused on the task and getting it finished.
- comment on the **ideas**, not the **person**
- listen to each other to clarify your own thinking
- trust each other
- always look for the positive ('That's a good idea', 'to make it even better we could . . .'): eliminate the negative ('No way will that work . . .).

Now use the project management techniques to:

- break this project down into **smaller tasks**
- identify the **help** and **resources** you might need
- identify the **time** needed for each part
- identify the **order** to do the parts in, i.e. the **sequence**
- decide **who** is going to do **what** (Remember, some of you can do several little tasks while others can do one big task).

Use this to produce a **schedule** and **plan** for the project.

Step Four – Design your contribution

Now you know what your role is and what your tasks are, and when they've got to be completed, the next step is to watch your contribution to the group. The success of this project relies on everyone pulling his or her weight. Sometimes people only evaluate their performance in a team after the project has been completed. This, of course, is leaving it too late.

As you go along, rate yourself for the following. Give yourself a mark between 1 and 5, where 1 = 'fully supportive of my team – they couldn't do it without me', to 5 = 'played absolutely no part in this at all'. A score of 3 would be about average effort. Ask yourself the following questions.

To what extent am I helping my team to:

- break down the task into smaller parts?
- identify ideas, resources, skills to help with the task?
- put the tasks into a working order?
- allocate tasks to team members?
- complete my own tasks?
- help others to complete their tasks?
- bring the whole thing together at the end?
- present the completed project?

This will help you to work out where you made the largest, and the least, contribution. Then you can build on this knowledge and work on your skills.

You might also find it useful to rate the whole team's contribution. Compare your results with the results of other team members and discuss your findings.

Step Five: Where now?

My largest contribution	My least contribution	My group's largest contribution	My group's least contribution	Action to be taken

Now you are well on your way to becoming a great team player! Remember, you can use this Five Step Plan on every occasion that you have a project to complete in a team.

It works in other subjects, too!

Ideas handling techniques for teams

The following two pages give you a range of team techniques. Use the box at the top of page 32 to decide which to use.

Making sure that your work is of high quality

Continuous improvement is a fundamental principle in this course: it means always trying to improve the quality of your work. This section offers practical advice on how you can do this.

What is meant by quality?

The word 'quality' is often used in everyday language. It is often unqualified and used on its own to describe 'designer' clothes, expensive cars and even football players – 'he is a real quality player'. In this sense 'quality products' are of the highest possible standards and with no expense spared. This view of quality has two clear features: 'rarity' and 'expense'. Most of us admire it, many of us want it, few of us can afford it! This is often referred to as **absolute quality**. It has little to do with **Total Quality Management (TQM)** or **Continuous Improvement (CI)**. These are ideas that can be used to improve quality in the real world and are far more useful to us.

Using a **relative approach** to quality is much more useful. The quality of a product or service is matched against a specification and is often described as **fitness for purpose**. This view of quality can be used to judge any product or service and has two clear features:

1 Measuring against the specification
2 Meeting customer requirements.

A customer definition of quality. Who describes the quality of a product or service – the producer/supplier or the customer? They may have quite different opinions. Perfectly good products are rejected by customers because they do not meet their requirements. Making a product to meet a specification does not guarantee sales. There is a need for a customer definition of quality. TQM involves the supplier of a product or service and the customer; the level of quality and the cost required is agreed between them. This leads to a clear specification describing the requirements of the product or service.

Quality can then be defined as **'that which best satisfies and exceeds customer needs and wants'**.

Generating ideas

Use a SWOT analysis to work out how to use your team in the most effective way

Is your team full of lively, energetic people who all like to contribute to the activity?

YES

Use a brainstorm session

NO

Use a **Nominal Group Technique** or **Trigger session**, these are more structured and help to make sure that everyone is involved. Ask your teacher for details of these.

This will give you a list of ideas to work on

Sorting out your ideas

Do you want to group ideas together?

Use an **Affinity network**

Do you want to reduce the list?

Use **Multi-voting**

Ask your teacher for the details of the technique that you have chosen.

Working out the most important or useful ideas

Pareto analysis
This is a statistical method for finding the most important idea or the one likely to be most effective

Force Field analysis
In this technique you identify the things in favour and against each idea

Using a Champion
This involves asking one member of the team to try to persuade you that a particular idea is best

You should now have an idea to work on

Nominal Group Technique (NGT)

1 Make sure that everyone is clear about the subject and the purpose of the session.

2 Each team member then writes down their ideas (5–10 minutes) in order; their "best" idea first (5 minutes extra).

3 Ask each person for the item on the top of their list. Record all of these.

4 Go around again and repeat this until all of the ideas have been recorded.

5 Reduce the list by combining similar items. (Use an affinity network).

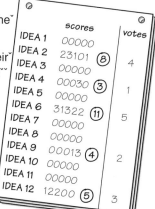

Scoring Ideas

Give each idea a score:

3 for the best idea, 2 for the next and 1 for the third.

Record the scores and the number of votes for each item.

The points for each item are then added up. This then gives an order of priority for the items.

Trigger sessions

1 The problem is defined and clarified.

2 Each member of the group writes down a series of "two word ideas" (3–4 minutes).

3 One person reads out their list. Listen carefully. The others cross out any ideas that are also on their list and write down new ideas as they listen. This is known as "hitch-hiking".

This is a civilised game. No calling out "that was my best idea" or other comments.

4 Each person reads out the ideas on their list that have not been crossed out and others cross out and hitch-hike as before.

5 The last person to read out may have few or no ideas left but may have a "hitch-hike" list.

6 Go around the group in reverse, crossing out and hitch-hiking as before. You might manage several passes like this.

The best ideas may well come from the hitch-hiked lists as the first set of ideas become developed and refined.

Affinity networks

This is a way of grouping together similar or related ideas to deal with a session where a lot of ideas have been created.
It can be done by:

- grouping ideas using coloured pens,

- making a new list with the related ideas grouped together,

- drawing 'spider' diagrams

Multi-voting

This is a way of selecting the most popular or most promising ideas.

1 Use the 'affinity network' to combine the similar and related ideas.

2 Give each of the ideas a number.

3 Ask everyone to choose some ideas that they want to discuss further.

   This should be about a third of the total number; for example, if you have 23 ideas everyone should choose about 7 or 8.

4 For each item on your full list note down how many people chose it for further discussion.

5 Reduce the list by eliminating those items with the lowest number of votes.

   Repeat steps 3 to 5 until only a few items are left. If you want the best idea have one final vote.

Pareto chart

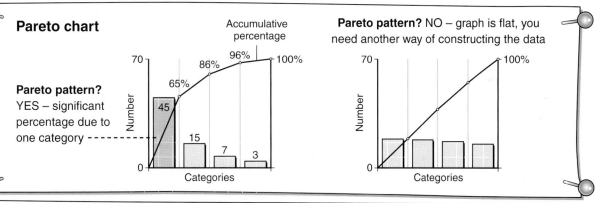

Pareto pattern?
YES – significant percentage due to one category

Pareto pattern? NO – graph is flat, you need another way of constructing the data

Force field analysis

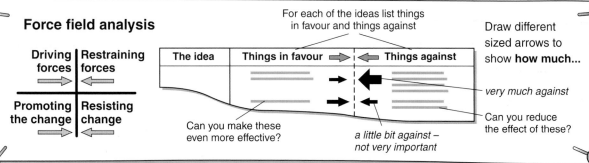

Driving forces	Restraining forces
Promoting the change	Resisting change

For each of the ideas list things in favour and things against

Draw different sized arrows to show **how much...**

very much against

Can you reduce the effect of these?

Can you make these even more effective?

a little bit against – not very important

Using 'champions'

For each of the top three ideas find someone who is prepared to be a 'champion' – this is someone who finds the idea interesting and is prepared to talk in its favour.

Allow PREPARATION TIME (about 10 minutes). Other supporters of the idea could help with this.

Then present the ideas: TALKING TIME 5 minutes each.

Useful techniques for team players.

Research has shown that if a customer complains, and that complaint is handled skilfully by the company, then the customer is **five times more loyal** to that company than a non-complaining customer. This is important to quality. It means you can turn the complaint (a negative thing) into customer loyalty (a positive thing).

Setting quality standards

Standards of products and services include:

- conforming to the specification
- fitness for purpose
- zero defects
- right first time, every time.

Customer standards include:

- customer satisfaction
- exceeding customer expectations
- delighting the customer.

Stop and think

How will you establish the specification for the quality of your product?

The key features of quality systems

Quality control (QC) can be summarised as 'techniques for checking quality against a set standard or within tolerances'. It involves inspection and the detection of products not up to standard. The inspection takes place 'after the event' (after the relevant stage in the manufacture or when the product is complete) and is carried out by trained inspectors.

Quality assurance (QA) is a series of planned and systematic actions and procedures designed to ensure that the product or service meets the quality standards. It takes place 'before, during and after' and the aim is to prevent failure – **right first time, every time**. QA is the responsibility of everyone, it is a process used to build quality into every stage in the product development and manufacturing process.

Total quality management (TQM) extends QA, creating a 'quality culture' where the aim of the organisation is to 'delight its customers'. TQM embraces a philosophy of continuous improvement where the aim is to continually improve the performance of the organisation and its products and services – always trying to make things better.

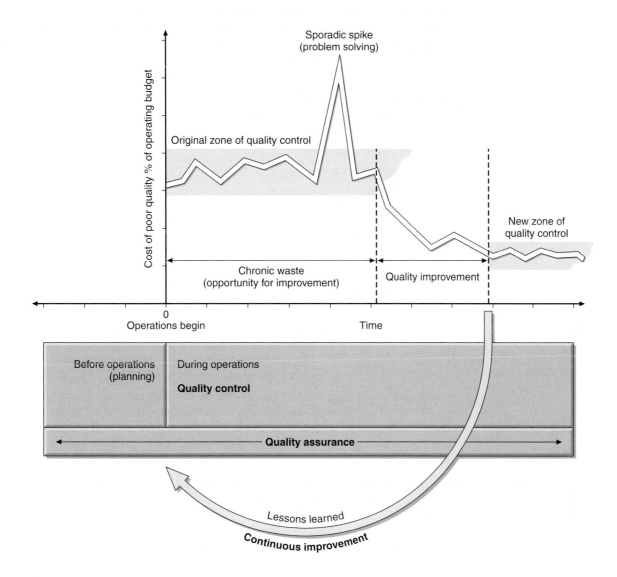

This diagram shows the use and impact of different quality systems.

Focused task: Improving the quality of your work

1 Delighting your customers
When you are trying to assess quality in any situation, there are two fundamental questions to ask:

- What is the product or service being offered?
- Who is the customer and what do they expect?

Apply these two questions to an aspect of your work; this could be:

- a coursework assignment that you have completed
- a lesson you have attended
- a group activity you have undertaken
- an industrial visit or visitor whilst involved with your own work.

Try to judge whether the outcome of the activity met, or even exceeded, the requirements of the customer.

Which of the quality systems described above would be most useful in improving the quality in that situation?

2 Setting quality milestones
Designing and manufacturing a product is not a linear process, however it is possible to establish a series of key stages or milestones throughout the process. These milestones are used by companies to provide 'check points' for planning projects and can also be used as points when set quality standards can be checked.

Apply the approach given in the table below to your own project.

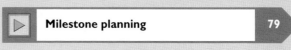

Milestone planning   79

3 Setting your own quality standards

Complete the checklist below.

Discuss your answers with some friends to agree that your answers are fair and correct. Use your answers to set one or two targets for yourself to improve the quality of your work.

You should do this regularly throughout your course in order to continuously improve the quality of your work.

Quality checklist

Give one of these responses to each of the following questions:

a all of the time
b most of the time
c just some of the time
d occasionally
e never.

1 Do you aim for error-free work?
2 Do you know what standards of quality are expected from your work?
3 Do you check the quality of your work against the standards expected?
4 Does your work meet the expected standard of quality?
5 Are you proud of your work?

Are there variations in your answers for different stages of your work; for example, during research, designing, making, writing reports?

4 Continuous improvement

The key feature of continuous improvement is moving from an attitude of 'there is no alternative' to one where you believe 'there must be a better way'. It involves continually asking questions such as:

- Why am I doing this?
- What am I trying to achieve?
- Why am I trying to achieve this?
- Why am I doing it this way?
- What other ways are there of doing this?
- How can I do it better?
- How do I know if it is better?

Ask yourself questions like these when you are planning your work, before you start on a key part of the work, and at key stages in a project or assignment. You should always try to improve on the last time you did that type of activity. This could be improving a particular skill or developing a deeper understanding.

MILESTONE	QUALITY STANDARD
Design brief	The level of quality required for the product set in broad terms
Specification	Specific quality indicators set
Conceptual designs	Quality indicators used when producing design proposals
Presentation and evaluation of conceptual designs/design proposals	Evaluate against the quality indicators
Final design specification	Includes clear criteria for: • quality of the design to meet the specification • quality of manufacture.
Design for manufacturing	Includes checking against the quality indicators and risk assessment
Production plan and schedule	Includes quality check points
Production	Quality Control

Research: How and where to get the information you need

Research is vital to the success of your course work. Your research and investigation will underpin the whole project and will reveal your underlying thinking. Your information gathering will require careful planning and thoughtful application. It is important that you do not waste valuable time collecting information that you do not need.

Advanced level studies require primary research gathered from a range of sources. This means that the work should be drawn from sources unique to you and not those provided by your tutor/lecturer.

It is important to understand the differences and comparative value of primary and secondary sources. Up to now most of your research is likely to have been based on secondary sources with some reference to primary research in the best of your course work.

Primary sources

Primary research involves collecting information yourself, from various sources, including:

- direct contact with experts by phone or making a visit
- communication with a client or user
- fieldwork – going out and physically collecting data
- questionnaires which are carefully constructed and offered to a representative sample
- exhibitions and displays
- testing and experimentation
- modelling, including computer simulations.

In other words, primary sources are original contributions, and not gathered in quite this form before by anyone else. As you can see from the list, many primary sources are people, others are direct observation, recording and measurement. The best research is based on what new information people have given to you.

Remember though, you always have to make judgements about the data you obtain.

Secondary sources

Secondary sources are easier to obtain and can provide good background information. Secondary sources include:

- articles from books magazines and journals
- items from catalogues
- printed matter issued by companies
- handouts
- data sheets
- world-wide web.

If you write to a company seeking information about a product or system and they respond by sending you a lot of information, this is not primary research. Although you have written a letter and the company may be unique to you, the resulting material is printed matter which is sent out to other people too. It may support a degree of design activity or written case work but it may not relate directly to the task. Your job is to sift it rigorously, dispose of the chaff and then show how your designing is informed by the information you choose to use.

66 *I have a good idea of where computers are going – but it's very difficult for customers to know that. If you just went with what people liked, you'd never develop. In fact if everyone felt really comfortable with what I showed them, you could probably guarantee that it's not the right thing to do."*

Jonathan Ive, Design Director Apple Computer in Computer Arts, April/May 97

Planning your research

When planning your research you will need to establish a clear course of action. This will prevent you from collecting too much information and consequently wasting time.

- Identify the information needed and produce a research brief.
- Clarify how you expect to use the findings to improve your designing or case work.
- State the sources from which you intend to gather the information.
- State which information will be drawn from primary or secondary sources.
- Collect and analyse the data.
- Evaluate your action – check against the research brief.

Keep a summary list of the useful information you obtained and how it influenced your designing or manufacturing decisions. Planning is made easy by using a simple table.

Case Study: Researching on the world-wide web, Helen Socha, Beauchamp College

Yahoo! Search Results   http://av.yahoo.com/bin/query?p=starch+company&hc=0&hs=0

Yahoo! Chat -- NBA - NHL Playoffs -- UPS™ Worldwide Services

Categories - Sites - Net Events - Headlines - **AltaVista Web Pages**

AltaVista Web Pages

Found 28910 matches containing **starch company**. Displaying matches 1-20.

- National **Starch** & Chemical **Company**: Regional Centers - Regional Centers | Countries | Regional Centers. World Headquarters *01 Telephone Fax National **Starch** and Chemical **Company** 908-685-5000 908-685-5005 10...
  --*http://www.nationalstarch.com/usaindex/national/regional_centers.html*

- National **Starch** & Chemical **Company**: By Country - Countries | Regional Centers | Locations By Country. Argentina | Australia | Belgium | Brazil | Canada. Chile | Czech Republic | Finland | France. Germany.
  --*http://www.nationalstarch.com/americas/usa/national/by_country.html*

- National **Starch** & Chemical **Company**: Australia - Regional Centers | Countries. Australia. Australia. 61ý Telephone. Fax. *A. R. S. National **Starch** & 2624-6022 2624-1468 MS MS S Chemical Pty.,Ltd 7-9.
  --*http://www.nationalstarch.com/usaindex/countries/australia.html*

The National Starch listing that Helen found through Yahoo!

"I was given the task to complete a case study on modified starch and one of my aims was to find a company that could be used as a basis for my research.

"To begin my research I went into the Internet browser to search the world-wide web. I chose the directory *Yahoo*, using a search engine (in this case AltaVista) which looks up the information that you require. I typed in my key words 'starch' and 'modified' and pressed the search button and the host then came up with a list of matches.

"I also tried 'starch' and 'company' and one match included the name of a US company called The National Starch Company with sites around the world. This seemed to be particularly relevant so I went into their home page and found a lot of useful information. I also found that it included a response page, so I sent an e-mail explaining who I was and what I was doing, and asked them to send me some information. Within two weeks I had received two booklets and four or five useful leaflets explaining their products. From these, and the web information, I was able to complete my case study very efficiently."

Using your research findings

You will gather lots of information as you progress. Keeping this work under control is potentially difficult. Knowing what to include in your portfolio and what to leave out requires skill and judgement. Only include the information that influences your work directly and annotate your work to show how your research findings have affected your decisions.

Checklist

- identify the information needed
- plan your information gathering
- use a range of primary and secondary sources
- consult experts or your client/user
- keep accurate records
- evaluate your research activity
- don't include all your findings in your portfolio
- include tests, modelling and experimentation
- show how your research has been helpful.

How to communicate

Earlier in this chapter, communication skills were included in the list of key skills considered to be vital by employers and Higher Education. This section will help you to develop these communication skills.

Writing reports

Reports are an important form of communication — you will be expected to write reports about your work. They are widely used in industry and being able to write a report is a key skill. This section provides some advice on how to structure and write a report.

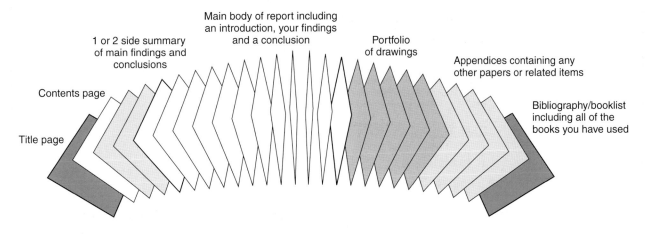

The main components of a report.

There are five main stages to preparing a report.

I Planning
- Write down the purpose of the report in 1 or 2 sentences.
- Identify the audience for the report.
- Decide on the format for the report.

2 Organising

- Select the raw material for the report
  - discard material not necessary or irrelevant for that audience
  - identify the material that is best put into appendices.
- Arrange the material under the main headings
  - attach the raw material to each relevant heading
  - write suggested sub-headings on the paper under each main heading
  - put the main headings with their raw material, into a logical order.
- Consider how using IT will help with this process (Does your word processor have an outlining feature?).

3 Writing the report

- Consider the layout and appearance – keep the audience in mind.
- Include illustrations: use well-annotated drawings and sketches and flow charts.
- Write clearly and logically.
- Consider how to use IT to help you – word processing, draw/paint software, CAD, use of spreadsheets to show data, presentation packages – make sure that using IT is the most effective way of producing that part of the report.
- Will you include a summary? Where will you put it?

4 Producing the report – things to think about

- How will you bind the report?
- What sort of cover will you use?
- Will you put all of the report in one 'package' or keep some parts, such as drawings, separate?
- What size and shape should it be – for example, does landscape or portrait work best?

5 Checking your report

You should use two checks:

- Check the report as the **author**
  - have you answered the questions you set out to answer?
  - have you included all of the key points you wanted to make?
  - can you improve the report in any way?
  - are you happy with the presentation and format?
- Check the report as the **intended audience** – this could be an examiner – does it contain everything that is expected?

A useful checklist

- Does it make sense?
- Does it flow?
- Are there any obvious mistakes?
- Is it well presented?

Making presentations

When you have to make a presentation, the actual presentation is only about 10% of the process. The remaining 90% is preparation – this is unseen by the audience but is vital for an effective presentation. This is sometimes known as the **Iceberg Principle**.

What can you use to help with a presentation?
Using a variety of techniques will help to break up the flow and keep the attention of the audience. Select the methods most suitable for what you are trying to get across and for the audience.

Overhead or LCD projector

- Very useful for putting up key points, summaries, charts and graphs, flow charts.
- Acts as a useful *aide-mémoire* for you – do not put too much on the screen at once.
- Screen displays take the attention away from you.
- Check that the screen is clear from the back of the room.
- Colour photographs can be turned into overhead transparencies using a colour photocopier (a local print shop can do this for you).
- LCD projected presentations can include scanned images.

Poster display

- Provides a useful background.
- Can show key stages in a project (use colour posters and large photographs).

Slides (photographic transparencies or digital stills)

- Show stages in the development of a product.
- Show the product in use with intended users.
- Can be used to show evaluation sessions.

Video

- A short video sequence could be used to show a dynamic aspect of your work (useful to break up the flow).

Using IT

- Use presentation software to produce high quality OHTs.
- Display the presentation on-screen, through an LCD projector or on an electronic whiteboard.
- Make use of all of the IT available to you.
- Don't rely on live links to the World Wide Web – download the pages onto your hard drive.

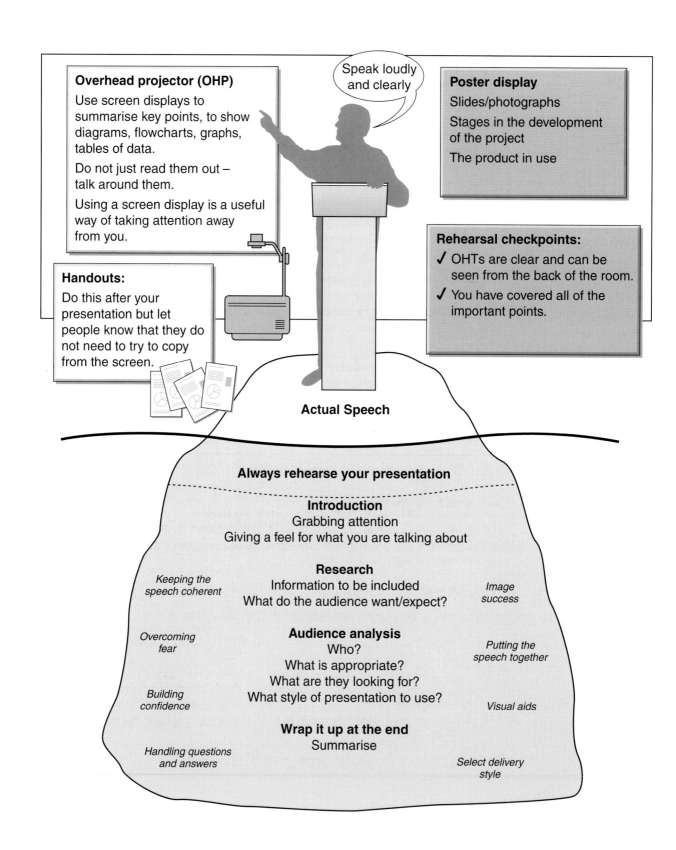

Overhead projector (OHP)

Use screen displays to summarise key points, to show diagrams, flowcharts, graphs, tables of data.

Do not just read them out – talk around them.

Using a screen display is a useful way of taking attention away from you.

Speak loudly and clearly

Poster display

Slides/photographs

Stages in the development of the project

The product in use

Rehearsal checkpoints:

✓ OHTs are clear and can be seen from the back of the room.

✓ You have covered all of the important points.

Handouts:

Do this after your presentation but let people know that they do not need to try to copy from the screen.

Actual Speech

Always rehearse your presentation

Introduction
Grabbing attention
Giving a feel for what you are talking about

Keeping the speech coherent

Research
Information to be included
What do the audience want/expect?

Image success

Overcoming fear

Audience analysis
Who?
What is appropriate?
What are they looking for?
What style of presentation to use?

Putting the speech together

Building confidence

Visual aids

Wrap it up at the end
Summarise

Handling questions and answers

Select delivery style

Making use of what you know – applying your knowledge

This section is designed to help you make use of the knowledge and skills you gained in other subjects and in other activities when you are working on your manufacturing or design and technology course.

Getting the information you need to help you with a task in design and technology has been described as **eclectic pillaging**. This means making use of any and every possible source: books (not just D&T books); other people; TV; computer databases; CD ROM etc. You will also find that you may have much of the information already but you learnt it through another subject, outside school or college, watching TV or reading a magazine or newspaper. You may not even realise you know it! The important thing is turning this into *knowledge for practical action*; in other words, knowledge that you can apply to the task in hand.

What do you want to do?

Before you can decide what relevant knowledge you have, you need to work out exactly what you want or need, to achieve. You need a clear statement of the task. Using questions like What? Who? Where? When? How? and Why? can help you become clear about the task.

Some examples of students' task statements:

- I need an electronic circuit that will enable me to monitor changes in temperature in moist soil.
- I need a method of producing this sauce in large quantities keeping the same consistency.
- I need a collapsible mechanism that provides the rigidity, stability and strength required and which locks in the upright position.
- I need a way of making parts of the textile conduct electricity.
- I need a method for machining this component in large quantities to a high level of accuracy every time.

What do you know that could help with the task?

What do I already know about this?

- Write down a key word or phrase about the task in the middle of a piece of paper.
- Write down other related words to form a **spider diagram**.
- Use another colour to add things you already know linked to the words on your diagram.
- When you have added as much as you can, check it against the task you were working on.

You might need to repeat this using some other key words.

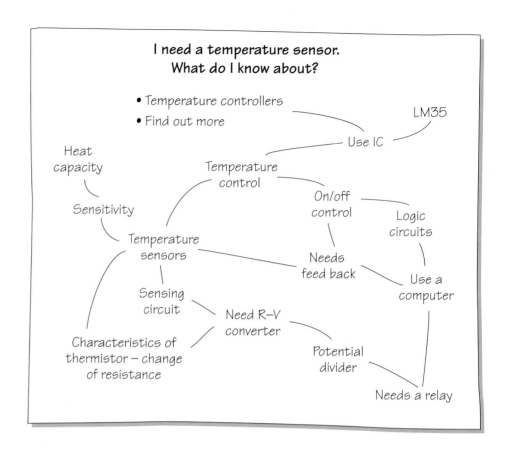

I need a temperature sensor.
What do I know about?

- Temperature controllers
- Find out more

LM35

Use IC

Heat capacity

Temperature control

On/off control

Logic circuits

Sensitivity

Temperature sensors

Needs feed back

Use a computer

Sensing circuit

Need R–V converter

Characteristics of thermistor – change of resistance

Potential divider

Needs a relay

Lateral thinking

The approach used above will help you sort out things you know that could help you, but will probably be limited by your dominant ideas – these are the obvious ideas that come relatively easily. Using other techniques will help you to find out about other things that you know which, at first sight, may not appear to be useful to the task but turn out to be the *most* useful.

Applying what you know to the task

The knowledge you have may not be available immediately, you may need to work on it before you can make use of it, by turning it into 'knowledge for practical action'. For example, you may know Ohms Law ($V = I \times R$) from your GCSE Science course, but can you use it to work out the size of resistor you need in part of an electronic circuit?

It is useful to produce a table like the one given below, it does not need to be neat, it is just a tool to help you.

- Write down the task or the part of the task you are working on.
- Write down next to it what you know about the task.
- Write down what you need to do to apply what you know to the task.

You might find it useful to group the things you know as:

- essential to the task
- looks as though it will be useful
- could be useful but not yet clear how.

You will often find it useful to work with one or more other people when you use these techniques. Forming a small support group of your friends will help. You can then call on each other to help out when you get stuck on a task.

The task	What do I know?	How can I apply this?
Designing my temperature control circuit	ON/OFF feedback control	Use a systems electronics kit to model my ideas
	Using sensors in a potential divider	
	Using a comparator	
	Using a relay to switch the heater on and off	
	Using logic circuits	
	I know there are ICs I can use	Find out how they work

Some suggestions for sorting out your ideas.

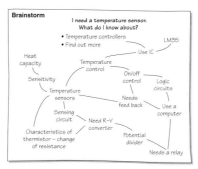

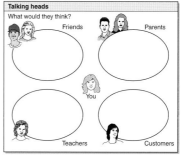

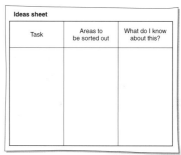

Try to fit an idea into every square

Making full use of partnerships with industry

There are many people outside of school/college who can help you with your work; this section will help you make the best use of these people.

Making contacts with industry and commerce will allow you an insight into the world of work. It is important that you identify a useful industrial partner at some time during your post-16 studies. It is a requirement of both GNVQ and A/AS Level GCE courses that you carry out some of your work in collaboration with an industrial partner. You will find working with industry useful and informative and it will give your work added relevance. You might need help from industry with:

- writing case studies
- GNVQ units
- complex manufacturing operations that cannot be done at school.

GCE syllabuses and GNVQ specifications increasingly expect students to build good relationships with industry to the point where you will be unable to achieve high grades without doing so. Undertaking a case study can be a good way into a relationship, not least because you will have to talk to company personnel at length and come to understand the company's activities.

GNVQ Advanced Manufacturing

Element 11.2: Investigate monitoring and control methods

PERFORMANCE CRITERIA

A student must:

1 describe the **methods** of sampling used for monitoring and control

2 describe the **purpose** of acceptance sampling

3 construct decision trees to illustrate **types** of acceptance sampling plans

4 identify the **quality indicators** monitored by control charts used for acceptance **sampling by variables**

5 identify the **quality indicators** monitored by control charts used for acceptance **sampling by attributes**

RANGE

Methods: variable, attribute

Purpose: recommend action, accept, reject, accumulate information (internal, external)

Types: single, double, sequential

Quality indicators for sampling by variable natural variability, assignable depth, diameter) compo

Attribute (PC1 range) sampling by attributes is concerned with setting limits within which the product is judged to be acceptable or defective.

Purpose (PC2) it should be understood that the purpose of acceptance sampling is to recommend a specific action (ie accept or reject, go or not go, good or bad). It is not intended to control quality directly..

Sampling Plans (PC3) students should be able to differentiate between the three types and understand their practical application through the use of given examples. Theoretical treatment of the related underpinning knowledge involving distributions and operating characteristic curves is not required.

Quality indicators (PC5) students need to be aware tha natural or chance variables are likely to occur in a r manner and are a function of the overall acc process: they largely determine wheth meet the requirements of the outp

Assignable causes tend to variation which is tra errors in tool sett

GUIDA

You cannot meet these Performance Criteria without going out to consult the experts in industry and commerce.

Planning for a work placement or industrial contact

Whatever course you are following, a work placement is a valuable experience. We are not looking here at the type of work experience that might involve working at a repetitive task over a period of time but one where you look at the firm and spend time in departments gathering information that is useful and relevant to your course.

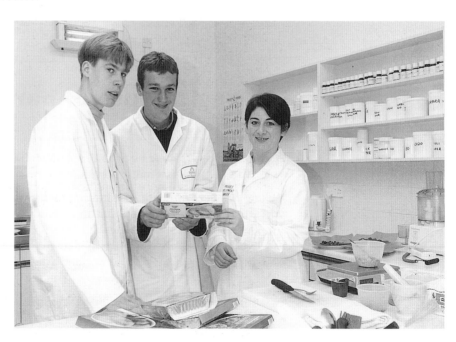

You should visit as many departments as possible so that you get an overview of the firm.

When seeking help from companies you need to be prepared. Working people are usually busy and will want to deal with your requests as efficiently and effectively as possible. Many people working in industry like to help students by encouraging them to show interest in the company. By doing this they might pick up a good employee in the future.

Choosing a company or industrial contact

You will need to select your company. There are many ways of going about this.

Try to make a contact through someone you know. It is unlikely that anyone else will use the same source if you make a link in this way and it prevents some firms from being over-run by enthusiastic students. Your tutor can usually provide a list of firms who have been helpful in the past. They might be a good choice again. The careers adviser may be able to help. They spend a lot of time talking to industrialists and their knowledge is current. You may know of a successful and reputable company in your region but have no formal contact. Find the company's phone number and phone them with a polite request. The worst that can happen is that they will say no (probably politely!).

Do the right thing!

Before first contact:

- Establish a clear purpose for your industrial contact.
- Make a list of things that you will need to know.
- Write a list of carefully thought out questions designed to gather the information that you need.
- Prioritise your questions in case there is too little time to get them all answered.

Arranging and carrying out your visit.

- Make telephone contact with the company. Fix a date and time for the visit. Record who you spoke to and who to contact when you arrive.
- Prepare the questions you want answered on your visit.
- Arrive at your company 10 minutes before you are expected in the department. Report to reception where you will be told what to do.
- Show a positive interest throughout the visit even if some of the information might be too detailed or boring.
- Make notes as you proceed. You will forget a lot of the information if you do not record your findings.
- Establish a contact in the company if you need to return. It can be any of the staff who have proved most helpful or it might be a member of a department or section in which you have a particular interest. Get a contact number and try to set up an arrangement where you can call back to ask questions that emerge later or that you did not get time to look at.
- Write a letter of thanks saying a few words about how the visit helped you with your project.

Work experience

Work experience is quite different from a work placement or industrial visit. On work experience you will be more likely to specialise in one task or a number of focused operations.

If you have been on a work placement, you will know the company already.

- They may be able to help you with information about the industry.
- They might have a special skill or process that is not available at school.
- You might be able to make part of a project in an industrial situation or you might get access to good quality presentation facilities.
- They may know of a company that can help you.

Questions to ask when visiting Hamilton

Subject: Plant Layout

What type of plant layout do you have?

....

....

What were the factors that affected you choice of plant layout?

....

....

Why did you choose this type of plant layout?

....

....

What scale of production is in progress here?

....

....

How did this affect your choice of layout?

....

....

How do you feel the scale of production affects the choice of plant layout?

....

....

Have you got a plant layout plan?

Ask to take photos, to illustrate where the machinery is and why it is there.

When going in to industry it is best to plan the questions that you are going to ask. Your information gathering will be more focused avoiding the necessity for repeat visits.

There are many benefits to be gained from collaborations between schools/colleges and companies – benefits for the company, the student and the school. Your partnership with industry is a two-way process so it is important that you foster good relations with your mentors.

The benefits *you* will gain include:

- an opportunity to investigate different industries and different scales of production
- a good source for relevant primary research
- support for the knowledge component of your course
- development of communication skills
- direct help with difficult processes and operations
- advice from real experts
- a chance to look into employment opportunities.

The benefits to *companies* will include:

- building goodwill in the community
- the possibility to recruit quality employees
- a chance to spend time developing a new system or product variation without dedicating expensive research and development time
- the opportunity to gain effective publicity
- gaining a view of the education system
- a possible input to school curriculum development.

PAPER 2   (50 marks)

Case Study

Candidates are required to submit a case study for assessment by an examiner appointed by the awarding body. The study must be submitted to the examiner by **30 April** in the year of the examination. The main written content should consist of some 2000 to 2500 words and is expected to take approximately 40 hours. Part of the work will be school-based and part industrial/commercial liaison. Where centres operate a work experience scheme it would be entirely appropriate to associate the case study with the work experience should they wish to do so.

The topic may be based either on a system/ process or on a product. In either case the study must be based on a proposition that can be explored, and from which conclusions can be drawn and recommendations made. The case study is not to be seen as simply an historical survey but a demanding intellectual investigation.

Some courses require an industrial case study. Work placements can be excellent opportunities to resource such a study.

Working with a client

It is possible that on your course you may want to design a product for a particular client; this will add purpose and focus to your work. Here is some advice on working with a client.

- Arrange a meeting with your client so that you can discuss all aspects of the work.
- Take a note book and make notes of important or agreed points. Check these with the client at the end of the meeting to make sure that you both agree.
- Be as creative as you can in your questions – this will help you find out what the client really wants. Plan these questions in advance.
- Make sure that both you and the client are clear about deadlines for each key stage of the project.
- Make sure that your client knows about any constraints on you — for example, requirements of your course, equipment available, resources available, time available.
- Arrange the time, date and place for the next meeting — the purpose of this meeting will be to discuss initial design ideas.
- After the meeting, draw up a design brief and a schedule for the project and send these to your client for agreement and clarification.
- At the second meeting agree how you will continue. This may be a further meeting to discuss the specification, your developed design, look at a mock-up etc.
- You will need *continual* discussions with your client; this may mean further meetings or agreed times when it is convenient to telephone, when you could fax design ideas and so on.

CHAPTER TWO   Designing and manufacturing: Customer need to customer satisfaction

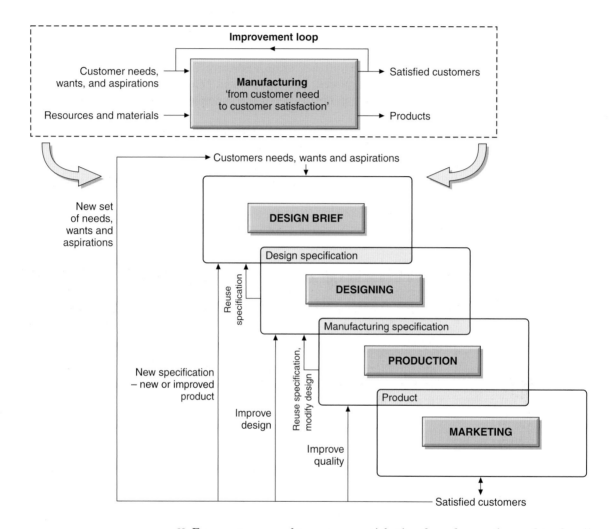

❝ *From customer need to customer satisfaction through manufactured products*''

This phrase encapsulates the complete process of product development and manufacturing. It also shows how important it is for all of the manufacturing functions – marketing, design, production, engineering, and finance – to work together.

Designing and manufacturing can be considered as a system. All systems involve **inputs** which are **processed** to achieve the outcomes required. The fundamental output of a manufacturing system is **satisfied customers**. One of the key driving forces or inputs will be customers' needs. The process of designing and manufacturing is to meet these needs through manufactured products. The needs of customers can arise in a variety of ways, therefore the reasons why products are developed are wide and various. Companies often try to exceed the needs and expectations of their customers – in this way they can build customer loyalty and it will often lead to new or improved products. All of this is explored in more detail later in this book.

Why customers are so important

Without customers there is no point in making products. The customer also plays a key role throughout the product development process. Customers are the life blood of any company — without them in sufficient numbers a business will close. To retain their customers, companies need to ensure that they are producing goods that meet customers' requirements at the right quality, time and price. Feedback from customers and customer care is crucial to satisfying these key requirements.

Many companies use total quality management (TQM) systems to ensure that they meet these key requirements. TQM has a number of key features related to customers:

- TQM involves the supplier of a product or service and the customer. The level of quality and the cost required is agreed between them.
- Quality can be defined as 'that which best satisfies and exceeds customer needs and wants'.
- Products should conform to the specification, be fit for the intended purpose, have zero defects and be 'right first time, every time'.
- Setting customer standards that lead to customer satisfaction, exceeding customer expectations wherever and whenever possible, and delighting the customer.
- Establishing a philosophy of continuous improvement – of products, services, relationship with customers and all other aspects of the company.

Identifying customer requirements

Close contact between the manufacturer and the customer or user is essential. The focus of this relationship should be on critical design issues and will:

- help to establish the optimum performance/price balance which in turn will optimise the design specification
- establish an improvement loop.

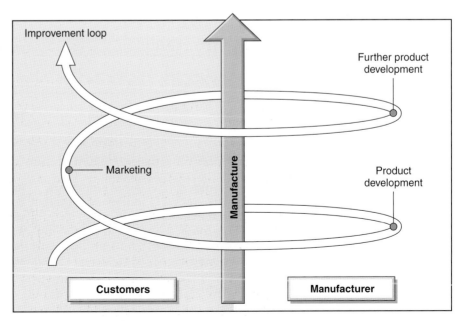

A product improvement loop.

Perfectly good products are rejected by customers because they do not meet their requirements. Making a product to meet a specification does not guarantee sales. Market research is used to establish customer's values and tastes and their perceived needs and wants; customer clinics are often used to provide feedback on design proposals, mock-ups and prototypes. The difficult task is to be able to predict what customers are going to like that they do not already know about – meeting latent needs!

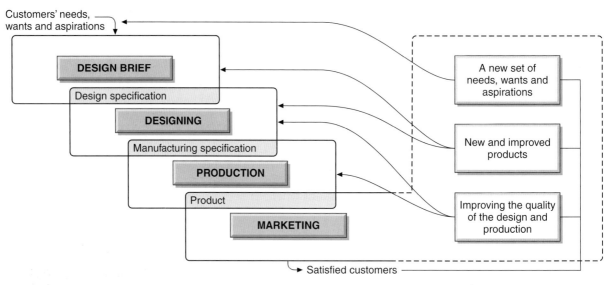

Customers can be involved at all stages of the manufacturing process; marketing provides a key link between products and customers.

Price factors	**Technical factors**	**Service factors**
price	performance	quality of after care
life cycle costs –	reliability	delivery/availability
running costs,	ease of use	user training/instruction manual
servicing costs,	ergonomic (human) factors	
breakdown costs,	maintenance	
cost of parts,	safety	
depreciation	appearance	
	flexibility and adaptability	

Factors affecting customer choice.

Before purchase	Purchase	Initial use	Long term use
(brochure characteristics)	(showroom characteristics)	(performance characteristics)	
Manufacturers specification, advertised performance and appearance, test results, image of the company's products list price.	Overall design and quality, special features, materials, colour, finish, first impressions of performance, purchase price	Actual performance, ease of use and safety.	Reliability durability and ease of maintenance, running and servicing costs.

How the design of a product affects the customer's view of it.

Case Study: **Folding pushchairs**

The pushchair is an example of a product with at least two users to consider – the child and the parent or carer.

Criteria to meet the needs of the child	Criteria to meet the needs of the adult
• held safely and comfortably • feet clear of the floor • comfortable to sit on for quite long periods • no sharp edges or corners • no features that could trap or harm • be adjustable to allow for growth • be adjustable for sleeping or awake and alert child	• ease of use • size – to fit doorways and cars • suitable for a range of heights of user • ease of cleaning and maintenance • strength, rigidity • lightweight • attractive – range of colours and patterns of material used • durability, weather resistance

Consider how:
• each of these criteria would be established
• the 'customer' would be involved in the development of the criteria – and the product
• potential customers could be consulted
• the design might satisfy specialist needs e.g. joggers, twins

Can you predict 'what customers need or are going to like, that they do not already know about'? (latent needs)

Do the right thing!

When you are developing your own products:

• Who are your customers?
• What are their needs? Can you identify any latent needs?
• How do you know?
• Can you exceed their needs and expectations?

How will you establish a working relationship with your customer or client?

How will you make best use of this relationship?

The commercial imperative for new products

The world of business and industry is changing rapidly. Just think of all of the new products and services that have been developed in your own lifetime: video and computer games; biotechnology developing new medicines; telephone and PC banking; home shopping on your computer or television, and the world-wide web/internet. All of these new products and services have developed because the technology was there and the customer wanted it – even though they may not have realised it beforehand!

In the past, slower communications and local, rather than international competition, meant that product development was slower. Products tended to change in response to developments in technology or improvements in manufacturing processes. Now the time taken to develop a new product has been reduced from years to months. This means that the life of the product is often also reduced. You only need to look at the pace of change in computers, for example, how long is a new personal computer 'state of the art'?

Customers now want newer and better quality products. Companies exist in a global market place. Information about the cost and quality of products can be passed instantaneously between customers and alternative suppliers – often in very different parts of the world!

To meet these challenges companies need to continuously create new and improved products if they are to survive.

 The UK Technology Foresight Programme | **92**

Focused task: Competition

1 Choose a product that exists in a very competitive market — that is a product where the customer has a wide range of alternative products from different companies.
2 Survey the range of products available.
3 Identify how some manufacturers have attempted to make their product appeal to a wide range of customers through particular features.
4 Identify how other manufacturers have developed their products to meet the needs of niche markets.

5 Find out about how the product has developed over time. Look for:

- the use of new technologies, manufacturing methods and materials
- additional features to meet developing customer needs
- additional features that have been used to create new needs and aspirations
- any improvements in quality and how they have been achieved
- how these items have made the product successful (or not!).

Mapping new products against customer attributes and profiles

The first requirement of any successful product is that it must be matched to satisfying customer needs. This is more easily said than done. There is already a vast range of products of all types on the market to service almost all and any consumer needs. Innovative design needs to go one stage further by attempting to stimulate subconscious needs – so-called **latent needs**. As stated by one company: "You must get into the mind of the customer even when the customer does not know their own mind!" Innovative products can stimulate new consumer wants.

The reverse can also be true – consumer needs can stimulate innovative products being developed. This happens in the fashion industry where the marketing people tell the materials scientists and technologists what new fibres and fabrics they need, to create the products the designer and their customers want.

Case Study: The Casual Traveller from Sony

The Casual Traveller is a radio cassette alarm clock. The idea stemmed from design concepts produced in 1992 and based on a survey of European lifestyles. The designers thought of audio products to suit bikers, hikers, campers and even footballers! This provided discussion material for a brainstorming session involving designers, marketing staff, engineers and product planners. At this stage the company encouraged younger, more junior employees to become involved to maximise the creative input. From this meeting emerged the idea of a portable radio cassette designed for what was dubbed the 'Eurokid' – the frequent travelling, inter-railing student. It would need to be a personal stereo, a clock and an alarm, but also have a built-in high quality speaker to share music with friends. The other key requirements were for it to be tough, durable and light-weight.

At this stage a target price is also agreed – this is a estimate of what the likely customer can afford and would be willing to pay. This provides a ceiling to the production cost which may restrict the designers to using less expensive features or materials. For the Casual Traveller, a target price of around £60 was agreed between the marketing and design staff. After several months of discussion and generating design ideas it was also agreed that the product had sales potential in Japan as well as Europe.

Once the product was approved, design, engineering and manufacturing staff had to turn drawings into high volume production. Because of the extensive use of teamwork, this process was achieved in a year – which is very fast. The Casual Traveller has been a commercial success in both Japan and Europe.

♦ Explain how the Casual Traveller meets the needs of the market and customers identified for it.
♦ Explain how it meets the latent needs of customers.

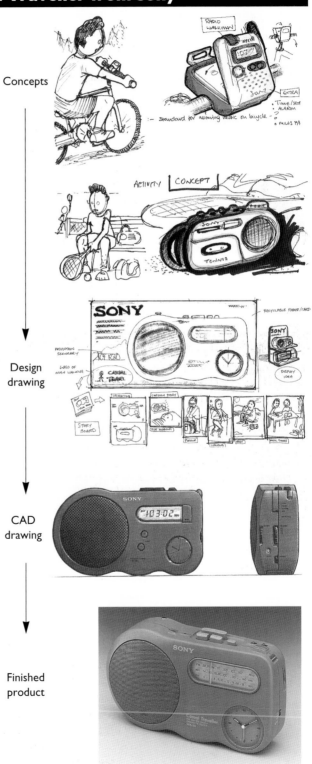

Concepts

Design drawing

CAD drawing

Finished product

Case Study: Apples – consumer preferences and product attributes

The Institute of Food Science and Technology is an independent professional body for food scientists and technologists. The Institute aims to promote the creation, production and control of safe, wholesome and nutritious food and drink products. The increasing use of sensory analysis within the food industry has led to the development of The Sensory Interest Group which aims to expand the knowledge, understanding and use of sensory evaluation techniques within the food industry. The long term aim is to establish a professional qualification in sensory science.

The development of more rigorous sensory analysis procedures in the food industry becomes more important as consumers' expectations of new food products become more refined. Therefore mapping consumer preferences with product attributes is a way of identifying and developing a new product specification.

At the Institute, Professor Hal MacFie has researched into the preferences of consumers for different varieties of eating apples and then mapped this against the attributes of eating apples to establish the criteria for developing a new variety.

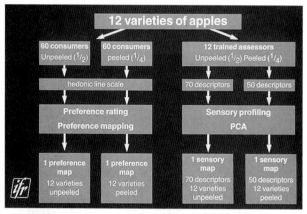

12 varieties of apples tested by 60 consumers and 12 trained assessors.

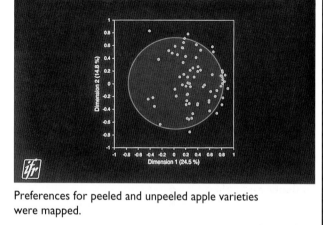

Preferences for peeled and unpeeled apple varieties were mapped.

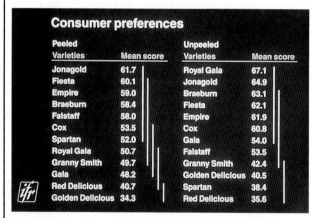

Consumer preferences

Peeled Varieties	Mean score	Unpeeled Varieties	Mean score
Jonagold	61.7	Royal Gala	67.1
Fiesta	60.1	Jonagold	64.9
Empire	59.0	Braeburn	63.1
Braeburn	58.4	Fiesta	62.1
Falstaff	58.0	Empire	61.9
Cox	53.5	Cox	60.8
Spartan	52.0	Gala	54.0
Royal Gala	50.7	Falstaff	53.5
Granny Smith	49.7	Granny Smith	42.4
Gala	48.2	Golden Delicious	40.5
Red Delicious	40.7	Spartan	38.4
Golden Delicious	34.3	Red Delicious	35.6

Consumers' preferences for peeled and unpeeled apple varieties were recorded.

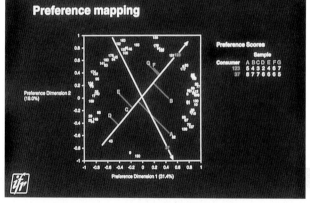

Attributes of the most popular variety of apples were identified and used for the development of a new variety of English apple.

Case Study: Product design at IDEO

This case study was written by John Stoddard, IDEO (Innovation, Design and Engineering Organisation).

Some IDEO products

At IDEO a five stage process is used for developing products.

Understand
- ◆ the relevant technologies
- ◆ the market
- ◆ the pressures for change
- ◆ the aims and missions of clients

Observe
- ◆ users of existing products (clients)
- ◆ extrapolate to predict needs in 5 years time
- ◆ brainstorming ideas – involves the whole team

Visualise and predict
- ◆ innovative ideas
- ◆ use of drawings, mock-ups, cardboard models, prototypes, computer simulations

Evaluate and refine
- ◆ with users
- ◆ technical evaluation

Implement

There is often a **feedback loop** between **implement** and **understand** leading to product improvement and ideas for new products.

IDEO make extensive use of teamworking with engineers, designers and people with expertise in 'human factors' working in parallel throughout the process.

Focused task: The IDEO design process

- • How does this process ensure that products are mapped to customer needs and expectations?
- • How will this process uncover latent needs?
- • Explain how the OBSERVE phase could uncover latent needs?

Focused task: Matching design features to the market

A range of kettles from different times and designers.

A Victorian cast-iron kettle.

A premier electric kettle, 1920.

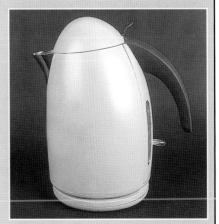

A 1990's plastic jug kettle.

Focused task: Matching design features to the market *continued*

Hot Bertaa, aluminium kettle designed by Philip Starck, 1991.

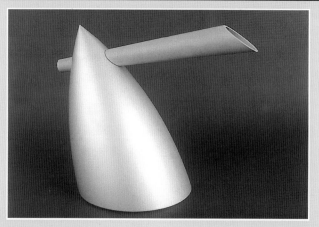

Philips–Alessi line kettle, 1994.

For each of the kettles shown:

1 Identify its key design features.
2 Identify the market you think it was aimed at.
3 Decide how the design features match the needs of the customers in that market niche.

Read the UKettle case study on page 209.

- What key design features did the UKettle have?
- How are these linked to the market it was aimed at?

Work in a small group for this activity.

- How do you think kettles will develop in the future?
- What new needs will customers have? Try to think of latent needs as well.
- What new technologies could be incorporated in kettle design?
- Brainstorm ideas for a new type of kettle aimed at a particular market niche.

Market research

Market research is involved with the identification of **needs** and **wants**. Philip Kotler, in his book, *Principles of Marketing*, defines a need as 'a state of felt deprivation in a person' while wants are 'needs as shaped by our culture and personality'. In other words, everyone *needs* to eat, but each person may *want* to eat a different food. Wants only become **demands** when people have the resources to acquire what they want. What most people want is usually more than what they need and more than they can afford.

The marketing mix: the customers – and how the market is divided up

Market research provides clues as to the kinds of people who are likely to buy a product. Several distinct groups of customers are revealed who make up **segments** within the total market. Once the characteristics and buying behaviour of these groups is known, the marketing can be directed at particular **target groups**. These will contain the most potential customers. A company establishes its **market position** by concentrating its marketing effort on the segment of the market most likely to provide the best sales for its products.

One of the most common ways of dividing up the market is to use **socio-economic groups**. This divides up people by the type of job they do and their earning power. It relies on these groups showing similarities in the types of products they buy.

Maslow's hierarchy of needs. People have different levels of need; they respond differently in the way they satisfy a particular need according to their attitudes and the values they hold. People do not buy a product, they buy solutions to their perceived needs or problems. How does this affect the way products are marketed?

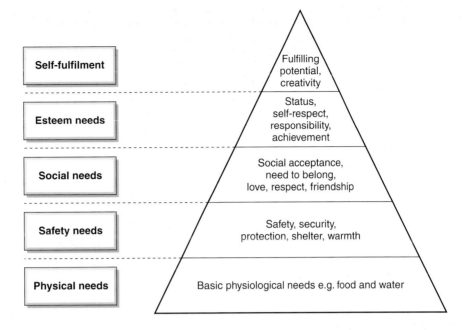

Self-fulfilment	Fulfilling potential, creativity
Esteem needs	Status, self-respect, responsibility, achievement
Social needs	Social acceptance, need to belong, love, respect, friendship
Safety needs	Safety, security, protection, shelter, warmth
Physical needs	Basic physiological needs e.g. food and water

Some companies find it easier to break into a specific segment of a larger market – **niche marketing**.

Explain how each of these products fits a niche in the market.
Be as precise as possible in describing the niche.

Any marketing strategy is based on the **four Ps**:

- **Product** – the product that is being marketed.
- **Price** – setting the price at the right level.
- **Promotion** – advertising.
- **Place** – who are you selling to? How will the product be distributed? How will the product be sold: through retailers, directly to the customer, or through a catalogue?

These are not independent — each affects the other and they must fit together and be consistent.

Of course, only a handful of products become winners. If a new product is to succeed, it must have features that make it stand out from the competition – **unique selling points (USP)**.

Focused task: Identifying USPs

Read the asthma inhaler case study on page 212 and compare the Handihaler with the more traditional product. What are the unique features of the Handihaler?	Choose an item where there are many competing products on the market and identify the USP for those that are most successful.

A process for market research

1 Decide on the purpose of the market research: What information is needed? what will it be used for? What market segments will be researched?
2 What information can be obtained from secondary data (data that already exists)?
3 What information requires primary research (information collected specifically for the purpose in hand)?
4 Decide on the most appropriate method taking into account the time and money available.
5 Decide on the size and nature of the sample needed.
6 Carry out the market research.
7 Gather and analyse the data.
8 Present the findings, summarise key points and make recommendations on appropriate actions.

Market research methods. The diagram shows **quantitative methods**. **Qualitative methods** are also used such as group discussions, focus groups, in-depth interviews – these are useful to establish who buys what and why.

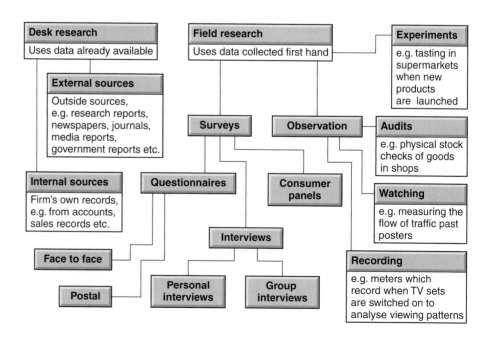

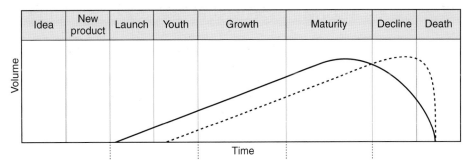

Idea	New product	Launch	Youth	Growth	Maturity	Decline	Death

Development

Technical innovation, research and development (R&D). Firm will decide if it is worthwhile continuing with new product.

Launch

Most expensive phase. Costs of R&D, production and marketing not yet recovered. Informative advertising used. Firm will assess commercial viability of product.

Growth

Product establishes its position in the market, and retail outlets become easier to obtain as sales increase. There is a shift from informative to persuasive advertising. Competitors begin to enter the field and prices fall.

Maturity

Product reaches its peak. More competitors enter and market reaches saturation point. Increased advertising needed to maintain market share. Efforts made to maintain product's position by adopting extension strategies.

Decline

Sales fall dramatically. Efforts may be made to slow down this process or product may be milked, if the firm has new products to take over from it. Product may be taken off the market if it starts to damage the company's image and prejudice the introduction of new products.

The product life cycle: a product passes through a series of stages in its life cycle. How would the product be marketed at each stage?

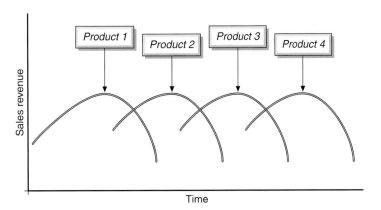

Giving a product a new lease of life: the product can be re-launched at key times. This could be an improved or modified version of the same product. How would the product be marketed at each re-launch?

 Profit margin and product cycle | 163

Case Study: MFI – customers and continuous improvement

Many companies realise that they can no longer compete on the basis of their products and prices alone; satisfying their customers is vital.

According to MFI:

'Customers are the natural resource upon which the success of the company depends. It has been estimated that it costs five times as much to attract new customers as it does to keep an existing one. The relationship between the organisation and the customer is critical for success. Here are some fundamental points about this relationship:

◆ Repeat business is the backbone of selling.
◆ Organisations are dependent upon their customers (not the other way around).
◆ Customers help an organisation to achieve everything a business aims for.
◆ Without customers an organisation would simply not exist.

Focusing on customers involves providing them with what they want, when and how they want it. Customer requirements are constantly changing and it is therefore necessary to understand customer fashions and needs in order to design and deliver products which exceed customer expectations. Intelligent organisations have therefore developed a strategy of providing superior customer care to differentiate their products and services. By doing this, organisations can meet their objectives, grow more quickly than their rivals and benefit from increased market share.'

MFI are also committed to the idea of continuous improvement — for them Continuous Improvement Process Management is a system which ensures that quality service is not a one-off initiative designed to temporarily improve customer service. It is a continuous programme which helps to emphasise that all employees within an organisation are part of a quality chain which is improved with better teamwork, employee care and efficient communication procedures. To do this MFI has created a customer service policy which sets out a statement of intent as to the standards to be achieved.

The MFI Service Policy, Statement of Intent

'MFI is committed to setting the benchmark for service within its marketplace. To achieve this, the company will, on an ongoing basis, measure and upgrade its internal and external requirements for the provision of quality service. This will ensure that the service benchmarks applied within the company consistently meet the service requirements of our customers.'

When developing a relationship with customers an organisation needs to consider how this relationship is managed. This is part of what is known as **relationship marketing**. This means that an organisation has to develop its activities in a way which takes into account how these activities affect its relationships with customers. For example, order times, reputation, goods exchange and refunds, dealing with faults, customer waiting times and the overall efficiency of the organisation. As part of its customer care profile MFI goes to great lengths to discover customer opinion from:

◆ customer forums (clinics)
◆ service evaluation
◆ mystery shopping
◆ exit interviews
◆ suggestion schemes
◆ branch-specific questionnaires
◆ internal attitude surveys
◆ internal improvement groups and teams.

Case Study: Corporate identity – Ben and Jerry's

This case study was written by Hannah Driver, a post-16 student at Beauchamp College in Leicestershire. Hannah found the information included in the case study on the world wide web.

Corporate identity refers to the image a company is trying to portray. The image is based on the values and beliefs that a company establishes, and is then characterised by using a common theme which allows the company to be easily recognised. Logos, advertising material, packaging, product decoration, trademarks, graphic designs and the use of particular fonts are ways that a specific image may be represented.

Ben and Jerry's is an American company specialising in ice cream and frozen yoghurt. The company has a very strong corporate image. They use traditional, but extremely successful marketing strategies.

Ben and Jerry's mission consists of three interrelated parts:

Product
To make, distribute and sell the finest quality 'all natural' ice cream and related products in a wide variety of innovative flavours made from Vermont dairy products.

Economic
To operate the company on a sound financial basis of profitable growth, increasing value for shareholders and creating career opportunities and financial rewards for employees.

Social
To operate the company in a way that actively recognises the central role that business plays in the structure of society by initiating innovative ways to improve the quality of life of a broad community – local, national and international.

Underlying the mission of Ben and Jerry's is the determination to seek new and creative ways of addressing all three parts, while holding a deep respect for the individuals, inside and outside the company, and for the communities of which they are a part.

Ben and Jerry's have established a Foundation that offers grants to organisations to facilitate progressive social change in the following areas:

◆ children and families
◆ disenfranchised groups
◆ the environment.

Ben and Jerry's environmental awareness is apparent in every aspect of the company. Every ingredient used for their products is carefully selected. The milk used in the products is not allowed to have any impurities. The cows that produce the milk are looked after by the company. This environmental image is backed up by the motto used as part of the their corporate identity: **reduce**, **re-use**, **recycle**.

The corporate image of the company is represented by the packaging used for their products. They are packaged in a standard cardboard tub used for all flavours. This stresses the company's environmental concerns.

 Reducing environmental impact through design 96

Why do some products remain successful?

Some products seem to stay on the market for ever; others seem to come and go very quickly even though they seemed to be a good idea at the time. In some cases the products seem to survive even though they have some obvious faults. This would seem to suggest that consumers respond to products in both logical and emotional ways. Emotionally, we can become very attached to products – sometimes for reasons we are aware of and sometimes for reasons that are buried deep in our sub-conscious (consider the teddy bear!).

These bottles have some very good design features. The spray mechanism can be re-used so that only refills need to be bought and you can spray different types of surface effectively. They also have one problem: they fall over very easily, especially when they are less than half-full. Why do you think that this product continues to be successful?

The original plastics 'stackable chair' was designed by Robin Day of the Royal College of Art in the 1960s. Look around your school, public buildings and offices – you will find very similar chairs in many places. This product was relaunched in 1999 – what makes this design so successful?

A new power in personal transport

Congratulations. You're among the first owners of the remarkable Sinclair C5 – the world's first *practical* personal transport powered by electricity.

No petrol, no driving licence, no pollution: and an energy cost of around a penny for five miles (or nearly 1,000 miles for the price of a gallon of petrol).

Easy to use, easy to maintain, the C5 is a resource for the entire family. The more you use it, the more uses you'll find.

But whatever you do, wherever you go, one thing about the C5 never changes: the sheer fun of driving it!

A vehicle for today – and tomorrow.

The Sinclair C5 is constructed from top quality components, many newly developed specifically for the C5 using state-of-the-art techniques. Each has been rigorously tested and proven.

Every C5 is thoroughly checked before despatch, and is backed by a nationwide parts and service organisation.

I hope, and expect, that your C5 will give you years of service and pleasure.

CLIVE SINCLAIR

Many people considered the Sinclair C5 to be an innovative product but it was not a great success. What were the problems: the design, the marketing. . . ?

Focused task: Product design lives

Find other products that:

- have been on the market for a long time
- came and went very quickly.

In each case explain why the product was successful or not.

Innovation — new product development

How and why do new products arise?

Innovation is the process of taking new ideas **effectively** and **profitably** through to satisfied customers. It is about **predicting** and **anticipating** customers' wants and needs and **satisfying** them, about achieving new developments in science and new technologies and turning them into products that people want and need. It not only leads to increased prosperity but also should improve the quality of people's lives.

People – designers, manufacturers, buyers and users – often have deep relationships with their products. Cultures express themselves through artefacts as well as thoughts, music, drama etc. Most of us 'get a buzz' from a new purchase or gift. Designers often tend to be very involved in their work, finishing a product on a high (or a low!). Companies involved in product design and manufacture can be said to be simply in business, developing new products for commercial reasons, but to do this successfully they are unavoidably working with rational reasoning and intuitive, difficult-to-articulate, emotive, even spiritual factors.

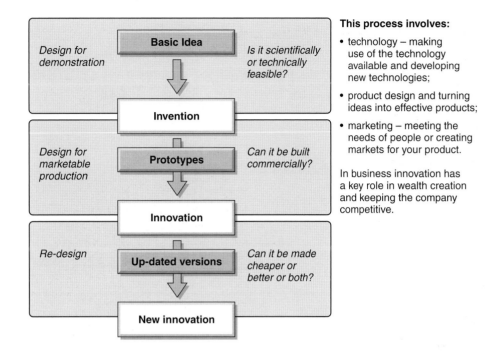

This process involves:

- technology – making use of the technology available and developing new technologies;

- product design and turning ideas into effective products;

- marketing – meeting the needs of people or creating markets for your product.

In business innovation has a key role in wealth creation and keeping the company competitive.

New products come about for an enormous variety of reasons, mostly driven by commercial considerations but also because those responsible for them are imbued with an enthusiasm they want to share with the world. Almost all products embody both these motivations in differing quantities – they are attractive, exciting perhaps, affordable (at least by some) and fulfil human needs. At the least rational end of this spectrum are art objects, and at the other those items (most of which we take for granted) which satisfy humdrum, pragmatic needs such as light bulbs and toilet paper. And yet, the most mundane items can often be shown to work for us in the emotional domain, for example many toilet rolls are bought as a response to cuddly puppies on the television appealing to our emotions.

For these reasons, there is a complex relationship between a product and the market it serves. It can be true that manufactured products succeed where a focused customer need can be identified and responded to well. However many issues come to bear on the way in which products arise, develop and eventually reach people and particularly on whether they are successful.

There is a commercial imperative for companies to develop new products or improve existing ones if they are to remain competitive, retaining or increasing market share. Otherwise catastrophe can befall them, for example the world-leading British motor-cycle industry of the 1950s died in the late 1960s because innovations had become minimal and they were not exploiting new technological possibilities. The Japanese did both.

Two major categories of reasons for new products to be developed are sometimes referred to: **market pull** and **technology push**. The first refers to the requirements of the marketplace 'pulling' companies into action to produce what the market wants. By contrast, the development of new technologies leads to product innovations being 'pushed' out to establish a new market.

As with all classification schemes this is somewhat artificial, usually a combination of both can be identified, for example desk lamps have existed for decades but only recently did they appear with bright little halogen bulbs.

Consumer expectations are constantly rising. Such mundane venues as supermarkets have recently become architectural masterpieces with an extremely high quality of design evident throughout. (See Asda case study page 220.)

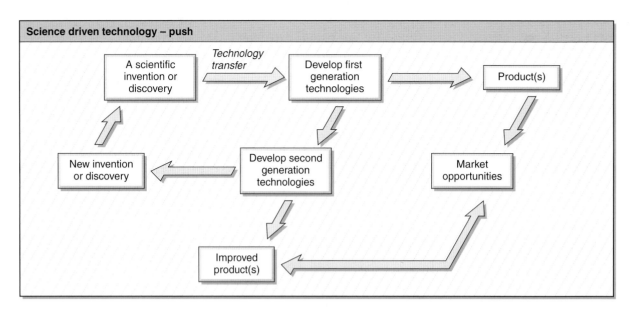

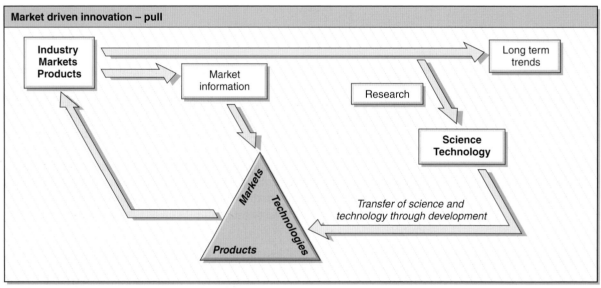

High quality products set the pace for the competition and raise expectations across the board. The more people experience ultra high quality products, the more they expect every product to be of that quality. (See Handihaler case study page 212.)

New technologies expand the range of facilities that products can provide e.g. inter-active digital terrestrial television versus broadcast TV. (Previously seen in the replacement of black and white TV with colour, mono with stereo etc.)

In technologically advanced societies people have come to expect sophisticated products and will not tolerate poor ones and commercial competition exploits this.

It is perhaps true that market pull is becoming increasingly concerned with smaller questions e.g. product differentiation and refinement rather than prompting new products. But changing lifestyles make people open to new variations of products to support their new way of living, such as automatic lawnmowers and mountain bikes, though sometimes a new product springs entirely from market knowledge. (See Canon Creative case study page 69.)

The Husqvarna automatic lawnmower – established cutting technology with a new power source and control system. Solar-powered when adequately charged, it cuts a random area of grass within boundaries marked with metal strips.

It is probably equally true that technology push is becoming increasingly common, perhaps the dominant stimulus for new product development. In the electronics field this is particularly true, especially the whole audio-visual entertainment area e.g. Sega and Nintendo games machines.

The re-working of established designs often incorporates both forms of impetus, as market information is usually drawn on and the opportunity is taken to consider possible technological innovations.

Market pull
- Responding to changing lifestyles e.g. chill-cook meals, (Sony Portable Radio page 55).
- Changing consumer attitudes change design priorities (Tencel case study page 113, Ben & Jerry's Ice Cream page 63).
- New products closely mapped against customer attributes and profiles (Frubes page 68, Domida kitchens page 190).
- Mapping to small groups of customers' preferences 'the market niche', broad product ranges, e.g. telephones from £10 to £200.
- New products developed from existing ones e.g. CD Walkman.
- A new product to promote or support an existing one e.g. Canon Creative page 69.
- People like new things!

Technology push
- New technologies make products that were previously impossible, possible e.g. mobile phones.
- New products developed long before the old ones wear out, e.g. computers.
- New ways of producing old products are developed (Teknit/Shima Seiki page 183).
- The new technology may have to wait until the need for resulting products is apparent or it becomes commercially viable.
- New technologies are sometimes driven by environmental pressures, e.g. biodegradable detergents.
- New technologies are used as a way of achieving an advantage in the market. Hi-tech is attractive and often offers real improvements, e.g. digital tuning for radios.
- Continuous improvement in the design and manufacture of a product can lead to improved quality and/or reduced price, e.g. cheaper air fares from more powerful aero-engines.
- The quality of products is constantly improved as a result of new developments in materials and processing. Sometimes however, manufacturers go back to 'old technology' for a variety of reasons, for example the tailgate for the Jeep Cherokee which went from GRP (Glass Reinforced Plastics) to steel when manufacturing volumes increased dramatically.
- A complex set of factors sometimes work in combination – often over a long time scale (the Biopol case study page 112), scientific research, developing the technology, economic factors (oil crisis), and environmental pressures.

Key features of innovative (and successful) product design

The development of a competitive product depends on:

- how well its market and technical specifications are defined and then translated into a commercially viable and economically manufacturable design (Handihaler, page 212, McLaren, page 198, PDSA, page 224)
- customer appeal (Jaguar, page 201)
- good communications with customers and with external sources of ideas (Sony, page 55)
- setting performance targets and **milestones of achievement** during the complete product development process (Psion, page 77)
- sorting out potential problems before the product is launched (UKettle, page 209).

Focused task: Design innovation and teamwork

Each of the points above has been linked to one or more case studies. Read through these case studies to understand how each illustrates that particular point.

In many of the case studies the importance of the use of a team approach including technical, design, production, research and development (R&D), financial, marketing and quality functions is stressed.

- Explain when and why this is important.
- When do these functions have to be performed by the same people?
- How can you learn from this to improve your own projects? Note down 2 or 3 key points.

Case studies: Starting points for new product development

I Petits Filous 'Frubes'

Fromage frais accounts for two-thirds of the children's fresh dairy products market but only 6.3% of children's fromage frais is consumed as a snack. Promotions, media coverage and free gifts, aimed at the target groups have been used successfully to promote these products. For example the Petits Filous company worked with a manufacturer to design a lunch box with a double, vacuum shell and a slot for an icepack, providing a container that maintains an inside temperature of 5°C for at least 5 hours. This illustrates how a manufacturer can promote their product and at the same time encourage the consumer to use the correct storage procedures, preventing spoilage of the product. Use of the cool lunch box would also enable Petits Filous fromage frais to be used for packed lunches, even though it does not contain preservatives, thus extending sales and its market share.

Market research highlighted that there was a potential gap in the 'snack' fresh dairy products market, so Yoplait developed 'Frubes' – fromage frais in a tube – to increase sales. The idea was developed by Yoplait in France as a way to move fromage frais into the snack market, with Frubes being seen as a healthy alternative to other snacks. It would also extend the Petits Filous franchise into the older 4–10 year old target group (57% of the 60g pot range is consumed by the under 5 years age group). The Frubes design had to be fun, bright and colourful to appeal to children (the consumers) but had to include details of the nutritional benefits and usage ideas in order to gain adult approval (the purchasers). This was achieved by using a checklist approach, informative pack copy and an eating shot. Children appear on the outer packaging, but only 'fruit' appears on the actual Frubes tube to make it acceptable to any age group. Adults were also found to be reassured by the Petits Filous branding, and would remain loyal.

The convenience and snackability of Frubes means that children can enjoy fromage frais in a variety of new usage occasions – as a snack, for picnics and when travelling. The fact that no spoon is needed makes Frubes ideal for packed lunches (the primary reason given by mothers for not adding fromage frais to their child's lunch box was that the spoon was rarely returned at the end of the day). Frubes can also be frozen for a refreshing and nutritious snack – a healthy alternative to ice pops. This enables consumers to extend the shelf life themselves and a ready-frozen product incurs VAT.

2 Canon Creative – a new software product

Canon is a leading manufacturer of many high technology products and among many products it specialises in bubble-jet printer technology. Canon were interested in increasing the sales of the company's printers and specialist papers for printing on, which enhance the quality of the images. Together these technologies – printers, software and papers – offer a complex range of choices to consumers who can be slow to understand what they offer and so slow to take advantage. Canon therefore developed a new software product in Australia called **Canon Creative** to extend the use of their products.

Based on two CD-ROM discs, it is a package designed to enable you to produce stationery, certificates, stickers, newsletters, brochures, personalised greetings cards, frames, and even T-shirts, quilts and cross stitch embroidery templates. It provides interactive help to guide the user through the range of possible and potential outcomes. At the heart of the package is a program called **Design Essentials** which contains a wide range of templates to assist in the production of quality outcomes. As a manufacturer of printers, by producing this **accessory** software Canon promote their printers, and increase the consumption of speciality papers, films and inks. This is an unusual case whereby a manufacturer has examined systematically the reasons for limited use of existing products and has used their creativity to develop an **add-on** which enhances the potential of an existing product through the production of a complementary product. Can you think of other similar examples?

3 CD racks – product evaluation and development

When compact discs arrived on the market they were similar to some products already available but they were also new in many ways. They were, basically, aimed at the same market as vinyl records which had established traditions in their sleeve labels and, to a lesser extent, supporting racks. Record racks were not very common as the large twelve inch LPs would stack easily on a shelf. They were large and made of card which soon became tatty so they were not often displayed.

With the arrival of CDs all this changed, despite their cases being very similar to those for records. They are smaller but more durable and visually stimulating, as they are made of a crystal plastic. We must acknowledge that a new product genre has emerged since there are now so many CD racks on the market. All share the basic function of providing for storage and retrieval, but many also become decorative objects in their own right.

Following are two comparative reviews of commercially available products from a panel of critics, organised by a national newspaper. They are compared with another radically different approach from a Royal College of Art student.

The Epoch CD storage box

Holds 20, costs £12 (1997)
Box second from right in photo (page 70).

The male voices on the panel greeted this elegant stacking box with shouts of derision and disgust on discovering its price. 'I could get a box file for a quarter of the price,' claimed Mike Eagleton (jazz promoter and record producer). 'Only a nutty millionaire would buy it. I would solely use it as a carrying box.' Opera Director Adrian Hilton's opinion was similarly coloured by the price tag, reporting that 'it would only be eye catching if a corner of it poked me in the eye. Cardboard boxes are style-less.' . . . Caroline Harper (graphic designer) adored its neatness. 'I love little boxes and I like hiding things . . . I love the old fashioned way of putting things away'. Joan Thackray (a music student) called it a 'glorified shoebox'.

Case Study: **Starting points for new product development** *continued*

Avec Trio CD-rack

Holds 20, costs £9.95 (1997)

When it came to genuine enthusiasm from the panel, this rack collected it in stack-loads. 'It's very classy' . . . 'As close to being perfect as I think you'd find.' . . . 'Sixties jukebox, resembled a modern tower block . . . could remove the shelves and fit in doubles . . . came in three colours and was designed to stack easily . . . sturdy and durable . . . a conversation point.. architectural lines . . . masculine . . . a reliable and classy-looking rack which exuded quality'.

Extracts from *Independent on Sunday* magazine, compiled by Rachelle Thackray *Independent on Sunday* 20 July 1997.

Five commercial CD holders that were reviewed by a panel and Splat! – a design from an RCA student.

You can tell from the extracts of the panel's discussions that controversy was provoked by being asked to look at these products. Obviously they stirred the panel's emotions and part of the reason for this was the products' meanings, part their price and also other factors.

SPLAT! in the background, disposes of cases and shows the discs 'full-frontal', pressed onto teats on a sheet of self-skinned foam. The whole thing is designed to be held to the wall with low-tack adhesive. What product competes with *SPLAT!* – is it other CD-racks or pictures, photographs and mirrors?

▷ | **Design semantics** | 126 ▶

Focused task: Design criteria

- Starting with those revealed by the extracts above and then adding your own, list the criteria for a good CD storage product.
- Discuss the qualities wanted from CD storage products with your fellow students (everyone could be asked to bring in an example).
- Discuss *SPLAT!*. Would you buy it?
- Produce a sheet of ideas for fresh new designs of wall-mounted CD holders. Annotate your ideas to reveal the appeal each one might have.

4 Commercial product evaluation, Dixons Mastercare

Dixons Stores Group operate over 800 stores nationwide under the names Dixons, Currys, PCWorld and The Link. To support this organisation, they have a technical operation called the Mastercare Technical Centre which is a product evaluation laboratory where they examine closely the products their companies sell, repairing, servicing and testing them. They identified instruction books as products in their own right, which needed development. Mastercare now employ a graphic designer to re-write the manufacturers' often complex instructions to make them more effective.

John Wright, the Manager explained, 'We videoed a range of customers using products for the first time and the results were sometimes frightening. Customers usually wanted to see the product functioning before getting to grips with the more complex instructions.' To counteract this Paul Skone, their graphic designer, produced the necessary information in a more user friendly way, taking into account the minimum information a customer requires to operate the product without risking damage to themselves or the product.

He produced a very visual generic manual in two parts: start up procedures, and more complex usage instructions. The start-up booklet is called **Quick Start** and is folded in an unusual way. The first fold reveals what is in the box and why it would be useful to open the next fold. Then there are clear drawings showing important information such as where the batteries go and where the leads go. The final fold reveals all you need to get started such as tuning instructions. As few words as possible were used and easy-to-follow steps were given such as, 'If you press this button on the remote control the TV screen will look like this.' He uses simple, clear graphics and as little technical jargon as possible.

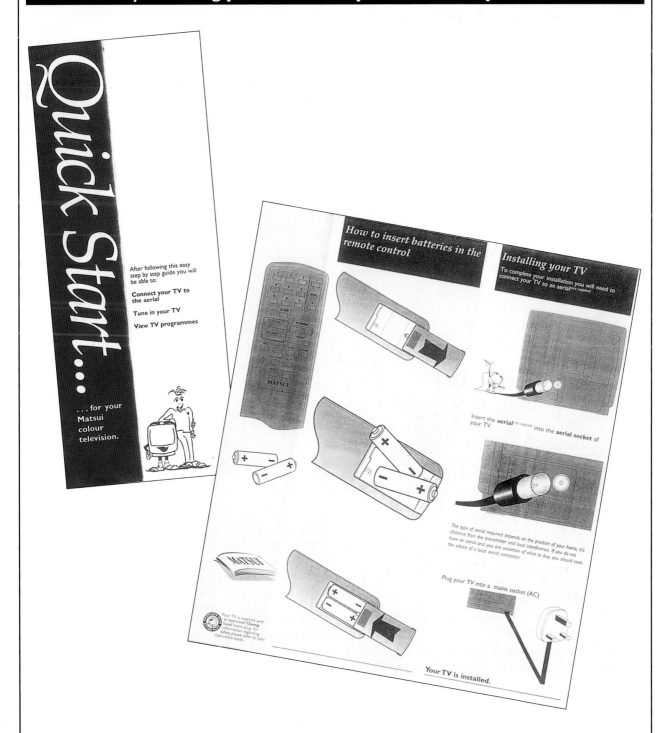

A Dixons Mastercare instruction leaflet.

A similar approach has been taken with the full manual. There are many legal requirements which must be met with this document. Safety warnings were rarely looked at when the customer trials were observed so Paul has used unusual symbols to draw attention to them. He has also used cartoon figures to give the manual a more user-friendly appearance.

The scheme has worked well. The design brief was to produce a better instruction book which would reduce the number of engineer call-outs. They have found that the number of 'Fault Found' calls has dropped dramatically saving the company thousands of pounds a year. More importantly, the customers have been more satisfied with their products. Paul's work has been so successful that he is advising other manufacturers about how to produce better manuals for their products. As he explains 'Ultimately, of course, the aim is to produce products that are so simple that they require little or no instruction, but that is unlikely to happen overnight'.

Case Study: **The role of scientific research in product development, Dalgetty**

This case study describes how Dalgetty, a major food group, builds on its strengths in research to add value through the effective application of technology. They therefore develop innovative products, which meet the requirements of today's customers in a highly competitive market.

Scientific research	The creation and knowledge of biological, chemical and physical processes that are required to develop enabling technologies. Scientific research is long term (over 3 years). It is normally carried out in research institutes and universities. Dalgetty accesses this research by funding some of the research and by keeping up to date with the published scientific literature.
Enabling technology	The key technologies that are important to Dalgetty in their new product development activities, are based on a full understanding of the scientific principles. In the case of Dalgetty, the key enabling technologies include: • Material functionality – correlating what a material does with its chemical and physical properties. • Flavour technology – extraction and analysis, chemical and biochemical synthesis, and delivery systems. • Process technology – extrusion, size management, preservation processing and applications. • Molecular biology. • Consumer sciences – matching consumer needs with material functionality.
New product development	The identification and development of new products to meet existing customer needs by raw materials selection, modification, combination and/or physical or chemical processing.
Brand maintenance and line extension	Changes to existing products by packaging, combination or simple modification of existing properties.

Types of technologies:

◆ **critical technologies** are the building blocks from which products develop
◆ **enabling technologies** are needed to make use of critical technologies
◆ **strategic technologies** are fundamental to develop new products in the future – in the long term they become the critical technologies.

For example, in developing new industrial robots:

◆ the critical technologies include the sensors and electronics that can be used in control systems
◆ the enabling technologies include drive motors and power control
◆ an example of a strategic technology is the development of artificial intelligence.

Focused task: Research and development

The Dalgetty case study provides an example of **technology push**. Choose one of the following case studies and draw up a similar table:

Psion, page 77.
Biotechnology, page 121.
Biopol, page 112.

You should also try to identify the critical, enabling and strategic technologies in that case study.

Designing and manufacturing – closing the gap

In this section we aim to clarify for you some of the major changes that are currently happening in commercial new product development that affect approaches to designing, manufacturing and to managing the whole process. Many of these changes are based on developments in the use of information and communications technologies (ICT).

Improving time-to-market

A major issue for manufacturing industry in the late twentieth century is the time it takes for new products to be developed and launched on the market. There are a number of reasons for this, not least being the increasingly competitive environment that companies find themselves working in and the accelerating pace of change. Consumers demand new products, expecting constant innovation.

The frequent release of new products stimulates an appetite for novelty and change. Fashions are created, for even the most unlikely products, by manufacturers and retailers wishing to stimulate demand. (Have you noticed what the latest fashion in domestic window frames is?) Companies in countries which are rising in competitiveness (e.g. Japan in the late 80s, Malaysia in the mid 90s) aggressively seek to take over market niches that have been previously dominated by others (e.g. Japanese cars in the late 80s, Malaysian cars in the 90s). Profit margins are trimmed, often to the point of being too small to sustain a period of slow sales, just as warehousing costs increase dramatically and the imperative for products to be shifted quicker increases.

Shareholders are less and less tolerant of drops in a company's performance, preferring to sell shares during lean times rather than wait for an upturn. Market situations are changing ever more rapidly, with the risk that the original specifications for a product are irrelevant by the time it reaches the market. (The Lotus Elan of the late 1980s lasted a very short time before being withdrawn, due to a recession causing a dramatic drop in demand for sports cars, only to be relaunched a few years later as the sports car market boomed – but by then it was out-of-date.)

This may sound like a nightmare scenario to you, but for many working in industrial management it is exactly what makes their job exciting and rewarding.

For the established, successful company to continue to survive, new product development is therefore essential and increasingly, this must happen at a faster rate. A well designed product hitting the market just as a slightly less well-designed one is establishing a good volume of sales, can be dead on arrival. Of course, the opposite is true – getting your product to market ahead of the opposition might be the single critical factor that makes it successful.

Of course, this scenario varies in different product sectors and in every sector there are products which seem to deny all the accepted wisdom and go successfully on for years. However, it is surprising to discover how critical time-to-market is in some apparently unlikely sectors. For example, this is true in the ten year 'race' to replace the Boeing 747 'Jumbo Jet' which had market dominance in the long haul sector for over twenty years, but then it takes a long time to design a new aeroplane.

The Dualit toaster – which has become a design classic, with a resurgence in sales in the 1990s, having originally been launched 50 years earlier in 1948.

▷ **Why do some products remain successful?**   63

Speed then, is of the essence in most designing, but equally important is getting things 'right first time' for mistakes cost money and cause delays, and delays as we have seen can cause total failure of a product. It has become very important therefore for the designing of a product to consider all the implications for how it will be manufactured, at as early a stage as possible. This would mean a smoother transition from idea to prototype to production item ensuring that the product is launched for sale earlier.

Consecutive engineering

A particular reason for product development time to become extended is the so-called 'over-the-wall' system of design and manufacture. This is characterised as a chain of departments contributing to the overall process, each of which carries out its part of the task and then 'hands it over' to the next.

| Identify the product opportunity | Produce concept drawings and models | Modify it to make it cost-effective to manufacture | Develop a production prototype (with changes) | ... it's too late |

The consecutive or 'over-the-wall' product development process.

It isn't unknown for one department to deliver their work to the next after those people have gone home on a Friday, to avoid difficult questions being raised immediately! Also, there is a widely acknowledged concept of 'degradation of information' which suggests that the more steps in a communication process, the more the quality of the information degrades. Chinese whispers are an example of this: try whispering a message around twenty people and see how different it can be by the time it reaches the end of the line. This can lead to an original design idea becoming very degraded as it passes through several separate departments on its way to production.

Relationships between the various departments involved in the same project can be very poor. Many designers working in this type of environment find themselves very frustrated because their beautiful designs end up spoilt by unsympathetic changes. Many production engineers regard their designers with contempt because they are always designing products that are over-complex or over-expensive to make. And the sales people are demoralised when expected to sell sub-standard products that they have no influence over.

In the case study of students working on the ASDA project (page 220) they reported that 'modifying the design to standard section materials changed the visual qualities and the proportions of the original design were lost.' This is just the sort of problem that arises when production considerations (e.g. standard sizes of material) are not given enough thought by designers. If someone in their team had been concerned with production from an early stage they might have designed from standard sizes rather than adapting to them later.

By contrast, the PDSA team (page 224) show how they consulted manufacturers initially at a very early stage and returned to them from time to time checking the evolution of their product's development ensuring that it was suitable for volume manufacture.

Coming to understand the limitations of their previous approaches, many companies have been developing processes known as **concurrent** (or **simultaneous**) **engineering**. This brings together different 'functions' (marketing, design, production, quality assurance etc.) to work concurrently, with frequent inter-communication, to speed the product development process, ensure 'manufacturability', improve the quality of the product and cut costs.

Concurrent engineering (CE)

In a commercial context almost anything can be measured in terms of its effect on the company's 'bottom-line', that is, its cost. Any of the failings inherent in consecutive engineering approaches that are characterised above can be seen to result in cost penalties to the company. These might be minor ones, such as when a design or production detail has to be changed, or catastrophic ones such as a new product on which the company's future depends reaching the market too late or being below quality expectations.

| ▷ | **The Ukettle case study** | **209** |

Clearly, the later in the product development process that changes have to be made the more they are likely to cost. This has been estimated as in the following diagram, the rule of thumb being that the cost of rectifying a design fault increases ten-fold as each step is completed. For example, the wrong specification of a steel instead of a brass washer, an item costing a few pence, involved one automotive manufacturer in calling back new cars already released into the market for it to be changed, at a cost of tens of thousands of pounds.

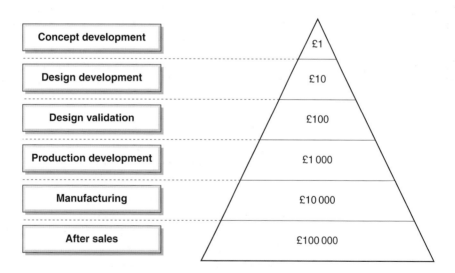

The escalating cost of rectification.

CE and information technology

Concurrent engineering is a way of organising and managing product development and these practices can be carried out using long established ways of designing, production engineering, marketing etc. However, information technology is ideally suited to supporting CE techniques. For example, a computer-aided design system utilises one database of information which can be made available at any number of workstations, distributed in any number of offices. For a concurrent engineering approach this is invaluable, as any member of a team at any company site can access the most up-to-date information as the design progresses – whereas traditional drawings can become out-of-date. However, the right to alter this database is strictly controlled as different people making changes to a complex design without co-ordination would soon lead to chaos.

Importantly for CE, information technology now supports much of the background administration of complex projects. This includes making communication between people working on the same project easier, through e-mail and other links, databases storing great quantities of information with quicker, simpler ways of accessing it, as well as the specific designing and manufacturing functions (CAD-CAM). CAD-CAM systems have been developed specifically to support concurrent engineering approaches especially by allowing highly sophisticated design modelling which can simulate the product in use and production processes. Modelling operational aspects can be illustrated through a car jack. The jack is designed to fit in a small niche in the car's boot. The designer can move it through its path from outside the car into the niche, on-screen, to check in three-dimensions, that sufficient clearance is available for the full range of movement – something that is very tricky, if not impossible to do in drawings. Problems discovered might be corrected by changes to the jack or to the niche in the main body, *before* a prototype is manufactured, ensuring that the time-to-market improvement potential of CE is further realised.

| ▷ | The impact of ICT on design and manufacture | 82 |

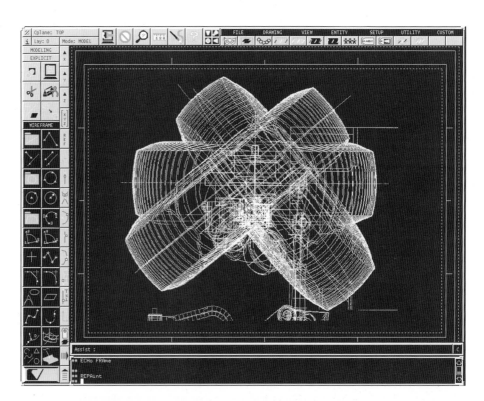

A dynamic computer model being used to check the 'wheel envelope' to ensure adequate clearance side to side and up and down for the front wheels of a car.

Manufacturing simulations allow the designer and production engineers to collaborate closely at an early stage considering manufacturing methods by, for example, 'running' a series of machining operations to check that tool paths do not clash with each other, that the sequence of operations is the most efficient achievable, or to time a series of operations to check for bottlenecks.

Rapid prototyping (the production of true three-dimensional models of complex components in a matter of hours, rather than days or weeks, using information technology) allows designers, engineers and others to discuss in detail how a part will be manufactured in volume as well as other design concerns.

| ▷ | Rapid prototyping | 178 |

Many other developments have been taking place since companies began to use CAD-CAM habitually. They have been able to exploit more fully the advantages of a database of design and production information held digitally within their CE approach. Known as **electronic product definition** (EPD), a digital database can be made use of in a greatly extended number of ways, each of which contributes to the overall efficiency of the product development process.

 Electronic product definition 85

Focused task: Consecutive and concurrent engineering

It is rare to see a company that uses concurrent approaches throughout its operations. Many move progressively from consecutive to concurrent over time, perhaps using the purchase of IT equipment to support significant changes of procedure (see the end of the Jaguar XK8 case study page 201). When you visit a manufacturing company consider how far they have progressed toward more concurrent engineering. Discuss with their managers what you are trying to design and ask for their guidance.

Here is a short checklist to help you:

When developing a new product or re-developing an old one, does the company:
- form a project team from different departments?
- include marketing and production inputs at an early stage in the design process?
- appoint a project manager?
- hold a series of project team meetings? (See Milestone Planning page 79.)
- have an IT system to assist communication within the team?
- investigate the manufacturing implications of each aspect of a the product e.g. material, fit with other parts, alternative manufacturing processes, in the design process?

Case Study: Product development for volume manufacture, Psion

This case study brings together many of the issues raised in the earlier parts of this chapter. Read the case study and carry out the focused task that follows to reinforce your own understanding of large scale manufacturing.

The case study looks at the development process used in Psion, a company that produces electronic organisers and palm-top computers. It illustrates the skills, processes and systems required by developments in industry. It has been adapted from a lecture given to the Institution of Electrical Engineers Electronic Education Conference by Dr David Potter, Founder and Chief Executive of Psion plc.

The roles of marketing, development and manufacturing

The creation of products to serve the market and meet people's needs is thrilling, creative, demanding, challenging and infinitely worthwhile. The creation of successful products is a holistic process involving large teams of people with many different skills working successfully together. While special skills are required, the most effective people are those who understand the team and the process as a whole. The creation of successful products involve those from:

- **Marketing** – identifying customer requirements.
- **Development** – designing and specifying the product to meet those requirements.
- **Manufacturing** – applying the tools, components and processes in production.

Our object is to serve the customer. In this competitive world, the successful companies will include only those who understand that they are there to serve the customer – not shareholders, employees, directors, suppliers or the government – the *customer*.

The Psion series 3 is an extremely versatile palm-top computer with a wide range of features including PC compatible applications such as: database, spreadsheet and word processor.

Case Study: **Product development for volume manufacture, Psion**
continued

This begs the question, 'Who is the customer?' The answer derives from the particular company's strategy, goals, skill-sets and market positioning. It is part of the role of **marketing** to identify the market segment and customer groups with precision and clarity. We need to understand the customers' needs, attitudes, income levels, work and social behaviour, demographic and indeed, psychological profiles. From this information we can construct product proposals which meet the requirements of the customer and products which therefore, have value, sell and create wealth.

Product development

In Psion, we use a five phase model for the creation of new products:

◆ The product proposal
◆ The design
◆ The specification
◆ Tooling and prototyping
◆ Piloting and release to manufacture.

Phase 1: The product proposal

The first phase is a consultative and discussion phase culminating in a proposal. The origination may come from anywhere in the company, but more typically will derive from **marketing** in identifying a clear, unfilled market need, or from **development** who may recognise that new technology may enable a new product. Either way, discussion, research and analysis will occur between these departments. The culmination of this process is a **proposal** which defines the requirements of the product, the market justification (volumes, unit costs, pricing), competitor analysis, a project timetable and cost.

This proposal will be reviewed extensively by management and, in Psion's case, by a formally constituted development committee of up to ten people. At this stage, we do not know that the conceptual product can be delivered according to the proposal, but with Development involvement, we believe it is possible.

Phase 2: Design

Once the proposal is accepted, a budget is authorised and people and resources are allocated. The next phase is the development of the **design** to meet or exceed the requirements of the proposal. The proposal is broken down into different aspects relying on different skill-sets. In the case of the Psion Series 3, these included operating system, applications software, digital electronic design, power management, mechanical design and ASIC development. But these different teams all had to liaise and work together.

It is during this phase that the overall design is developed, prototype components are evolved conceptually, breadboard designs raised to the working stage and a proved design developed.

At the completion of this phase the design is reviewed with the aid of block models, conceptual circuits, drawings and prototype components.

Phase 3: The specification

The third phase is the **specification** for the product, all components and the processes of manufacturing. This means the complete agreed definition of all components with chosen suppliers; comprehensive engineering drawings; the complete specification of all software components and drawings for tools etc.

The output from this phase consists of:

◆ a **bill of materials** – the specification for all of the components
◆ the **routings** – the processes or methods of manufacture.

In the case of the Series 3:

◆ The bill of materials is a list of about 200 components including detail specifications, tolerances and engineering drawings, the suppliers for each component and the unit cost of each component.

Availability:	with the user at all times size less than 300 cm³ weight less than 300 g battery life: 4 weeks use	Hardware:	solid-state disks graphic screen industry compatible Intel processor communications with PCs
Software:	windows metaphor (1988) agenda, database, spreadsheet, word processor file-compatible to PCs	Ergonomics:	use in the hand use on desk optimise navigation instantaneous, always live, multi-tasking
		Market:	high volume unit cost less than £100 list price £200–£400

Example of a product proposal: part of the proposal for the Psion Series 3.

Case Study: Product development for volume manufacture, Psion
continued

◆ The process includes the method of surface mount assembly for two circuit boards, the test procedures of in-circuit and functional test, the assembly of keyboards and screens and final assembly and test procedures.

To arrive at this stage, the process is iterative and aspects of the original conceptual product will have changed; the result may be substantially different from the original proposal or design.

Until now, the costs are all development costs, but from here on the scale of investment increases substantially.

Phase 4: Tooling and prototyping

Phase four implements the specification to construct the components. Where these are standard parts, this is simply a negotiation with suppliers. However, many parts will be **custom** and must now be 'tooled' for volume manufacture. This is the stage where **capital investment** is committed. For example, the forms for the castings will be machined out of steel in a complex and highly skilled process. Custom chips are produced and the software specifications finally programmed and tested.

At the end of this phase, the first real tooled prototypes are available for commercial and engineering review. The company can now see the real product and can therefore review, with some clarity, the extent to which the goals of the product have been met. Again a comprehensive review is required before the company commits itself to inventory, production and commercial distribution.

Phase 5: Piloting and release to manufacture

With high-volume manufacture, a further comprehensive phase is required to prove the design in production and to meet the requirements of the customer. This phase involves **volume pilot production**, **product quality evaluation**, **accelerated life tests** and **standard approvals**. For example, in the electronics industry products have to meet the requirements of the 'CE mark'. This includes very low-levels of radio emission to avoid interference. In addition, the product must be able to withstand static voltage discharges of up to 8 kV without impairment of function. During this phase, modifications may be made to tools and processes until the product has been proven for volume production.

Project management, working in groups

This five phase model relies on the extensive use of teamwork using multi-disciplinary teams. The key issues are the joint working of development, marketing and manufacturing teams, and the use of an iterative, rather than a linear, approach. The product is not technically led – it is **market led**. The value is not in the technical solution: the value is in meeting customer need.

Focused task: Case study analysis

In groups, consider how this case study illustrates the complete manufacturing process 'from customer need to customer satisfaction through manufactured products'. Then report back and discuss your conclusions as a class.

- How does the company identify ideas for new products?
- How does it exploit and develop latent needs?

- How does the company use **milestone planning** and a **multi-functional team** in product development? Explain what each of the functions is and the importance of each function at different stages in the product development process.
- Draw up a milestone plan for the product. You do not need to worry about details of timings but try to include some idea of the relative amount of time for each stage and where these stages overlap.

Milestone planning

Milestone planning is a key to the management of concurrent engineering, involving the setting of a series of goals or milestones and targets for achieving these throughout the development of the product. The use of milestone planning reduces the time taken to bring a new product on to the market.

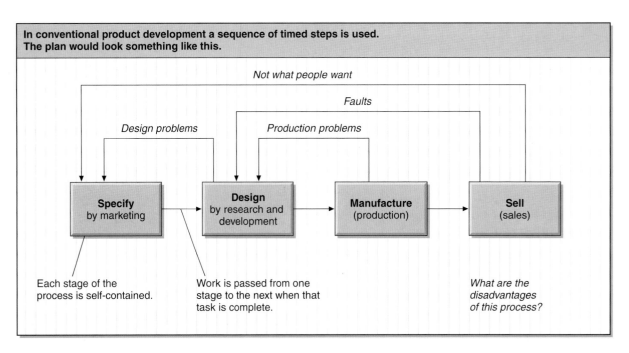

In conventional product development a sequence of timed steps is used.
The plan would look something like this.

Not what people want

Faults

Design problems

Production problems

Specify
by marketing

Design
by research and development

Manufacture
(production)

Sell
(sales)

Each stage of the process is self-contained.

Work is passed from one stage to the next when that task is complete.

What are the disadvantages of this process?

A sequential planning system.

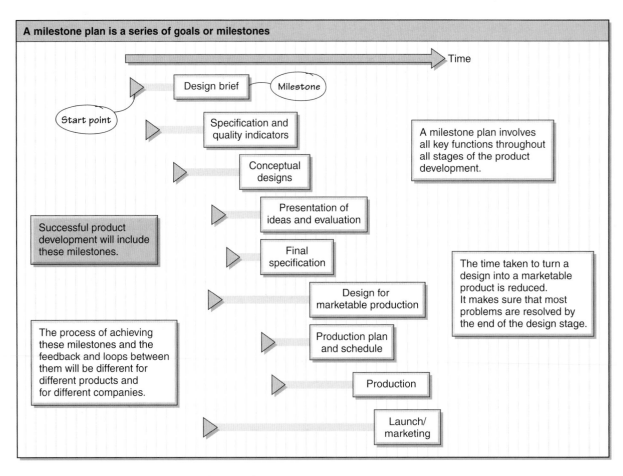

A milestone plan is a series of goals or milestones

Time

Design brief

Milestone

Start point

Specification and quality indicators

Conceptual designs

A milestone plan involves all key functions throughout all stages of the product development.

Presentation of ideas and evaluation

Successful product development will include these milestones.

Final specification

Design for marketable production

The time taken to turn a design into a marketable product is reduced.
It makes sure that most problems are resolved by the end of the design stage.

Production plan and schedule

The process of achieving these milestones and the feedback and loops between them will be different for different products and for different companies.

Production

Launch/ marketing

The use of product development teams in milestone planning.

MILESTONE PLAN
Product development team – responsibilities

SPECIFICATION	
Design brief	**Specification and quality indicators**
A typical product development team would include design, technical, production, financial, marketing, purchasing and quality functions. Although quality may be a separate function it is also the responsibility of everyone.	Developing the specification from the design brief involves the whole team.

DESIGN			
Conceptual design	**Presentation of ideas and evaluation**	**Final specification**	**Design for marketable production**
Producing conceptual designs will be led by design. Inputs from production, marketing, finance and quality are important if the designs are to be capable of production at the right level of quality and are marketable at the right price.	The presentation will be made by the design team. All other members of the team will evaluate the designs using their own expertise. The evaluation could also involve external agencies, customers, clients, senior management within the company and so on. *Is it marketable? Is it within budget? Will it meet the target price? Does it meet the quality standard? Can it be made within target cost? Does it use standard pre-manufactured components?*	The evaluation of the conceptual designs will help refine and improve the specification. At this stage production and purchasing issues become important. Quality indicators for manufacture can start to be developed alongside quality indicators for the final design.	A 'design for marketable production' has to be produced. The key issues are production and marketability. At this stage design, production and marketing considerations are all important. The **quality of the design** in meeting the specification and quality indicators has to be assessed.

MANUFACTURE	
Production plan and schedule	**Production**
This is the responsibility of the production team but the financial, purchasing and quality functions within the team will also play an important part. Also, planning for production may involve changes in the design. The design function therefore has a continuing role.	Overseeing the production is the responsibility of the production team liaising with purchasing. But the whole team still has a continuing monitoring role. The quality control and assurance role is also vital.

LAUNCH TO MARKET

▷ **Designing for manufacture**   128

You can apply the process of milestone planning to your own project. The main parts of the process are:

- to be clear about the key stages in your project or assignment
- to identify what the outcomes of each of these stages will be
- to be clear about how you will evaluate whether you have achieved the planned outcomes
- to build all these points into your schedule.

One of the key features of milestone planning and concurrency is the use of a 'project team' covering all of the functions needed. This team stays together throughout the life of the project. Different members of the team will take more important roles and spend more time on the project at different stages. In industry it is likely that some team members will be working on more than one project changing their priorities as the projects continue.

When you are working on your own projects or assignments there will be some occasions when you can work as part of a team in this way. However, there will be times when you will be working on an individual piece of work. In this case you will have to carry out all of the functions yourself. Even in this situation it is useful to:

- be clear about all of the functions that are needed; for example, market research, production planning etc.
- work out at which stages of your plan these functions are required
- decide on the relative importance of the functions and the time and resources each requires
- use this information to help you with developing your work schedule.

The impact of information and communication technology (ICT)

The increased use of information technology has had an enormous impact on designing and manufacturing. For example, in the areas of computer-aided design (CAD) and manufacture (CAM). This section focuses on how this use of IT has moved well beyond CAD/CAM and transformed manufacturing at all stages. Much of this is dependent on access to extremely rapid electronic transfer of vast amounts of information. For example, even when digital telephone lines were introduced 4 Mb of information took 40 minutes to transfer. With ISDN lines this was reduced to 4 minutes. ATM reduced this to about 1 second. This is where we are in the late 1990s. Where will we be in 5, 10, 20 years time?

Electronic Data Interchange (EDI)

Electronic Data Interchange is a mechanism that allows computers to communicate directly without the need for human intervention to re-enter information from computer generated documents. It transfers data files between trading partners, for example, between a retailer and a manufacturer. It has the effect of shortening the supply chain and speeding up the time taken to initiate and fulfil orders.

EDI has three basic requirements:

- a standard way of representing the data to be transferred so that it is recognisable to both computers – this is known as a **message standard**
- computer software which interfaces with in-house systems, allowing in-house data to be converted to the message standard and vice versa – this is known as **translation software**
- a method of transmitting standard data from one computer to another. This makes use of a variety of media including magnetic tape, one-to-one direct telecommunications links and networks allowing multiple connections to trading partners – the method chosen is the **communication medium**.

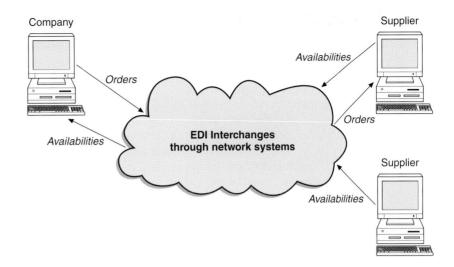

Company — Orders → EDI Interchanges through network systems ← Availabilities

Supplier — Availabilities ← / Orders ←

Supplier — Availabilities ←

Case Study: **Marks and Spencer**

Marks and Spencer pioneered Tradnet, the EDI communication system, and played a major role in setting up the standards that are essential for EDI. The company makes extensive use of IT and is a leader in high-tech retailing allowing them to retain a competitive edge and serve its customers better. The company has been using EDI since 1986.

Electronic point-of-sale tills

At the heart of Marks and Spencer's electronic revolution are the electronic point-of-sale (POS) tills. The IT systems which are transforming the company revolve around the detailed information which the POS tills gather about each store's sales. Every Saturday night the Company's central computers sort out the week's data from the POS tills and calculate what stock is needed by each store to replenish its sales. By Sunday afternoon, delivery instructions have gone out to suppliers, and the lorries start rolling. The first deliveries can be in the stores by Tuesday.

Keith Bogg, logistics divisional director, said "No other retailer has a distribution system that can collect information on what customers are buying one week and use it to organise deliveries into stores by the next week."

Do the right thing!

Before you read on be sure you are clear on these points:

- What are the implications of this system for the manufacturer?
- How will the information be used by the marketing department?
- How could the information be used by designers working for Marks and Spencer?

POS tills provide a better service to customers in other ways too.

- They are fast – they automatically look up prices, debit charge cards and print cheques.
- All POS tills are adapted to take both food and general merchandise – customers can pay for any purchase at any till; this provides flexibility in the store especially at peak time.
- The POS tills cut queuing time.

Speedier response – IT and the supply chain

Customer service is about having the right goods in the right place at the right time. Marks and Spencer head office can now base buying and distribution decisions on more accurate and up-to-date information.

The buying teams use desk top PCs fed with sales data from the POS tills giving them access to line-by-line and store-by-store product detail on how their departments are doing. They can respond to sales much sooner and if there is a need to revise estimates they can contact suppliers at an earlier stage in production when changes are easier to make. Each season, the first week's sales indicate which colours will be the best sellers. The indications come early enough to change the colour before the product comes off the production line. There is scope for extra allocation so that the supply chain can respond quickly providing extra production when sales change unexpectedly, for example, due to changes in the weather. Most suppliers use the computers to make their production schedules more flexible so that they can react sooner to sales in the stores. For example, if sales of men's suits are higher than expected for, say, 44" long fit jackets and 38" waist 33" leg trousers, Dewhirst – the manufacturer – knows instantly from its computer what cloth has been cut and in what sizes and can alter the ratios in production.

Case Study: **Marks and Spencer** *continued*

Buying departments must make sure that the suppliers are told quickly and accurately what to send where. During Wednesday night suppliers' computers send up-to-the-minute details of stock availability to head office computers. On Thursday morning the information is ready and waiting for the distribution teams to work out store allocations for the following week. If the distributors find themselves short of lines which are known to be in production, the computers are asked to up-date availability on Friday. Without this fast access to the latest information, stock which could be selling in stores might well be sitting at the suppliers.

The communication is two-way. Over the weekend, while head office is closed, buying department computers receive the previous weeks sales data from stores, calculate automatically the replenishment stock they need and feed the information to the suppliers' computers so that delivery instructions are ready on Sunday afternoon.

Stock control

The information from the electronic POS tills is used to monitor every store each day; the computers spot the warning signs of a possible sell-out, and respond rapidly by building up deliveries. If sales are below estimate, deliveries are cut back.

Hand-held terminals (HHTs) link sales assistants to a nationwide computer network which is revolutionising stock ordering and delivery. HHTs tell staff exactly what stock is in their warehouse, let them order what they want at the touch of a button, and guarantee that what they order is what they get.

Hand-held terminal as used for stock control.

Case Study: **How CAD can help research product ideas – Picture Portfolio by Gerber Garment Technology**

Designers need to research colour, style, current trends and what their competitors are doing. The database Picture Portfolio by Gerber Garment Technology is a powerful CAD system that allows designers to manage research data. Designers can input images, design drawings and style information into Picture Portfolio from colour scanners, digital cameras, Kodak Photo-CDs, video frames, AutoCAD drawings, 35 mm slides, spreadsheets and drawing software. Information can be collected in one location, stored in a digital camera, transferred to a laptop and sent to the design office via a modem.

Research data can be edited to produce the product image and technical data needed for the manufacture of the product.

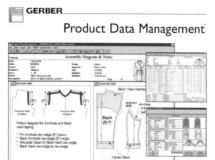

Stop and think!

Computer software enables designers to scan images from magazines, postcards, photographs or books and edit the images on screen. Is this a creative way of developing ideas? Is it necessary for designers to draw? Is it possible to learn visual skills electronically?

Do the right thing!

Use CAD to help you collect visual information.

- Take photographs with a standard camera, collect and draw images and use a hand-held or table-top scanner to input these images into a database.
- Import information from a CD-ROM.
- Use a still digital video camera to take photographs or pictures for a web page. Download this information into a PC or laptop computer.
- Experiment with and edit your chosen images to develop ideas and colourways.
- Print out your images to present ideas, import into DTP software or use presentation software to show your ideas on screen with music or text.

Electronic Product Definition (EPD)

EPD is a form of product development in which all of the product and process data is generated only once and then captured and stored electronically as one database. This database evolves as the new product is developed, with the data made available electronically to team members who add to it or use it for making decisions. This enables the manufacturer to take an integrated 'whole product' approach to product definition.

EPD makes use of a new approach to CAD/CAM known as **Total Product Modelling** (TPM). TPM captures the form, fit and function of a product and its constituent parts within a single computer model. This includes all of the mechanical, electrical and manufacturing disciplines. This is being taken even further through **Virtual Product Development** (VPD) or **Virtual Manufacturing**. This enables a new product to be developed, including defining its manufacturing processes, within a computer system. It integrates product development and manufacturing into a seamless process.

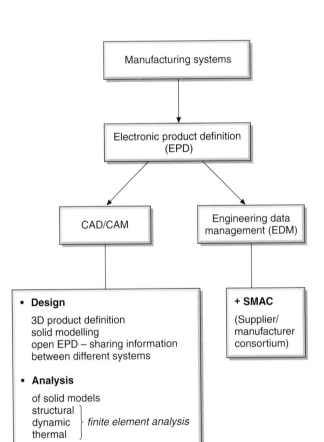

- **Concurrent engineering**

  What do you do when people and departments are in a different part of the country/world?
  ⇒ dependent on communications – information super highway

- **Engineering data management (EDM)**

  "Collecting together, structuring and storing all information about a product or component electronically"

- **Vault**

  Storage of all information about product development

- **Product Structure**

- **Release mechanisms**

  Control of access to information
  Automatically transmits information to appropriate people for action and monitors the action

- **Workflow**

  Who, when, sees information?
  What form is information in?

Case Study: The Advantages and benefits of EPD

The Rolls-Royce Trent 800 aero engine

Defining the external elements of the Trent 800 aero-engine in a single electronic database provided Rolls Royce with effective concurrent engineering with Boeing, the aircraft manufacturer, on the 777 long-haul jet aircraft.

◆ It eliminated the need for two of the usual three physical mock-ups saving millions of pounds.
◆ It reduced the need for rectification by making the pipes and harnesses fit first time.
◆ It saved twelve weeks in the design process.
◆ It reduced development costs by 35%.
◆ It allowed the development version of the engine to be built directly from the computer screen.

Trent 800 aero engine on a Boeing 777.

The Andersen Corporation

The Andersen engineering company introduced EPD for the following reasons:

◆ Electronic exchange of data with suppliers cuts turnaround times and costs.
◆ Quality is improved through minimising the re-creation of data.
◆ New process equipment designed using EPD will bring annual savings of $1 million through reduced waste material.
◆ Assembling components digitally has reduced re-working by 20% by improving the new product's form, fit and function on-screen first.
◆ Parts and the tooling that will be used to make them can be developed, simultaneously drawing on the same database, saving time.
◆ Rapid prototyping, using the information in the EPD database, reduces the prototyping process from days or weeks to hours.

SMAC (Supplier and Manufacturer in Automotive Consortia): extending EPD

SMAC have extended EPD to achieve even greater integration of processes through IT by allowing an engineer or designer to:

◆ select a component on screen
◆ check it meets the specification and quality criteria required and the purchasing arrangements
◆ check test data and study a video sequence of the test being carried out to make sure it conforms to the test requirements
◆ check availability, cost etc.
◆ video conference with the supplier to discuss other details if necessary
◆ 'slot' the component into the assembly on screen
◆ order and provide stock control information.

The Rover Group

The Land Rover Discovery was brought to market in less than three years against a European average of seven years.

Rover find that using EPD:

◆ brings design and manufacturing closer by using one set of data to drive both.
◆ integrates the supply chain and facilitates concurrent engineering through rapid exchange of data in a common electronic form.
◆ reduces risk, time to market and cost through validating designs via digital on-screen assembly and rapid prototyping. This reduces quality problems that could arise downstream in the manufacturing process.
◆ enables a 'products not parts' approach providing the ability to manipulate and develop the product design as a single entity.
◆ allows manufacturing and logistics processes to be developed simultaneously with the product, by making use of the same database.
◆ builds an electronic products and processes database that will act as the company's knowledge base for developing future products.

Textiles and product data

Gerber Garment Technology

Gerber Garment Technology, Inc. develops **computer integrated manufacturing systems** (CIMs) for the textiles, automotive, aerospace and industrial fabric product markets. Gerber Information Systems provide electronic product definition (EPD) software to enable manufacturers world-wide to automate the design and manufacture of up-to-the-minute products, so that they 'get it right first time on time'. The Gerber EPD system is called Product Data Management.

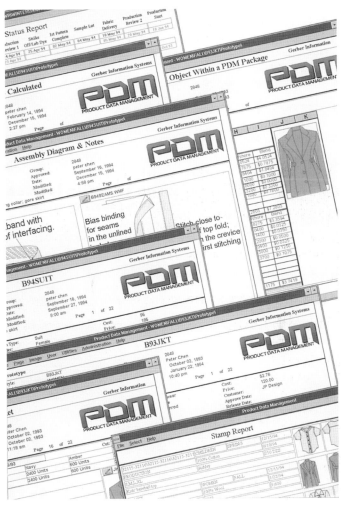

Stop and think

The use of IT systems enables manufacturers to make their products on a global scale, with the possibility of having a design office in one country and the production in another. What is the social impact of this 'globalisation' of manufacture on employment world-wide? Often manufacturing takes place in 'developing' countries, where land and labour is cheaper. How can companies that manufacture in 'developed' countries compete with so called low-wage economies?

PDM is an industry standard software package that organises and communicates accurate, up-to-date information for manufacturers and retailers. The PDM database is like an electronic filing cabinet, with access for each individual in the product development team. When changes are made in design, fabric or costing the information can be automatically sent to the designer, pattern-maker, costing department and materials planner who need this accurate up-to-date information. Information can be exchanged via a network of computer systems or stand-alone workstations using local-area networks (LAN) or global telecommunications.

For example, designers can research style information in one country and download from a laptop computer via a modem to the central design office in another, where product development can begin. The final product specification can be sent to the manufacturing site and quality can be monitored on the production line using digital cameras, linked to the design office.

Littlewoods Home Shopping and Product Data Management

Littlewoods Home Shopping makes use of PDM to manage the production of clothing and footwear for their customer base in the UK. PDM enables Littlewoods to standardise manufacturing procedures and documentation. Paper records have been replaced by data files which provide clear, instantly accessible information for Littlewoods suppliers and for the whole product team.

The benefits for textile manufacturers of using Product Data Management

Starting with a design illustration, the designer can build product information around it.

PDM allows manufacturers to:

- Start with a design illustration and build product information around it, keeping track of design changes, style numbers and costs.
- Customise specification sheets to suit their manufacturing needs, including construction details.
- Use a digital camera to add colour images to specification sheets, so pictures with notes can be sent to the production site anywhere in the world, showing how a garment is to be constructed.
- Manage concurrent product design, development, merchandising and production.
- Communicate manufacturing data to the office next door, between cities, or throughout the world.
- Record and monitor costs including fabrics, accessories, labour costs, freight, overheads.
- Monitor quality assurance by automatically calculating grading and measuring information for each garment.
- Monitor quality control on the production line by using digital cameras linked to the central office.
- Reduce product time-to-market.
- Successfully use quick response manufacturing techniques.

Textiles is a fast moving industry which needs to produce quality products that the consumer wants. Some manufacturers can have five or more 'seasons' a year, so the right information is vital to sell the right product at the right time. Companies that want to stay competitive need to manage this information so that product development is fast, resulting in a quality product that may have been designed in one country and manufactured in another. Electronic product definition enables manufacturers to manage information in a complex global economy.

Do the right thing!

Using ICT in your work

- How do you use ICT in your own designing and manufacturing?
- What ICT is available to you in school?
- How much of this do you use?
- Are you using the ICT to its full potential?
- How could you make more effective use of the ICT available in your school?
- What ICT is available to you outside of school?
- Can any of this be accessed from within the school?
- What ICT is available through links you have with local companies and other organisations?
- How could you make use of this?

Focused task: Using ICT

Use ICT systems to help your product development.

- Design a pro-forma specification sheet that can be used to specify the requirements of the products you make.

- Keep a database file of all your product specifications to help you monitor product development and quality control.

Case Study: ICT in schools' Design and Technology

Denfords remote manufacturing

Once a company (or school) is using CAD and CAM, the distance between the sites of these two functions can be extended – as long as excellent communication is maintained – through telecommunications. However, for complex designs to be machined on any particular piece of CNC machinery, it almost always involves some conversation between designer and production controller or machinist despite the main design information being contained in the CAD file.

Information and communication technology (ICT) opens this possibility as more channels of communication can be carried together with the CAD data. Video conferencing sends video pictures, sound and data along telephone lines allowing operators at each end to see and speak to each other, to send notes and to share control of applications programs such as computer-aided design.

A student and her teacher connected to the technician at the remote manufacturing centre through video conferencing.

A classroom video-conferencing screen showing a notebook section and a CNC machine at the remote manufacturing centre.

With the price of PCs and software falling this has now become possible for schools. Designs are created at one end on a PC and the CAD/CAM software then creates the special file ready for the CAM operation. Connecting with a manufacturing centre, live video conferencing allows the student designer to download their CAM file, talk to the technicians there to agree any modifications or special instructions and then watch their design being produced on a CNC machine. The part can then be checked by the technicians, and on-screen by the student, and sent to them by post.

For industrial companies remote manufacturing can reduce dramatically the amount of transportation of goods required, movement of personnel and duplication of expensive manufacturing facilities allowing a global company to integrate its new product development, world-wide. To achieve this depends on five factors:

◆ A digital design model (CAD).
◆ Computer controlled manufacture (CNC or CAM).
◆ Compatible file standards for data transfer.
◆ CAD/CAM integration (CIM) through efficient direct telecommunications between design and manufacturing sites.
◆ Software to share the communications channels effectively and provide user-friendly access and control (e.g. video conferencing).

In schools, this system offers students a taste of the latest industrial approaches to manufacturing, development of their communication skills and a much lower cost way of ensuring that all schools can access CAD/CAM.

Evaluation in designing

Evaluative judgements are made throughout designing. First decisions might be 'this is *worth* doing' or 'we *could* . . .' or 'this *needs* to . . .' all of which are **evaluations**. The reasons why a company may start on a design project are likely to be based on commercial evaluations – that the product is likely to sell well and make profits for the company. Design projects also come about because of people's needs. Every need is a judgement – if only that one need is greater than another – so will be given priority attention.

The aesthetics of a product will be based on aesthetic judgements, and perhaps commercial ones too, 'this way will sell'. In all these judgements, the feelings, prejudices and bias of individuals will come into play, but the conscious and professional designer will become more aware of these influences and will increasingly make judgements based on more objective criteria. For example, these would include 'This is the right aesthetic for the client group' rather than 'I like it this way'.

The professional, systematic, aware designer might still design products which have outcomes which are unforeseen. This is not least because of the complexity of the world in which those products are used, they may be used in contexts that were unforeseen or unknown to the designer or the contexts may change as time moves on and the product continues to exist. Particular responsibility rests on those who develop new ways of doing things – new technologies. The history of the world is littered with ideas that created products which had consequences that were unforeseen, from dynamite (developed for peaceful purposes by Alfred Nobel) to the ballpoint pen-top that a child choked on (before the design was changed to incorporate a hole). As the capacity of humankind increases and the scale and consequences of human actions have greater and greater implications it has become necessary for us to be more systematic in predicting, and controlling the outcomes of our innovations.

At the national and international level: evaluating technologies

We have come to realise that we have a collective, global, responsibility to look ahead and plan for the future. However, this responsibility may often be in direct conflict with immediate, local, political, economic, social or other needs. Although the evaluation of potentials and risks in new technologies is as old as technology itself, systematic methods to predict the potential outcomes from technological developments did not evolve until the late 1960s and early 1970s. The initial methods are largely credited to the US space programme.

Technology assessment looks at, amongst other things, issues in:

- concepts of quality
- opportunity assessment (including commercial opportunities)
- risk assessment
- evaluation of environmental and social impact.

Focused task: International impacts

Suppose someone develops a strain of wheat which yields outstandingly heavy crops even in drought-like or over-wet conditions but the seeds of this wheat are genetically engineered so that they cannot be used to grow further crops – and this strain of wheat is sold world-wide.

- What might be the social impact?
- What might be the economic impact?
- What value-system does such a development imply?
- Can a technological development like this be justified?

Some argue that the pace and breadth of current and future technological change are so great that systematic assessment is impossible. Others say that the risks for the future of the human race and our planet are so great that we can not possibly afford to let technological development go ahead unregulated.

Technology assessment will inevitably be heavily influenced by the viewpoint of the assessor; whether they are concerned with maximising economic or social benefits or minimising negative impacts; whether they are focused on the short or long term; whether they are objective; what influences bear on them and whether they are aware of the values they bring to the process.

In reading the following three sections you will see how varied approaches to technological assessment can be, how they are influenced by the perspective they come from and something of the difficulties governments face in assessing technologies.

The first part describes a technology assessment programme at governmental level in the UK – the Foresight Programme. The second outlines the current situation in the USA, and the third is from a West Indies perspective.

Technology Assessment, UK: The Foresight Programme

A report from Ruth Wright, England

The Technology Foresight Programme was set up in 1993 and co-ordinated by the Office of Science and Technology (part of the Cabinet Office) on behalf of the Government. The main objectives of this programme were to:

- consider how the UK can take best advantage of the markets and technologies likely to emerge during the next decade or two
- identify the investments and actions needed to exploit these markets and technologies
- inform on Government spending decisions.

The Foresight Programme was set up within a UK context which felt that knowledge and skills in Science, Engineering and Technology would be vital to future national competitiveness. It was expected that companies in the UK would become more and more dependent on knowledge-based products and processes. One of the main purposes of the programme is to help engineers, business people and scientists to get to know more about what each other are doing. So networks of partnerships were established to work together, looking at the possible future. The programme was also to help to ensure that resources were used to best effect in support of wealth creation and improving the quality of life. The results of the Foresight Programme are made available to small and medium sized enterprises [SMEs] who may not have the resources to undertake foresight work themselves.

The sectors covered by the programme are shown below:

Agriculture, horticulture & forestry	Transport	Chemicals
Construction	Defence & aerospace	Energy
Financial services	Food & drink	Health & life sciences
Retail & distribution	IT, electronics & communications	Leisure & learning
Manufacturing, production & business processes	Marine	Materials
Natural resources & environment		

Although the main focus of the programme is on the contribution that science, engineering and technology can make to wealth creation, the sector panels involved also consider other factors. These include:

- a work-force with relevant skills and market awareness
- technologically aware management
- social, economic and regulatory policies that are conducive to innovation.

The Foresight Programme: cross-sector themes

1 Communications and computing power: applications here will be pervasive in all sectors of the economy.
2 New organisms, products and processes from genetics: these have enormous potential in health, agriculture, food and environmental protection.
3 Advances in materials science, engineering and technology: development of materials — processing technology and of lightweight, recyclable, 'smart' and environmentally-friendly materials.
4 Getting production processes and services right: through developing and harnessing technologies in fields like sensors, automation and security.
5 The need for a cleaner, more sustainable world: embracing pollution monitoring and control technologies, as well as technologies for conserving energy and resources.
6 Social trends: e.g. the impact of demographic change in creating new markets and the acceptability of new technology in the workplace and home. Improving the understanding of the human factors involved in markets and scientific advance will be just as important as the advances themselves.

(Source: Department of Science and Technology, August 1995.)

The United States' Office of Technology Assessment

A report from Patti Hutchinson, The College of New Jersey, USA

In 1966, Congress undertook a study of the need for expert and non-partisan help in assessing technologies about which they would increasingly be asked to make decisions. Congress members felt ill-equipped to manage government funds for the huge projects being envisaged. They knew that the American public shared a general distrust of science and felt a need to raise public consciousness about the potential and limitations of science and technology. Meanwhile, their own experience with informational hearings had demonstrated that scientific experts, like other mortals, were subject to bias in their assessments. In 1972, to strengthen their position against the decision-making power of the executive branch (the President), they established the Office of Technology Assessment (OTA). It was seen as a mechanism for inhibiting the introduction of policies likely to be harmful in environmental or social terms. By 1975, the OTA had a working budget of $8 million and a staff of 100 people.

The OTA's job was to provide congressional committees with objective analyses of emerging, difficult and often highly technical issues, specifically to:

- identify existing or probable impacts of technology or technological programs
- where possible, ascertain cause and effect relationships
- identify alternative technological methods of implementing specific programs
- identify alternative programs for achieving requisite goals
- make estimates and comparisons of the impacts of alternative methods and programs
- present findings of completed analyses to the appropriate legislative authorities
- identify areas where additional research or data collection is required to provide adequate support for the assessments and estimates described above
- undertake such additional associated activities as the appropriate authorities may direct.

To do this, the agency operated with a multi-disciplinary staff who drew extensively on the technical and professional resources of universities, industry, public interest and citizen groups, state and local officials and individuals. OTA reports were published by the US Government Printing Office, and summaries of reports were available free of charge from the OTA. (Source: General Information Brochure, January, 1990.)

The OTA was widely respected for the thoroughness and impartiality of their reports on such diverse topics as security issues, governmental efficiency, education and commerce. However, in 1994, a congressional task force headed by Representative Pete Domenici (Republican, New Mexico) recommended eliminating the OTA as a $22 million/year cost-cutting measure. After 23 years and 750 reports, the OTA closed its doors on September 30, 1995.

Assessing Technology in Trinidad: a 'developing' country's perspective

A report from Glenda Prime, The University of the West Indies

The classification of a country as either *developed*, or *developing* is based on the extent to which certain socio-economic indicators exist in that country. These indicators are always directly or indirectly linked to technology. To a large extent, it is the ability to create and use technologies and until recently this meant specifically the manufacturing technologies, which determined the presence of those socio-economic indicators.

The terms *developed* and *developing* are not however neutral and carry with them implicit value-laden status differences, which suggest that *developing* countries aspire to become, or will one day be, like the *developed* ones are now. Since technology is so central to this notion, the acquisition of technologies, most often the products rather than the processes, has come to be regarded as a symbol of a country having moved closer to the preferred developed status.

In this way developing countries (some people prefer the term 'majority countries' to remind us that such countries are in the majority in the world) have come to acquire a taste for products and technologies that originate in metropolitan countries. Thus the country of origin has come to be an important value by which the worth of a technology is judged. This situation also has roots in the history of the relationship that existed between metropolitan countries and their colonies, in which the metropole controlled the economies of the colonies by limiting production in the colonies to those goods which catered to metropolitan tastes. In this post-colonial era, it is those former colonies that are now the developing countries, and the legacy of taste for things foreign continues to influence consumption patterns.

The evaluation of a technology almost always involves the balancing of a range of values which are sometimes in conflict with one another. In such cases it is the context that should determine the relative importance of those values. This is the concept of **appropriateness** in technology. It is the extent to which contextual factors are taken into account in determining which values are given the greatest emphasis in the creation and use of technologies.

Given the historical and contemporary relationships between the developed and majority world countries mentioned earlier, values that relate to the environment, to the social and cultural context and even to the economy often come second – in favour of foreign goods and foreign technologies. Most of the majority world countries are plagued by problems of high unemployment, food insecurity and under-application of technologies in areas such as agriculture and manufacturing. Attention to these problems seems to indicate that labour-intensive technologies using indigenous materials and technologies that are suited to the prevailing social and cultural peculiarities, are more appropriate than imported foreign technologies. These are capital-intensive and provide few jobs.

Trinidad and Tobago is a twin-island state of just over one million people situated at the most southerly end of the chain of Caribbean Islands. An example from here illustrates the dominance and persuasiveness of the **foreignness value** on the technological development of the country. The economy in Trinidad and Tobago is petroleum-based and thus the period of high oil prices on the world market (the mid-seventies to the mid-eighties), was a period of economic prosperity for the country. It was a time when surplus funds generated by the oil sector should have been used to foster developments in other sectors of the economy. The Government chose to develop a steel manufacturing industry but this failed to produce the benefits that were expected and the industry was for a long time a drain on the country's economy. The reasons were not hard to find. It was a time when the world market for steel was declining and Trinidad and Tobago was but a poor competitor on the shrinking market. Further, the industry used raw materials that were not available locally and provided relatively few jobs.

The foreignness value seemed to be a major factor in the decision to develop a steel industry. Steel manufacturing was associated with developed countries and was a symbol of prosperity. The end of the story however, is instructive. The industry has become a major contributor to the nation's revenue, but only since a considerable portion of its shareholding was invested with a foreign company, under whose expertise it is now managed.

The argument is that it is not just appropriate to use indigenous technologies. The countries of the developing world cannot avoid dependence on imported technologies. To do so, would be to sacrifice efficiency, competitiveness and quality of life. What is necessary is a careful weighing of values, costs and benefits – in spiritual, social, cultural and environmental, as well as technical and economic terms – so as to select those technologies which are most appropriate. Furthermore, the conditions within the majority world countries should be such that maximum benefits could be derived from the foreign technologies with a minimum of dependence on the country from which the technology originates.

 Neocreole cooking pot   126

The evaluation of technologies is always a matter of resolving conflicting values, and the concept of appropriateness, is equally applicable to the developed as the developing countries. There is always the danger that technical and economic values will be given more prominence than social, cultural, spiritual and environmental ones resulting in inappropriate choices. Whenever this happens, in developed or developing countries, we are all losers.

At the company level: social responsibilities

For some time it remained unargued that companies are in business for commercial reasons – to make money – and that is their sole concern. Almost all countries have comprehensive safeguards in place to check on the soundness of companies' financial behaviour, requiring them to produce financial accounts, have them regularly audited and make them public.

Various action groups have tried hard to make companies also audit and account for their behaviour in respect of non-financial criteria such as environmental (e.g. reducing pollution) and social (e.g. improving the quality of life for their workers).

Events such as animal liberation activists invading companies' laboratories and the prevention of the disposal of the redundant Brent Spar oil rig (in 1996) as Shell intended (with Government support) have been highly confrontational. However, some companies and their shareholders have been adopting more collaborative approaches. **Social accounting** (and **social auditing**) acknowledges the fact that the impacts of a company's activities on people can be influential on the success of the company in similar ways to the financial accounts (see the 'mission statement' at www.benjerry.com).

Other companies are actively working with pressure groups to ensure that their actions are appropriate – environmentally and socially. An example of this is the collaboration between do-it-yourself chain B&Q and the World Wildlife Fund. B&Q was a founder member, in 1995, of the WWF 'Tick-tree' scheme which marked their timber as having come from a source which had been certificated as environmentally sustainable. Following this they expanded their links to network people throughout B&Q and WWF to work together. The company's experiences offered WWF a valuable insight into the realities of trying to balance commercial and conservation success, while WWF contributed conservation expertise and encouragement.

The central question is how a company which aims to meet customers' demands for consumption can be reconciled with an organisation whose purpose is to conserve those same resources. Arguably, we are not going to change the world back to a low population-low consumption situation, neither are we likely to see many companies exist which regard financial success as of secondary importance to environmentally appropriate activities. Finding ways to achieve a publicly accepted balance between these competing criteria will therefore be important.

Reducing environmental impact through design

Developed countries, by definition, enjoy a high standard of living supported by the use of modern technology. This has a range of environmental impacts such as: the wastes and by-products from the manufacturing process; those from the disposal of products at the end of their useful life and the pollution caused by burning fossil fuels.

In designing and manufacturing products account should be taken of the need for:

- more efficient use of energy and other natural resources, and the increased use of sustainable resources
- more effective use of materials, including a reduction in amounts used, and the re-use and recycling of waste materials and by-products
- minimal environmental impact from the products and the processes used to manufacture them and the safe disposal of waste
- all future technology is designed taking full account of environmental criteria.

As with all design decisions, the optimal approach is looked for, achieving a balance between the benefits and costs. This is often referred to as 'making trade-offs'. Balancing the needs of consumers against the environmental impact of the product or the processes used in manufacturing it can be tricky.

CHAPTER THREE   **Designing**

The preceding chapter has focused on broad design and manufacturing issues from the international and national levels down to how particular companies (which might be international) should operate. However, it is not always easy for a company or a design team working for it to keep in mind these broad, sometimes grand, ethical issues when concerned with a particular product. It is even harder for you as a student designer/ manufacturer. The intention of this chapter therefore is to provide you with a range of strategies, illustrated with examples of their use by companies, which you may be able to apply to your own product design process. We start by continuing the theme of environmental impacts and go on to other design considerations including new materials and technologies, detailing and using standard components. All this is to help you with your design projects.

Firstly, as a caution, the example below shows how a product which was legitimately designed to exploit a new technology in a valuable way may provoke conflicts with broader environmental considerations.

Case Study: **The cold drinks can**

The **cold drinks can** developed by an American company will chill the contents of a can without a refrigerator in less than two minutes. In doing this it releases into the atmosphere a gas (HFC 134a) which is over 1000 times more potent than carbon dioxide in contributing to global warming – sometimes referred to as the 'greenhouse effect'. When the can was revealed Britain urged the European Union nations to ban it because of these harmful environmental effects. The British company which makes the gas HFC 134a for use in sealed refrigeration units, has refused to supply the gas to the can manufacturer.

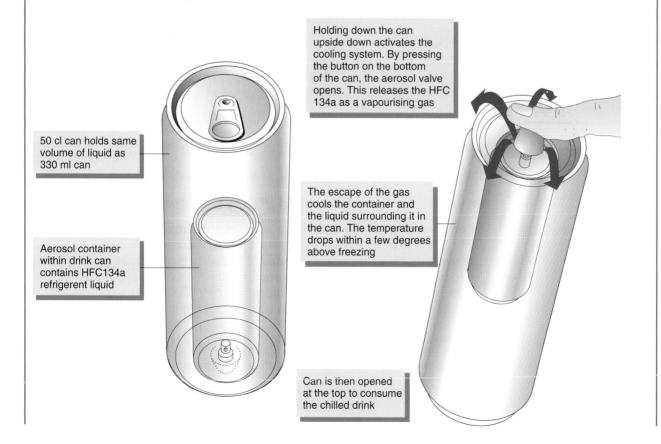

Holding down the can upside down activates the cooling system. By pressing the button on the bottom of the can, the aerosol valve opens. This releases the HFC 134a as a vapourising gas

50 cl can holds same volume of liquid as 330 ml can

The escape of the gas cools the container and the liquid surrounding it in the can. The temperature drops within a few degrees above freezing

Aerosol container within drink can contains HFC134a refrigerent liquid

Can is then opened at the top to consume the chilled drink

Reduce, re-use and recycle

The amount of material used in a product, and therefore the resources and energy used in extracting and processing that material, should be **reduced** as far as possible. A process known as **life-cycle assessment** (LCA) can be used to evaluate this impact 'from the cradle to the grave' – the complete life cycle of the product from raw materials to final disposal.

Wherever possible products should be designed so that the product or parts of the product can be **re-used**. Designers should also consider in the design of a product, the use of materials that can be **recycled**. At the end of the product's life these materials can be processed into a form that can be used in other products. Products can also be designed for **easy maintenance** so that parts can replaced rather than having to throw away the complete product.

In Germany manufacturers and retail stores are required to take back all packaging materials such as cardboard boxes and styrofoam. The plan is that consumers will be able to return sales packaging to the point of purchase for disposal; by 1996 manufacturers were responsible for collecting about 80% of packaging waste. A private company, Duales System Deutschland, has distributed collection bins to virtually all of Germany's 80 million population.

The bag on the left is disposable but can be **recycled** to produce bags like the right hand one which is **re-usable**.

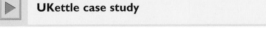
UKettle case study 209

Environmental audits and life-cycle assessments

An **environmental review** is the first step towards improving the environmental performance of a company, organisation or on-going activity. It involves a systematic review of impacts and should identify how performance can be improved. This should result in an environmental policy which is an overall statement of aims for environmental improvement. This should be capable of being translated into targets for improvement over a specified period of time. There should be a plan that states how the targets will be achieved.

Environmental audits involve regular and systematic monitoring and review of performance against the targets laid out in the environmental policy statement.

Environmental assessment is a technique for listing and analysing the environmental impacts of a new development or process against agreed criteria and attaching relative importance.

Life-cycle assessment (LCA) is one process for evaluating the environmental impact of a product 'from the cradle to the grave'. The environmental impact is assessed at every stage from extraction of raw materials to the final disposal of the product. It involves identifying and quantifying at every stage:

- the energy used
- the materials used
- any other resources used
- wastes released into the environment
- the effects on the environment and on people.

Financial costs would be considered alongside LCA to give the complete picture. **Value engineering** and **value marketing** are increasingly used by companies to maximise the usefulness of their products to customers. LCA can help to ensure that the **life-cycle value** of a product is not undermined by avoidable environmental impacts or costs. A crucial step in making sure that an LCA is both manageable and meaningful is setting the **system boundaries**. This defines what components and operations are to be included in the assessment.

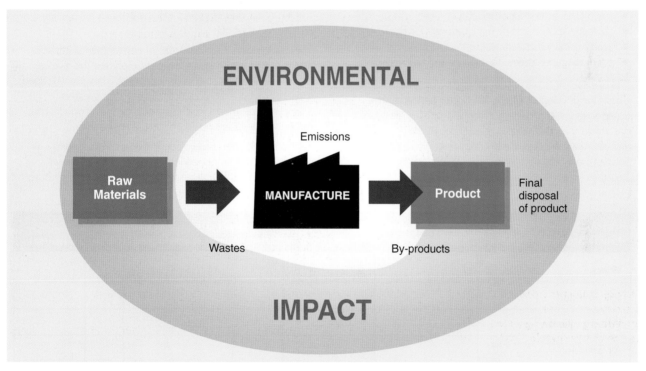

Life-cycle assessment.

Two other techniques used are:

BATNEEC **B**est **A**vailable **T**echniques **N**ot **E**ntailing **E**xcessive **C**ost
CATNIP **C**heapest **A**vailable **T**echniques **N**ot **I**nvolving **P**rosecution

Stop and think

Try to think of an example of a product which exhibits each of these approaches.

Case study: The ecolabelling scheme

The Ecolabel is awarded independently, only to products that pass strict Europe-wide environmental criteria.

The Ecolabelling scheme was set up in 1992. It aims to encourage manufacturers to make products less damaging to the environment, and provide consumers with independent information so they can make informed choices about the products they buy. The Board is responsible for:

- setting the criteria for products
- assessing applications by manufacturers for Ecolabelling
- licensing manufacturers to use the Ecolabel
- promoting the scheme to industry and to the public.

The Ecolabelling scheme uses life-cycle assessment (LCA) as a basis for developing criteria for judging products. This cradle-to-grave approach monitors a product's life-cycle. It starts with the raw materials, goes through the manufacturing process, the distribution and packaging, the product's use, and ends with disposal: the 'grave'.

It takes into account the following:

- use of natural resources and energy
- emissions to air, water and soil
- disposal of waste
- noise
- effects on ecosystems.

Examples of questions asked during a life-cycle assessment:

Production
- Are the raw materials renewable or non-renewable?
- How much energy is used during manufacture?

Use
- How much energy is involved during the use of the product?
- What kinds of pollutants does the product emit to air, water or land?

Disposal
- What kind of impact will the product have when it is disposed of?

The chart shows the main areas of environmental impacts. When put together with the life-cycle phases, this gives a total of 40 different checks on a product. These can be used to identify where the product may have the greatest environmental impact, so the criteria for that product group can be set to ensure less harm to the environment.

In March 1998, the UK Ecolabelling Board was reported as costing £0.6 million per annum. In June 1998, as the UK's presidency of the EU neared an end, a review of the future direction of the scheme was started.

Product life-cycle assessment matrix					
Environmental impacts	Raw materials	Production	Distribution & packaging	Use	Disposal
Waste					
Soil pollution					
Water pollution					
Air pollution					
Noise pollution					
Energy consumption					
Natural resources					
Ecosystem effects					

The search for a single environmental indicator

To be able to understand and manage a system, one of the first things you need is a means of measuring its main **inputs**, **operations**, **outputs** and **impacts**. In many areas of science and technology this has already been achieved, for example the development of international units for physical quantities such as energy, electric current and forces. In evaluating environmental impact the measures are still evolving. One possible single indicator is **MIPS** (**M**aterial **I**ntensity **P**er unit **S**ervice or function) proposed by Professor Friedrich Schmitt-Bleek at the Wuppertal Institute in Germany.

MIPS focuses on 'the total material and energy throughput (in mass units – kg or tonne) per unit of goods from cradle-to-grave'. The approach is based on the recognition that environmental impact is, in large part, a knock-on effect from the extraction, processing and movement of materials around the world. As the units of service build up, so the MIPS invested in each unit of service fall, up to the point where the product begins to fail. The greater the product's durability, within limits, the fewer the MIPS needed per unit of service. Once it has reached the end of its apparent life-cycle, however, its useful life can then be extended by repair, re-manufacturing or recycling into a new product. Each of these will need a further injection of MIPS. So products will need injections of energy and materials as they move through their life-cycle. In Professor Schmitt-Bleek's terms, these are **manufacturing** MIPS, **use** MIPS, **collection and sorting** MIPS, **re-manufacturing** MIPS and/or **recycling** MIPS.

Behind the MIPS concept lies a more fundamental goal than simply measuring the material and energy intensity of industrial products and services. The Wuppertal Institute argues that the MIPS framework can be used to set targets for society in the pursuit of sustainability.

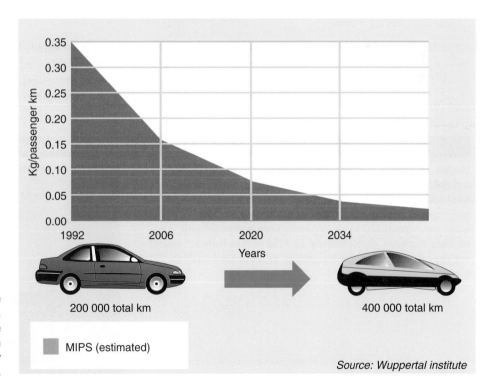

Applying MIPS to the development of private cars. The graph shows the life-cycle MIPS associated with each passenger-km falling dramatically over 40 to 50 years.

Life-cycle design

Although product design is not normally seen as part of the LCA process, the use of LCA in product design and re-design is becoming an extremely important activity. The MIPS approach indicates the way in which life-cycle thinking can be incorporated into product design.

To be effective, using life-cycle design to improve products will require exploring the use phase of the product in more detail. For many products, for example, washing machines and detergents, the major environmental impacts are associated with this stage of the life-cycle. Manufacturers and retailers will have to work more closely with customers and consumers to ensure that products are used in the most 'environmentally efficient' way.

Sustainable design and washing machines

Many homes have a washing machine and most people consider it to be an essential domestic appliance. Several years ago a life-cycle assessment was carried out on domestic washing machines to investigate their impact on the environment. The results showed some interesting findings.

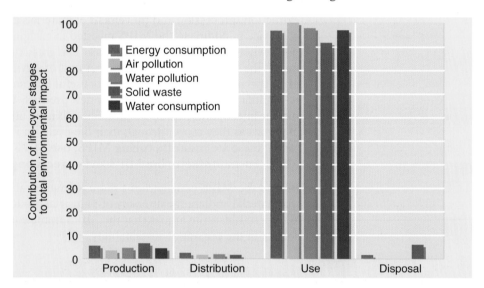

Life-cycle assessment of the domestic washing machine.

The day-to-day use of the washing machine shows by far the greatest environmental impact. Partly as a result of this study washing machines are now designed to use less water and detergents have been developed for use at lower temperatures leading to lower energy consumption and less harm when released with waste water.

Case Study: **Hoover washing machines**

Hoover recognised consumer concern about the environment and developed a new range of washing machines. The company was keen to gain the first EU ecolabel to help increase exports to Europe. Hoover calculated that its ecolabelled machine could save around £50 a year in running costs compared with standard machines. (Unfortunately, by 1998 neither Hoover nor any other manufacturer was making an Ecolabelled washing machine.)

The key criteria for washing machines covered energy, water and detergent consumption, the clarity of user instructions, performance criteria and consumer information. Revised criteria were published in 1996 which included a reduction in water consumption from 17 to 15 litres per kg of washload. The Ecolabelling scheme aimed to make the criteria more stringent each time they are revised to ensure that ecolabelled machines used the latest technology.

Focused task: Evaluating the environmental impact of industrial processes

In this activity you will consider environmental impact alongside technological and financial implications.

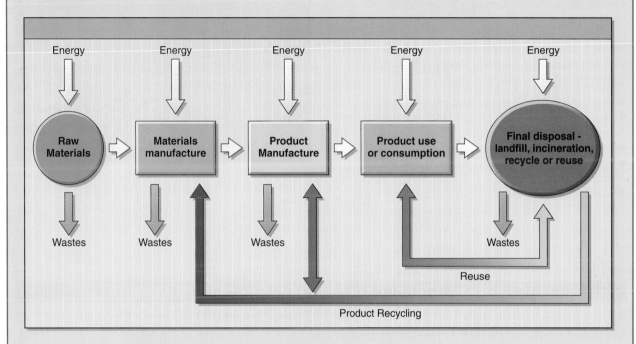

An overview of an industrial system.

Identify an industrial manufacturing process and find out everything you can about it. This could be done on a work placement or through a series of visits to a local company.

1 Put all of the stages of the manufacturing process into a flow chart.
2 Determine the inputs and outputs at each stage of the process including materials used, resources (water, energy etc.), chemicals, wastes and by-products.
3 Try to quantify these as far as possible.

4 Consider ways of:
   • making more use of renewable or sustainable resources
   • reducing dependence on non-renewable resources
   • improving the efficiency of the processes used
   • reducing wastes
   • making use of by-products
   • re-using or recycling materials
   • improving the design of the product to make it easier to maintain and repair.

Waste minimisation

The Environmental Technology Best Practice Programme promotes the use of better environmental practices that reduce costs for UK industry and commerce. The Programme promotes and supports waste minimisation and cost-effective cleaner technology. Even efficient companies produce waste and the true cost can be as high as 10% of business turnover. Waste minimisation is the process of systematically reducing waste at source. It covers:

• raw material and ingredient use
• water consumption and waste-water generation
• packaging, factory and office consumables
• energy consumption
• wasted effort.

Don't forget that waste and its disposal needs to be included in the cost of your product development.

Case Study: **Waste-water management – biostoning**

Stone-washed denim jeans are traditionally washed with abrasive pumice stones to produce the well-worn faded look. This process leaves dust and stones in garments and high levels of sludge deposits in waste-water. A new process called **biostoning** has been developed to finish denim garments, using cellulose enzymes. Biostoning is now used globally including being used by almost 100% of the specialist denim garment processors in Northern Europe. The benefits of changing to biostoning are:

◆ less damage to finished garments and machinery
◆ faster processing resulting in a 30–50% improvement in machine capacity
◆ higher product quality
◆ savings of time and labour in removing dust and stones from finished garments
◆ elimination of abrasive sludge deposits in waste-water.

Case Study: **Cleaner technology, Courtaulds Lyocell**

Half of all manufactured textile fibres are made from oil which is a non-renewable resource. Fibres can be produced from other sources, like viscose which is made from chemically-treated plant cellulose. The problem with most fibres produced in this way is that the manufacturing process is fairly expensive and doesn't use 'clean' technology.

A way of manufacturing has been developed by the Courtaulds company to make a new fibre called Lyocell. Lyocell is made from renewable wood pulp and is made using a clean manufacturing process. It can be used for technical textiles, non-woven fabrics and special papers. Examples of end-uses include protective clothing, tents, medical dressings, leather substitutes, tea-bags and smoke filters.

The major raw materials for Lyocell are water and wood cellulose, which comes from managed forests. Replanting rates exceed usage.

Wood pulp and a non-toxic solvent (N-methylmorpholine-N-oxide) are used to spin the fibre. NMMO is recovered, purified and recycled in a process that uses less energy, water and non-renewable resources.

Products made from Courtaulds Lyocell can be recycled, incinerated or digested in sewage. The fibre degrades in eight days in a sewage plant and generates a natural gas which can be used to power the plant. In landfill Lyocell breaks down to carbon dioxide and water.

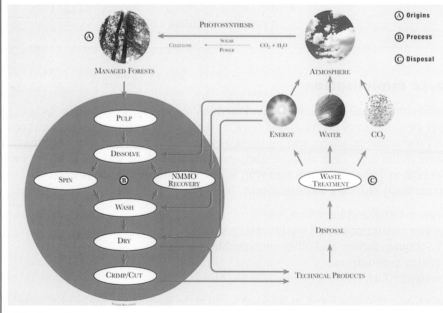

The Lyocell process.

Mouchel and Partners: The Hindhead tunnel

A detailed model of the Hindhead tunnel proposal.

The A3 is one of the busiest trunk roads in the country. It runs from Portsmouth to London and is dual carriageway carrying fast moving traffic for most of its length. At Hindhead the A3 reverts to single carriageway, passing through part of the town and restricting traffic to 30 mph. This has caused congestion for many years and motorists and local residents have been calling for a solution to the problem.

A number of solutions have been studied but Hindhead is in an 'area of outstanding natural beauty' and proposals for normal surface by-passes have been strongly opposed. To minimise impact on the environment a tunnel was suggested with a complex and demanding brief. A detailed scale model was produced to assist in all aspects of the brief alongside other methods such as site surveys. The model was particularly useful during the public consultation exhibition as it gave ordinary people ready access to detailed information.

Mouchel and Partners: Brief

As the consulting engineers, Mouchel and Partners were asked to develop a scheme which:

1   provides minimal visual intrusion to Hindhead town centre
2   provides the least topographical disruption, i.e. minimum earth moving, cuttings and embankments
3   provides least disruption to wildlife and the ecology of the area
4   has the least impact on surface water drainage patterns and changes to groundwater levels helping to preserve features including ponds, ditches and streams
5   identifies suitable underlying rock to ensure stability
6   utilises best location for portals, where tunnels emerge, to minimise visual intrusion
7   avoids deep cuttings and high embankments at entrances to tunnels to reduce visual impact and facilitate construction
8   considers the impact of lighting, both the problems of motorists emerging from the tunnel into bright sunlight and the effects of a brightly lit tunnel entrance on the evening landscape
9   provides effective, detailed landscaping and planting schemes reinstating trees lost during construction and forming visual screens to residential and recreation areas
10   provides effective noise screening to ensure least noise impact upon residential and recreation areas
11   considers severance of local footpaths, side roads and the need to re-direct them over the tunnel
12   considers severance of local agricultural land and size, and scale of working farm units
13   considers the disposal of tunnelled material and use of surplus to mitigate the visual impact of approach roads by earth banks and screens.
14   considers public opinion and impact on communities (often ascertained by a public consultation exhibition).

A view of the model showing the tunnel entrance.

Focused task: Environmental impacts

The following case studies consider different environmental issues:

Life-cycle assessment in the Ecolabelling scheme page 100

Environmental issues – changing practices in waste management page 104

The Jaguar XK8 page 201

The cold drinks can page 97

Technology Assessment page 91

The Hindhead tunnel page 105

You should:

Read through the three-part task below, scan the case studies to get a feel for them and re-read the task description.

- Identify the key environmental issue in each of the case studies and state it.
- Relate the issue to the five principles explained above – reduce, re-use, recycle, ease of maintenance, life-cycle assessment.
- Identify and note any relevant points that you could consider during the development of your own product.

The most efficient way of completing this task may be to present your findings on a grid.

Evaluating the environmental impact of your own product

There are various stages in the product development process where you should consider environmental impact:

- Identification of need and balancing this against potential environmental impact. Determining the pros and cons of the product against possible environmental impact.
- Design specification. Establishing criteria for reducing environmental impact, using the principles of reduce, re-use, recycle, ease of maintenance.
- Assessment of environmental impact – in design proposals, manufacturing specification, manufacturing processes to be used, packaging etc.

New design projects: what should you take on?

The purpose of this section is to help you when you are planning a new designing and/or manufacturing project and to relate your ways of working to companies' approaches. You should also refer to the section on Innovation in the company context (page 64) which shows a number of reasons for and ways in which companies embark on new product development.

Whilst both you and a professional designer work in designing and manufacturing, there is a major difference between the two of you – other than the amount of experience you have not had! The prime purpose of a designer's work is to produce successful products. Your prime purpose is education; to learn. You are a learner who is acting as a designer, so have to balance design outcomes (successful products) and learning outcomes (successful education), including working for assessment.

Selecting a major project always involves an element of risk. Get it wrong and you may not give yourself the best chance to demonstrate your abilities or may fail to meet the expectations of the assessment system. The checklists below are to help you select the most promising ideas from a set of alternatives and for you to check again from time to time.

Characteristics of some of the best projects:
- ✔ originally identified by you, ensuring personal involvement and commitment
- ✔ originates in an identified need or purpose rather than a product idea
- ✔ clear purposes, preferably for a real client
- ✔ clear evidence of primary research influencing the design

✔ not over-demanding, to allow attention to detail (manageable size)
✔ systematic, well planned use of time
✔ time built-in for evaluation, and modification (at various stages)
✔ giving opportunity for a range of manufacturing skills
✔ develop known/established skills into a 'virtuoso performance'
✔ make good use of other people and facilities
✔ potential for commercial production (including spin-off products)
✔ comprehensive – good ideas in various aspects of the design
✔ use a variety of materials
✔ succinct folio, clear to follow, much use of relaxed sketches notes and photos
✔ are modelled and tested thoroughly (are the right facilities available?).

Characteristics of the worst projects:

✗ large and over-ambitious, requiring major constructional work
✗ involve repeat processes with no further learning (e.g. 48 welded joints!)
✗ look like D-I-Y projects
✗ lack attention to detail (because of shortage of time)
✗ few new ideas evident
✗ originate in an idea for an actual product rather than identifying user needs
✗ require too much work in unfamiliar aspects of D&T or new skills
✗ little evidence of research influencing the design outcome
✗ have far too much 'folder work' much of it of little real value, too much emphasis on presentation making the folio dry and artificial
✗ folio written in the past tense rather than being a lively and real planning tool
✗ just about manage to make the main item – no development, no detail, no 'finish'.

Knowing which of these descriptions will apply before you begin a project is not easy. The answer therefore is to conduct rapid **feasibility studies** on a very limited number of competing ideas. Ask 'Is the problem what I thought it was? Is there potential for original ideas? Are the right contacts available?'. Be prepared to drop a project – but do so quickly, do not waste too much time.

Use your teachers or tutors well: take the initiative and ensure that they help you to find a suitable project. Consult others too and listen to their experience. Look at previous projects including the ones in this book and the *D&T Routes* books.

Stakeholders: resolving conflicts

One of the preferences already mentioned is that you should work with a real client. This might be a single person (e.g. stair climbing assistance for a disabled person), an organisation (e.g. a corporate identity for a playgroup), someone who represents a group (e.g. all those who find stairs difficult to climb), or an individual or corporate client (e.g. Asda). You also have to take yourself into consideration: know what your learning needs are for the project, and for the examining board or awarding body that will give you a formal qualification.

All these people or organisations may have a stake in the success of your project – even examination boards want to see success, but they place constraints on you by having specific requirements or expectations. If you overlook this fact you may find yourself torn between conflicting influences, and both the quality of your work and your final assessment may suffer. To avoid this, the first rule is to make explicit what each stakeholder expects. If the reasons for you not meeting a stakeholder's expectation are made clear in advance, then you are likely to find them willing to compromise. Avoiding conflicts will be absolutely necessary for the overview of a whole project – it may also be useful for smaller decisions within the project.

Ultimately, as your prime purpose in school or college is your own education, you are likely to have to put yourself, and your grade first. However, you may avoid this if your bring all the pressures out into the open.

Stakeholder's requirements – resolving conflicts

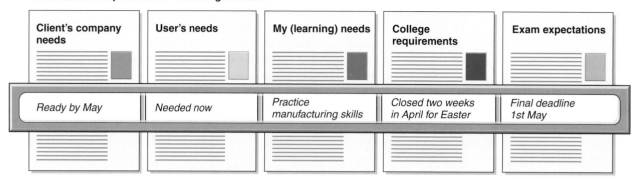

Client's company needs	User's needs	My (learning) needs	College requirements	Exam expectations
Ready by May	*Needed now*	*Practice manufacturing skills*	*Closed two weeks in April for Easter*	*Final deadline 1st May*

Preparing a list of each stakeholder's expectations will allow you to discuss conflicting pressures and resolve them in a spirit of co-operation. It will, most importantly, show what considerations you weighed, what decisions you took and why.

It might be important to carry out a similar exercise at some intermediate points when significant decisions are to be taken or when conflicts arise. The purpose of this might be to expose for discussion the opposing directions in which you are pulled. It is also a succinct way to report a decision in your folio.

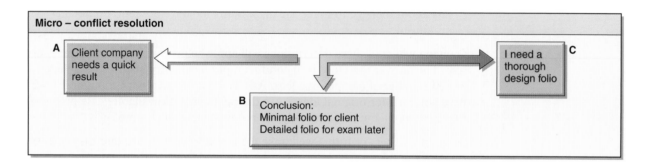

Micro – conflict resolution

A — Client company needs a quick result

B — Conclusion: Minimal folio for client Detailed folio for exam later

C — I need a thorough design folio

Checklists, D&T Routes Core Book   47–49

Design considerations

This section is intended to build on the Designing section of the *D&T Routes* series of books, especially the *Core Book*. Those books give help with many different detailed design considerations from function to aesthetics, ergonomics to product life. Here we give you a broader view offering further insights into contemporary approaches to designing with many further industrial examples.

Whatever the designer's personal approach, every design task has to take into account numerous considerations – both **constraints** and **opportunities**. This is why designing is complex, and it is complicated further by the fact that every consideration can affect every other. For example, changing the aesthetics of a product may change its ergonomics and might also require a change in the manufacturing method. This is why designing is often referred to in educational psychology as a 'higher order thinking skill'.

Moving through the designing process the designer has to go back and forth between different considerations. Keeping an eye on the interplay between them is as important as paying enough attention to any one design consideration. It is easy to make the mistake of becoming too involved in one or two aspects of a design only to lose the all-important over-view. It is the over-view of your progress and the interaction between different design considerations that ensures continuous improvement and keeps you moving forward. Then, you can keep options open as your design continues to develop and you close-in on your final decisions.

This can be represented in diagram form. It is important to remember, however, that no diagram (or model) of designing can ever tell the whole story, they can only draw attention to certain aspects. Designing is too complex an activity to be illustrated fully in a diagram.

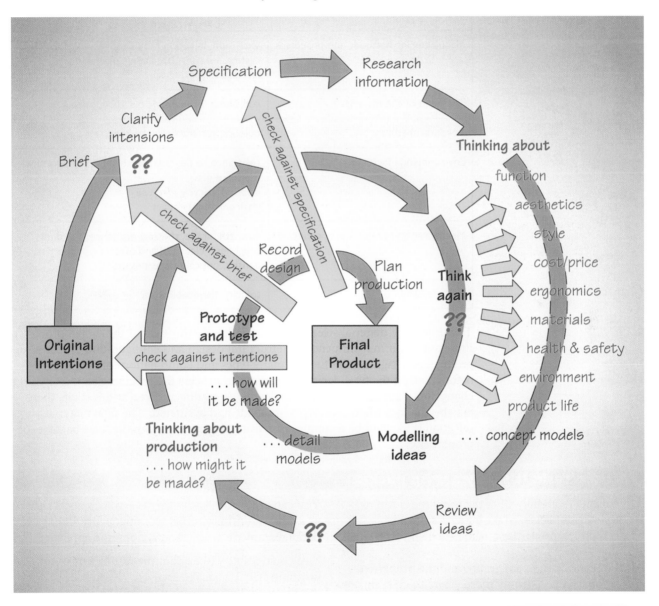

Closing in on a final design.

▶ Developing ideas, D&T Routes Core Book 64–114

Focused task: Designing processes

Read the section on consecutive engineering, pages 74–75, and re-draw the diagram to show how a consecutive approach would be different.

Materials

Designing or improving a product requires a knowledge of materials in order to select, process and finish them to meet the requirements of the product and manufacturing specifications. The table shows some of the key properties and characteristics of materials that should be considered during the materials selection process.

Key features	Example considerations
Cost and availability	raw materials processing equipment energy requirements disposal of waste and by-products
Manufacturing methods and processes	extrusion, injection moulding, vacuum-forming, casting, weaving, laminating, machining, fabrication/making-up
The form of the material	roll, sheet, fibre, foam, bar/tube, casting
Aesthetic features	colours, surface finish, texture
Environmental factors	resistance to degradation through temperature, moisture etc. disposal, recycling/re-use environmental impact
Mechanical and physical properties	strength, drape, thermal properties, hardness, toughness, electrical and magnetic properties, density, optical properties etc.
Risk assessment	toxicity, flammability etc.

The process of material selection has an influence throughout the design process. For example, it may influence the structural design and configuration of the product. A designer will often try many types and combinations of materials before making the final decision. During this process the specification is likely to change until a manufacturing specification is produced. Even at this stage, there may be changes when prototypes are made and evaluated. The final materials selection is likely to be a compromise using the material with the 'best balance' of properties.

Focused task: It's only a crisp packet!

1 Consider carefully all of the properties required for a crisp packet. Make a list.
2 Group the properties together to help you analyse them.
3 Look at the different groups and the properties within them – identify those where there seems to be a conflict.
4 Look at a range of crisp packets and explain how the material used meets the requirements you identified. Where do you think a compromise has been made?

You can repeat this with other everyday objects such as a fizzy soft drinks bottle, clothing, pens, other food packaging, medical containers, domestic appliances.

You could also try to explain the results from warming crisp packets in an oven. (Keep temperatures low, starting at about 120°C, and raising the temperature only if necessary to shrink the pack. Do not go above 190°C.)

Materials science, materials technology and product development

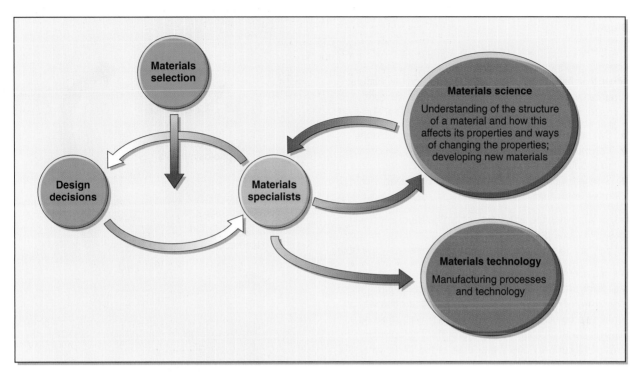

Materials science and materials technology.

Case Study: **The evolution of the tennis racket**

Sports equipment is one area where the development of new and improved materials has had a major influence on product development. In the competitive world of professional sport there is a high premium on performance. Equipment manufacturers, eager to have their products used by the top professionals, constantly experiment with new and improved materials. These developments then have a great influence on design at the cheaper end of the market.

The key requirements for the performance of a tennis racket are: strength, lightness, stiffness or flexibility and shock absorption.

◆ **Wooden rackets** Originally made from laminated wood — little real change in design took place over many years. Limited in stiffness and strength but good shock-absorbing properties.
◆ **Metal frames** Became feasible with the development of light alloys (aluminium or magnesium) using extruded or drawn tubing, competitively priced but relatively poor vibration damping.
◆ **Composite rackets** Now used by most professional players, the best performance rackets are the 'graphites' using carbon fibres in injection or compression mouldings. Compression moulding uses long fibres of carbon in an epoxy resin matrix. Injection moulding is cheaper and uses chopped carbon fibres in a matrix of nylon giving better vibration damping.

◆ **Strings** Racket strings have also changed from natural gut to monofilament nylon. However, most professionals still use natural gut because these strings retain their tension better than the synthetic strings.

Tennis rackets in wood and synthetic composites respectively.

Case study: Biopol – a material for its time

Pioneering research over 60 years ago by ICI led to the creation of the world's first truly biodegradable polymer, **Biopol**.

The trend over the last century has been the development of synthetic polymer (plastics) fibres such as nylon, and PVC rather than natural polymers such as wool and silk. Natural fibres can vary largely in quality, and the availability can fluctuate. The advantages of synthetics over natural fibres are:

◆ Synthetic fibres can be made to precise specifications.
◆ Polymers derived from petrochemicals (oil) are cheaper to produce than natural fibres.
◆ Synthetic fibres can be prepared and processed much more easily than natural ones.

Biopol combines the advantages of synthetic polymers with those of natural polymers, being biodegradable and suitable for bulk production, and the raw materials are easily available.

In 1926 scientists discovered that a number of micro-organisms produce a natural polymer known as PHB (polyhydroxybutyrate) as a 'food' store (in the same way as humans accumulate carbohydrate and fat). This could be mass-produced in a fermentation process. The polymer remained a curiosity until the oil crisis of the 1970s when ICI developed an innovative fermentation process which allowed alterations to the flexibility and toughness of PHB, creating a range of more useful plastic materials. Pressure from environmentalists in the late 1980s led to the development of Biopol and its use for the Wella 'Sanara' shampoo bottle. 'Sanara' is itself a biodegradable product so Wella were keen use biodegradable packaging.

Sanara shampoo in Biopol containers.

Biopol is fully biodegradable and can be made into a range of films and fibres as well as moulded to make more solid objects such as bottles. Current efforts are directed at reducing manufacturing and processing costs even further. This case study shows how a scientific discovery can be developed, often via lengthy processes, into an innovative and marketable product.

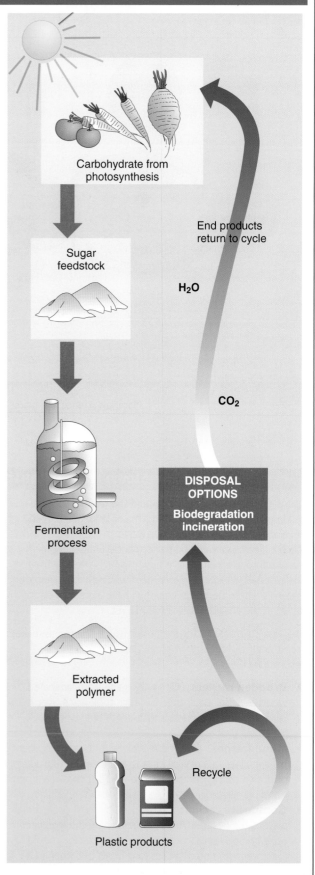

The production of PHB.

Focused task: Other uses for Biopol

Consider how the combination of the right economic and environmental conditions made it possible for Biopol to be turned into a marketable product.

What other products could be made from Biopol?

Selecting one or a range of products:
- Prepare a product proposal for presentation to a company suggesting the use of Biopol to manufacture your product idea.
- Prepare a briefing paper for their marketing department setting out how the advantages of Biopol might be presented to consumers.

(Information on Biopol is available on the world wide web — use a search engine to find the relevant information.)

Case Study: Courtaulds Tencel – A new fibre for the mass market

Courtaulds is an international specialist materials company producing a range of fibres and films. It was the first company in the world to produce viscose yarn (rayon) commercially, which is often known as a 'natural synthetic' because it is produced from cellulose – a natural polymer obtained from wood pulp consisting of hundreds of glucose molecules.

Glucose is the world's most abundant organic material, but dissolving wood to obtain it produces sulphurous waste. Courtaulds' challenge was to produce a new cellulose-based fibre that could be mass produced with less environmental impact. This took 14 years, resulting in Tencel, the first new synthetic fibre for the textiles market for 30 years. The process used to develop it involved three key stages:

1 Research – to produce the new fibre in the laboratory and turn it into a filament
2 Pilot plant – to develop the production process
3 Full-scale operational plant

The first filaments were developed in the laboratory within the first year of the project. It took over ten years to solve the problems of scaling up production.

Tencel can be made into fabrics that look as if they are made from rough denim but have the feel of a heavy velvet, they look like brushed cotton but with the 'floppiness' of silk and consumer reaction has been very positive.

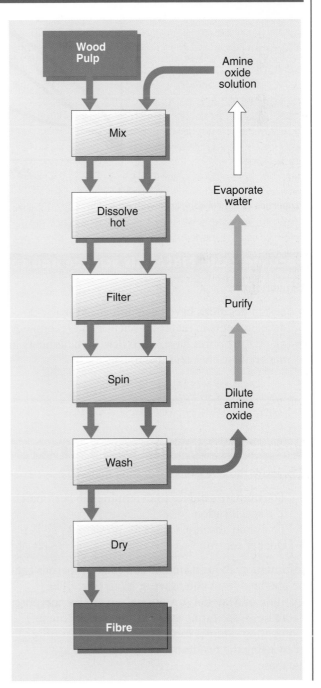

The production of Tencel. The key feature of this process is that the solvent used can be purified and concentrated and then used again. Over 99% of the solvent is reclaimed. This greatly reduces the amount of harmful effluent produced.

Case Study: **Courtaulds Tencel – A new fibre for the mass market**
continued

Property	Tencel	Viscose	Cotton	Polyester	
elongation under load%	14–16	20–25	7–9	25–30	Note: all of the materials have the same thickness
elongation when wet%	16–18	25–30	12–14	25–30	
water absorption%	65	90	50	3	

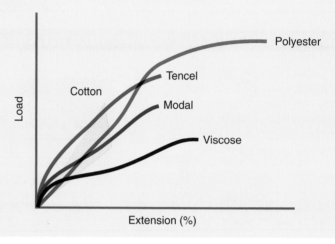

Properties of Tencel compared with other fibres.

Focused task: Materials science and technology

Explain how:

- design decisions have been influenced by developments in materials science and technology
- market pressures have led to new developments in materials science and technology.

Look for other examples of products where progress in material technology and market pressures have influenced product development. Good examples are footwear, fashion and outdoor clothing. New developments can also cause products to be improved and re-launched, for example; mountain bikes.

Focused task: Investigating the properties of materials

There are three reasons for testing materials:

1 To compare samples to determine the best match to a specification
2 To obtain absolute values for properties
3 Quality control.

Information about materials and their properties can be obtained from databases or by testing. (The Institute of Materials produce a very useful computer database — see http.//www.instmat.co.uk/eductn.) Comparing samples can be done either by testing or by using the results of previous tests on a database.

Obtaining absolute values is best done using a database as this information is usually available unless you are working with a new or modified material. Quality control will involve testing. These tests can be mechanical tests which determine properties by deformation or destruction or physical non-destructive tests.

Determine a test which is best for each the properties listed in the table.

Focused task: Investigating the properties of materials *continued*

Properties of materials.

Physical properties	Chemical and biological properties	Mechanical properties

Electrical and mechanical properties:
 	
  Electrical conductivity/insulation
  Magnetic properties
 	
Thermal properties:
  Thermal conductivity/insulation
 	
  Thermal expansion
  Melting point
 	
Optical properties
 	
Recycling e.g. by chopping up, melting down and remoulding
	Corrosion resistance
	
	Resistance to biological degradation e.g. insects, bacteria, fungi
	
	Resistance to degradation by water
	
	Biodegradability
	
	Recycling through chemical reactions
	Toxicity
	
	Flammability
		Strength – tensile, compressive, shear,
		torsional, bending
		
		Ductility (deformation by tension)
		
		Malleability (deformation by compression)
		
		Stiffness (how much the material bends under load)
		
		Hardness
		
		Toughness (resistance to sudden shocks or blows)
		
		Elasticity (goes back to its original shape after it has been deformed; all materials have an **elastic limit**)
		
		Plasticity (does not go back to its original shape after it has been deformed)

1 For each property required for a tennis racket frame, decide how you can best compare a range of possible materials.

2 Obtain the information you need and display your results.

3 Write a description of each material explaining its suitability and deficiencies.

Case Study: **Cars and plastics**

Most car bodies are highly stressed and made from pressed sheet steel. Because of the importance of the stress factors, changing the steel body is expensive. There has been a great increase in the use of plastics in cars over recent years but they have not yet been used much for stressed sections, though these parts are highly suitable for lower cost styling changes.

The front bumper of this Rover 100 is made from a thermosetting polymer, Propathene and the rear from an elastomer – modified Procom. Both of these were developed by ICI to meet the requirements specified by Rover. The bumpers only have to withstand low speed parking bumps and can be changed cost-effectively for cosmetic reasons.

Car manufacturers use plastics because of their low density, durability, toughness, resistance to corrosion and ease of manufacturing. Plastics materials can be processed into complex components often requiring little or no finishing. In many cases an expensive assembly process can be replaced by a simple, cheaper manufacturing operation. This means that lower levels of stocks are needed, allowing 'just in time' deliveries to be used to keep costs down.

For body panels, sheet steel has several major advantages over plastics as it is cheap, easy to form into body panels, has greater stiffness over large areas, can be easily assembled using spot welding and can be recycled. However, plastics also have several advantages, as they have excellent corrosion resistance, low weight and good damage resistance. There is also the problem of surface finish; steel bodies are spray painted and pass through high temperature ovens to 'bake' or 'stove' the paint. This has been difficult with plastics, particularly thermoplastics that can be easily moulded into complex shapes. Many plastics are also difficult to recycle.

ICI have developed a new material, imine polyurea, a polyurethane, that overcomes many of these problems. It can be injection moulded into complex shapes but can withstand stoving temperatures of up to 200°C when painted on the production line in the same way as steel components. This material is currently being evaluated for the front wings of cars and motor cycle bodies. It would also have environmental benefits in reducing overall weight and fuel consumption. Plastics were among the first materials to cause us to consider their environmental impact throughout their life-cycle. Imine polyurea is a thermosetting polymer and these have, in the past, been extremely difficult to recycle but ICI are optimistic about new recycling methods for the future.

▶ **Life cycle assessment** 98

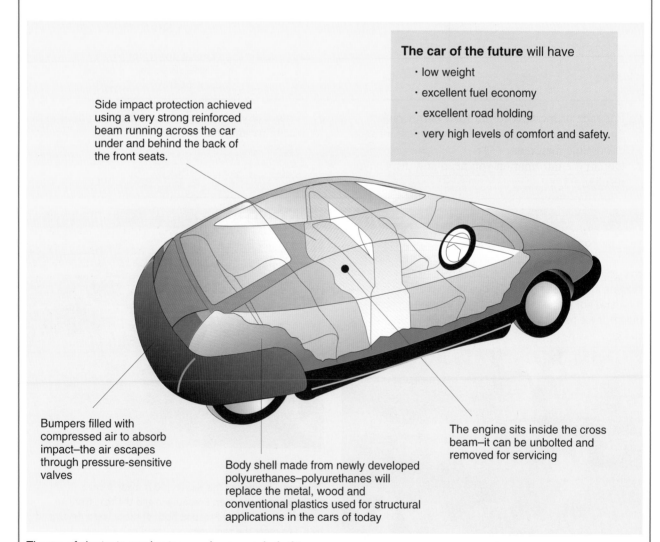

The car of the future will have

- low weight
- excellent fuel economy
- excellent road holding
- very high levels of comfort and safety.

Side impact protection achieved using a very strong reinforced beam running across the car under and behind the back of the front seats.

Bumpers filled with compressed air to absorb impact–the air escapes through pressure-sensitive valves

Body shell made from newly developed polyurethanes–polyurethanes will replace the metal, wood and conventional plastics used for structural applications in the cars of today

The engine sits inside the cross beam–it can be unbolted and removed for servicing

The use of plastics in cars has increased enormously. Is this the car of the future?

Focused task: Materials selection analysis – cars

Choosing from steel, aluminium alloy and a range of thermoplastics, thermosets and elastomers prepare and complete two tables as given below. Use a materials database to obtain the information you need and consider raw material costs, processing costs, manufacturing and production costs, disposal and recycling.

Part of a car	
Properties required of the material	
Possible materials	
Cost-benefit analysis	
Recommendation	

The advantages and disadvantages of using plastics.

Issues	Advantages	Disadvantages
Design		
Engineering/Production		
Environmental		
Safety/passenger protection		

Detailing a product's design

There is an old saying, 'The devil is in the details' which draws attention to the fact that a broad general idea can seem fine until looked at closely. This is an important concept for the designer as the overall quality, and success, of a design can be achieved or broken by the success of its detailing. This has implications for you when planning your project work – a surprising amount of time needs to be allocated to fine detailing, both in the designing and execution aspects. The photographs in the ASDA case study (page 220) show you how some careful detailing brought to life what might have been very conventional items, giving them some character. The saw illustrated overleaf does the same.

Case Study: **The Sandvik hand saw**

Hand saws for cutting wood are a traditional item that have been made for centuries. They date back to before the Industrial Revolution when they were made, as well as used, by hand. Many manufacturers produced them in their common volume-produced form throughout the 19th and 20th centuries with little difference between brands. More recently, as with many taken-for-granted items, they have been looked at more closely by designers to achieve **product differentiation** – i.e. to ensure that their brand stands out from the others. This can be achieved in relatively trivial ways such as a bright coloured handle (though it might be argued that this makes it easy to find in the clutter of tools on a site). However, even so simple an item as a saw can be subject to real innovation that improves the user's experience. Some of these will be less visible, concerning the exact materials used, heat treatments given and forming processes. Others are easily discovered by the discerning customer.

Protecting the teeth of the saw in transit and storage with a plastics sleeve was an innovation some years ago – previously saws were just wrapped in anti-rust brown paper. Early sleeves were simple U-shaped cross sections which would be slipped on from the end of the blade and pulled off at any angle. Removing them caused some minor accidents as the user's thumb scraped across the sharp teeth. This small problem has been elegantly solved by Sandvik. Careful re-design of the cross section of the plastics sleeve, still produced as a single extrusion, has created a locking hinge. This holds the sleeve firmly on the saw when not in use but releases sharply at a flick of the thumb allowing it to be withdrawn easily without risk to the user. It also allows the sleeve in its wide-open position to be mounted on the saw, again without risk as the user's thumb, is kept clear of the teeth until the sleeve is in place, when it is 'clicked' into position. Even the sharp precision of the shutting action is satisfying – the sleeve then stays firmly in place, gripping the blade because of its spring action. The company have patented the sleeve design.

Some of the design features of the Sandvik handsaw.
Main handle from rigid orange plastics.
Soft plastics handling surface for improved ergonomics.
This hole sits nicely under the forefinger (left or right handed).
45° and 90° angles on handle for use as mitre/try square.
Ideograms and text giving customer selection criteria.
Hole for hanging on a hook.
How-to-use ideograms for protective sleeve.
Clip-on protective sleeve.
Window in sleeve allowing examination of the teeth.

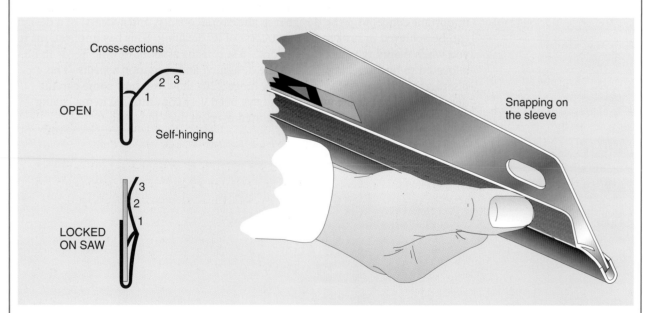

Careful attention to detail is evident in the design of this protective sleeve for a saw.

Here is a collaborative task to undertake with fellow students. This task will allow you to look more closely at the detailing of products and carry this approach into your own work.

1 Find an item which is significantly improved by careful detailing in the design – try to find something which you can be enthusiastic about.
2 Bring this to school/college and share your enthusiasm for it with your fellow students.
3 Discuss your conclusions.
   • Why are these products well detailed?
   • Who might have pushed the design beyond the mundane?
   • Against what criteria are you judging these to be well detailed – ergonomic, functional, aesthetic etc?
   • Are the good details on the main product or accessories/fittings?
   • What materials predominate in the group?
   • Are plastics products often better detailed? If so, why might this be?
   • What is the relationship between quality of detailing and volume of production?

Extension task:
Practice your drawing and communication skills by producing an annotated presentation of the details you are featuring – as in the Sandvik example. Mount a group display of these under the title 'Celebrating good detail design'.

Using standard components

Nobody makes their own nails, cotton thread or transistors, except companies specialising in these products. This is for two main reasons – the economies of scale that bring down unit costs dramatically when very high volumes of production (and sales) are achieved, and that companies concentrate their skills in their specialist field. It is for the latter reason that many organisations contract-out subsidiary activities like lunchtime canteens and delivery transportation to experts in those fields. Product designers often do the same, incorporating ready-made components from other companies in their designs.

The disadvantage can be that the overall integrity of a design can be spoiled by the appearance of 'bolt-on' extras. For this reason, and especially when the product is destined for high-volume production, even the smallest component may be custom designed for one application. Examples of this include the McLaren door hinge — low volume integrity (page 198) and a range of suitcases — high volume — which achieved product differentiation (making one design stand out from its competitors) through custom-designed zip pulls.

The electronics field in particular uses standardised components, of the utmost complexity and produced in ultra-high volumes for the lowest possible unit cost, such as computer central processor units (CPUs). However, mechanical engineering also gains similar advantages.

Case Study: Bicycles and standard components

Take a look at a standard bicycle. The components you see are common to most bikes: a frame, handlebars, brakes, saddles, gears and hubs, rims, spokes and tyres. Whilst all these components may appear on every type of bicycle their design can vary greatly due to the style of the bike or the use it is put to.

The common basic design that is used for most bikes evolved during a period of rapid development in the late 19th century when bikes were first developed as a consumer product. Many radical variations were tried (for example: wooden wheels, paddling on the ground for propulsion; pedals operating directly on the axles, one wheel much larger than the other etc.), before the optimum format was arrived at. This has remained substantially unchanged, despite some short-lived or low-production radical alternatives appearing from time to time. This phenomenon is referred to as **design stasis**. In the case of bicycles, the 'diamond frame' is the basis of about 95% of products with alternatives used only for very specialist applications such as racing, folding into a car boot etc. Breaking out from this stasis usually requires a major change in one or more relevant factors:

◆ the technology available, e.g. a new gear shift mechanism
◆ new materials, e.g. carbon fibre for frame/body
◆ new uses, e.g. BMX bikes
◆ lifestyles, e.g. off-road mountain bikes for leisure use.

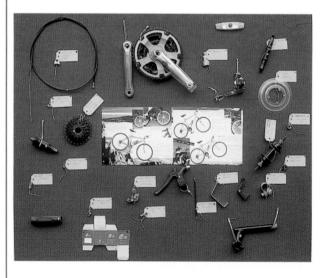

Styling changes to the basic bicycle design appeal to niches in the market. Product differentiation is often achieved by employing graphic designers to prepare colour schemes and transfers to stick on the frame, and also through trim changes such as plastic mudguards or luggage carriers.

The use envisaged for a bike is the other main influence on its design. For example, a mountain bike relies on the same key components, but in this context the demands placed on the component may vary considerably from a standard 'touring' bike. The exact position of the design in the market will be a major consideration. 'Up-market' designs may be used by serious competitive cyclists. These are discerning buyers to whom innovations in both design and technology will appeal, and who may be prepared to pay much more but will expect a more durable product. However, as designers work up a range of bikes they must be concerned to keep component changes cost-effective at each step in the market.

The designer has to consider whether it is necessary to modify *all* the parts of a bike to suit a new style or use, or at least, which components must be changed. Clearly there are cost advantages to re-using the same components across different bike designs but there will also be reasons for a manufacturer to design or buy-in different components for a new or variant product. These will include customer-appeal as well as functionality.

Putting yourself in the position of a designer of products like bikes, which use many standard components, you can imagine how important it would be to have efficient access to design information about them. This is a good use of electronic product definition which allows CAD files to be shared on the world wide web so a designer can source parts from anywhere. Also, the internal storage of this design information makes electronically equipped designers more efficient as they can call-up component designs from an in-house, or supplier's design library and assemble them, on-screen, into a new design. You could try searching the web for some of the main component manufacturers.

▶	Electronic product definition	85

In your work you should consider 'bought-in' components, even if only in the form of nuts and bolts and washers, for exactly the reasons that manufacturers do:

- cost-effectiveness
- draws in the benefits of reduced costs due to high volume manufacture
- the producer's design and manufacturing expertise comes with the component
- quality is assured
- reduces equipment and capital demands.

Additionally, you may benefit from saving time to concentrate on the overall task that is your project rather than trying to solve every single sub-problem.

Focused tasks: Standard components and product differentiation

1 Compare two bikes with different applications, see if you can identify common components, some may not be visible to the eye, bearings, clips and internal components such a shafts, gears and fasteners.

2 Using bicycles as your example, prepare two lists:
- Reasons for a designer to keep to the same components.
- Reasons for changing the components.

3 Now prepare a third list to include ways in which a bike can be varied within the same price range and style (e.g. racer, mountain, shopper etc.) to stand out from the competition (product differentiation).

4 If you are keen on bikes you might like to estimate the costs of the changes in components step-by-step up a range of similar bikes and compare these with the selling prices. Take into account all the boring bits like brackets and lugs – look for common usage – as well as the flashy, high profile parts like gear sets. You will undoubtedly identify an increasing profit margin i.e. more expensive bikes make proportionately more profit – the law of diminishing returns (for the buyer!).

New technology developments: Biotechnology

Many people have predicted (for well over a decade!) that biotechnology is the next most significant area of technological development following the 'micro-chip age'. This section will give you some background and insights into current uses of biotechnology.

What is biotechnology?

Our current society is the product of generations of rapid advances in scientific understanding and industrial innovation. Many technologies have contributed to this advance, including biotechnology, which makes use of living proteins called

enzymes to create industrial products and processes. An early application was the use of fermentation for producing and preserving bread and beer, then technologists developed enzymes that could be added to improve the cleaning properties of detergents and to improve waste treatment. Now enzymes are used to manufacture products such as antibiotics or dairy foods and in manufacturing, replacing mechanical processes, such as in the 'biostoning' of denim textiles.

You will see from this section how biotechnology has the potential to be benign, helping to hold human impacts on our eco-system in balance or, as many fear, having the potential to go disastrously out of control. You should cross-reference this section with that on environmental impacts elsewhere in this book.

▶ **Reducing environmental impact through design**   96

Quorn™ products are a range of meat alternatives that are a good source of dietary protein and fibre and are low in fat. The principle ingredient in Quorn™ is myco-protein which is derived from a distant relative of the mushroom using fermentation technology.

Food and drink

The food industry makes use of many biotechnological processes for products like bread, yoghurt or cheese which are made using living micro-organisms. Marmite yeast extract is a by-product of a biological process in the brewing industry. **Fermentation technology** provides the potential to grow foods, food ingredients and additives, such as the production of meat substitutes based on fungal protein or polyunsaturated fatty acids from fungi and algae. The brewing industry uses yeast to ferment the fruit and without this biotechnology, wine would be grape juice and cider, apple juice. Have you ever wondered how skin and pith are removed from fresh fruit cocktails? Until recently this was done by hand. Now enzymes called pectinases are used to 'dissolve away' the skins, leading to a higher quality and more hygienic end-product. Technologists have used an enzyme to develop a natural concentrated cheese flavouring that provides 25–30 times the flavour of cheese without added flavour enhancers. It can be used in processed and substitute cheese, dressings and dips, sauces and soups, pasta and snack products.

In agriculture the use of **gene technology** can produce crops that are resistant to pests, reducing the need for pesticides. It can also lead to crops with better nutritional properties and improved marketing characteristics, such as tomatoes with a better shelf-life. There is a great deal of concern about the possibility of gene technology in agriculture going out of control. No one can predict where changes that are now being made to our 'gene pool' might lead in the long term.

Textiles

Textiles treatments are currently a major centre of attention for biotechnology. The surface of a cotton shirt may look smooth but it is covered with tiny protruding fibres, which can go unpleasantly 'bobbly' after the shirt has been worn for a while. This is called 'pilling' and is one reason why cotton clothes are sometimes thrown away. However it can now be treated by **biopolishing**. The Danish company Novo Nordisk has developed an enzyme treatment called **Cellusoft** which 'chops off' the protruding fibres, leaving a softer, shinier fabric. One treatment, before the fabric is dyed, improves its quality so that it continues to look and feel new for the lifetime of the garment.

An important long-term use of biotechnology could be the production of fibres, polymers and dyestuffs to make textile manufacturing more economical and environmentally friendly. The development of naturally coloured (non-dyed) cottons is already possible and rust, green, brown, yellow and mauve varieties have been produced using conventional growing techniques.

New fibres such as polyester-cotton could be developed. Research is being carried out into the introduction of genes to the cotton plant to produce a bio-degradable polyester core inside the central channel of the fibre. The ability to grow Biopolyester-cotton could be one of the most amazing developments for the whole textile industry.

The fraudulent labelling of fibre content, country of origin of textiles and the copying of well-known brands is a major problem facing the textile industry. Techniques for the security marking of fabrics using marker molecules are under development. The markers are completely safe and the secure 'codes' can be detected by customs or trading standards officers using simple equipment. This kind of technique can be used for marking denim fabrics and can be used to protect brand names.

Cleaning clothes and treating waste

Alongside the mechanical and electronic improvements in washing machines, enzyme technology is used in biological washing powders to get whites whiter at lower temperatures, producing energy savings of around 30%. Modern enzymes in detergents decrease the use of sodium perborate by 25%, reducing the release of salt into the environment. The rapid urbanisation of populations world-wide has resulted in the need for effective sewage treatment systems. In many industrial countries sewage is treated by biotechnological processes in treatment plants using micro-organisms to break down the waste. Some developing countries cannot afford the technology needed to manage industrial or waste processes so we must consider:

- Who should pay the costs of clean technology?
- How can we help developing countries to afford new processes?
- Do these countries already have (perhaps low-tech) ways of their own for processing waste?

Focused task: Biotechnology and the environment

Cross-referencing to the Environmental Impact section of this book (page 96), write a short commentary identifying the developing uses of biotechnology which you see as most threatening to our environment and which seem most benign. Support your comments with good reasoning.

The research illustration on page 38 would suggest that the world-wide web would be a good source of further information for this assignment.

The 'Biotechnology Means Business Initiative' offers information and technical support to help understand the potential for biotechnology. The BMB publishes literature and case studies to show how biotechnology helps manufacturers to develop environmental solutions for industrial processes. For more information, contact BMB Initiative, Chemicals and Biotechnology Division, DTI, 151 Buckingham Palace Road, London SW1W 9SS.

Risk assessment

Safety by design must be assured To achieve this worthwhile aim, a concern for safety should permeate **all** stages of a product development process.

Risk can be described as 'the chance of an adverse event, the likelihood of a hazard being realised.' These risks could be:

- risk to the health and safety of people
- risk to the environment including pollution, damage to flora and fauna and soil erosion
- risk to the activity being carried out including damage to equipment, loss of output, resultant delays and penalties.

123

Added to this there is a cost factor which determines how much money, time and effort should be spent to bring the risks to acceptable levels. Who decides what is an acceptable level? Often this will be laid down through a British, European or International Standard, it may be through a professional Code of Conduct agreed by that industrial sector; it may be through legislation or local bye-laws or it may simply be the level of risk a company is aware of and is prepared to bear. Considerations such as these, including relevant standards must be taken into account in designing your products.

Safety by design must be assured.

Key stages in the product development process	Assuring safety
Idea/design brief	Feasibility (versus desirability) including an initial risk assessment Checking standards, regulations, legislation
Initial specification	Includes key safety considerations and features Quality features and quality control procedures established
Design proposals	Account taken of safety and quality features Risk assessment carried out for each proposal
Manufacturing specification	Includes safety features Procedures for quality control and testing safety
Prototypes	Tested against standards and safety features of specification, tested in operating conditions and exceeding these conditions
Manufacturing process	Risk assessment of processes and equipment used Quality control procedures
Product	Tested against standards and safety features of specification, tested in operating conditions and exceeding these conditions Continuous Improvement – always trying to improve the product including quality and safety features

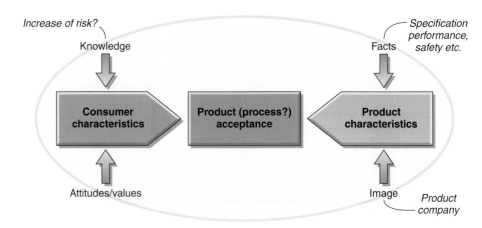

Product acceptance: Safety can be a key factor for customers.

In the food industry, HACCP (Hazard Analysis and Critical Control Points) is used by companies to:

- analyse the possibility of risk and its level of impact on the product
- decide how the risk will be managed and monitored.

The principles of HACCP can be applied to other products as shown by these students' work.

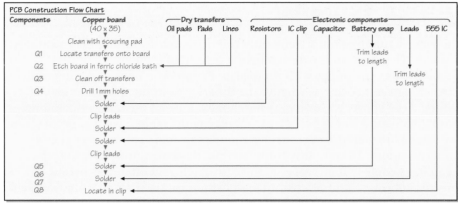

PCB Construction Flow Chart

PCB Construction Flow Chart with Components column, Copper board (40 x 35), Dry transfers (Oil pads, Pads, Lines), Resistors, IC clip, Electronic components (Capacitor, Battery snap, Leads, 555 IC)

Components | Copper board (40 x 35)
- Clean with scouring pad
- Q1 Locate transfers onto board
- Q2 Etch board in ferric chloride bath
- Q3 Clean off transfers
- Q4 Drill 1 mm holes
- Solder
- Clip leads
- Solder
- Solder
- Clip leads
- Q5 Solder
- Q6 Solder
- Q7
- Q8 Locate in clip

Trim leads to length
Trim leads to length

PCB Quality of Manufacture Check List

	Description	How to enforce	Job done	Teacher mark	Penalty marks
Q1	Copper board shining	Observation and use of scouring pad	✓		
Q2	Transfers correctly positioned	Check against circuit diagram			
Q3	All tracks etched properly	Use a multimeter to check continuity			
Q4	All holes drilled	Count – there should be 24 in total			
Q5	Are leads the correct length and in the correct holes?	Measure length of leads and compare with product plans			
Q6	Check components are in correct positions on board and battery connections are correct way round	Check board against circuit diagram and component overlay			
Q7	Check all soldering joints are shiny – check for 'dry' joints	Observation			
Q8	Check 555 is the correct way round	Check against plans			

If 'Job done' column is ticked and job has not actually been done properly

These examples show how students applied HACCP procedures to the development of electronic products.

FMEA – Failure Mode and Effects Analysis – is another useful technique. It involves asking yourself four questions at key stages in product development:

- What might go wrong?
- What effect would this have?
- What might cause it to go wrong?
- What can I do to prevent it going wrong?

 Health and safety, D&T Routes Core Book 144

Focused task: Risk assessment and garden equipment

The sales of lawnmowers and other powered garden equipment has increased dramatically in recent years as people have more leisure time. Unfortunately there has also been an alarming increase in the number of accidents resulting from incorrect use of equipment. For example: people cutting themselves on moving lawnmower blades, usually as a result of not unplugging the machine before turning it over; electrical shock caused by cutting through the lead and not using an circuit breaker; and people cutting their feet on rotary blades.

Manufacturers have used a variety of methods to avoid these accidents such as switches that require two hands to operate, trigger grips that switch the machine off when released, and movement indicators mounted on the top of mowers.

Heavy duty cables, double insulation and the use of fuses all help. Developments in materials technology have led to the use of plastic rather than steel blades.

1 Select a piece of electrical garden equipment.
2 Carry out a risk assessment, recording it in note form.
3 Survey the safety features used on a variety of equipment and use this to help you identify safety features to be included on your selected item.
4 Prepare an introductory sheet of information for new users.

 Dixons Mastercare case study 70

Design semantics

The term **semantics** most frequently refers to understanding the meanings of words. However, in the design field it is used to signal the fact that artefacts carry meanings with them also. People who have never heard the term 'design semantics' recognise the differences in the messages given by owning a red sports car or a grey hatchback. Like all meanings (including those attached to words), these can change with fashion: what's 'groovy' one day can be 'uncool' the next, or this month's trainers can be next year's embarrassment. Despite this complication, designers must consider the meanings people will interpret in their products and often this means considering your client or customer's position rather than pleasing yourself. Knowing the culture (or sub-culture) of the market into which your product is aimed becomes important, and often requires research.

Products bring meanings with them. They make up our **material culture** – the concrete ways in which we express ourselves and our values. If we are all surrounded by the same things we will lack variety and stimulus and will lose the richness of separate cultures and diverse individual identities. This has implications for the increasing dominance of high volume production. We are probably not concerned that all our lightbulbs look alike but in some things we want individuality. Fortunately, there are signs that flexible manufacturing technology, together with electronic product definition, is going to allow us to achieve the benefits of low unit cost (formerly given only by standardised mass production) with broad product variety (previously the preserve of custom — or one-off — production). Already we have come a long way from Henry Ford's famous 1920s dictum 'You can have any colour you want, as long as it's black'!

 Flexible manufacturing technology **174**

Case Study: **Neocreole cooking pot**

Cooking pot designed by RCA student Philip Marshall.

This project at the Royal College of Art was undertaken by a student from the Caribbean. He set about redesigning the most common cooking item in the world – the coal pot, a simple metal pot which contains a coal fire to cook over, similar to a barbecue.

To re-design a coal pot to be more efficient is not difficult – most barbecue grills have air vents to control the rate of burn, which make them more sophisticated designs. However, one of Philip's main concerns was the 'language' of the new design, that is the messages it would convey. He was keen to ensure that it would fit in the culture it was designed for, which is a product of a rich blend of European, Amerindian and African cultures, referred to as 'Creole'. To help him capture what otherwise might be unarticulated ideas he researched deeply into the nature of Caribbean Creole culture and its symbols. His research took him to Creole languages, beliefs derived from mixtures such as Roman Catholic and African, and products such as sandals and plant pots fashioned from old tyres and the 'shirtjack' – a shirt-come-jacket that evolved as a hot climate alternative to the European suit.

'The beauty of the creolised object lies in its duality; it is both familiar and novel to the cultures that spawned it ...'

Philip Marshall.

He was also anxious to contribute to the preservation of the Creole culture, feeling that "the Caribbean, like so much of the developing world, has attempted to emulate the first world and in doing so has adopted a consumerism that has all but annihilated all traces of its cultural autonomy. Our homes, our objects our very life-styles are in danger of becoming indistinct from that of the rest of the western world," he wrote.

 Assessing technology: Trinidad 94

Assessing technology: Trinidad — 94

Philip's analysis of Creole culture did not shirk from recognising that the main two continental contributions, European and African, brought with them traditions of clearly defined roles – master and slave. He linked to this a perception that even today, status and position in society remain vitally important and that led him toward a notion of 'aspirational objects' through which people attempt to achieve what is desired but with limited resources.

These then were the themes he worked with as he designed. To achieve a Creole feel to his objects he designed with multiple parts, though all were new, to achieve a redefinition of the Creole aesthetic. The materials he used needed to be assessed for their cultural feel and their aesthetics. Functional considerations included the primary function: cooking (airflow, pan supports, hygiene, fuel replenishment), and secondaries such as stability, lifting handles, warming spaces etc. All this had to be considered in the context of the demanding environment of highly concentrated heat, wide temperature ranges etc. So, typical of a design project, a complex range of demands was faced, some of which conflicted, all of which had to be brought to an optimal conclusion without losing track of the cultural significance of the artefact throughout it's life.

 CD racks case study 69–70

CD racks case study — 69–70

Some of the design sketches for the cooking pot.

Designing for manufacture

The purpose of this section is to help you whilst working on school/college projects to consider manufacturing considerations and to relate the issues that face you to those which companies face as shown in Chapter 2 Designing and Manufacturing, Customer need to customer satisfaction (page 50).

Every design task involves working within constraints, that is the limitations to what is possible imposed by such as costs, materials and consumer acceptance. A major set of these constraints concern suitability for manufacture, some of which might apply in any circumstance (e.g. every material has its inherent limits) and some of which are specific to a particular design under consideration (e.g. whether a machining process would be cost-effective for a particular product). In your designing and making projects you have, no doubt, had to consider the skills of the workforce as this has usually been you – i.e. whether you would be able to make what you designed. In doing so you have probably chosen a simpler manufacturing process at times to make sure you can carry it out successfully.

Some manufacturing processes impose constraints on the designer, an example being vacuum forming. Moulds for these products must taper slightly and avoid sharp corners, whether or not this is desirable for other reasons, or else consistent quality of product is impossible.

As well as imposing constraints, there are times when a production process is an opportunity, or a stimulus for new ideas. For example, if a part has previously been fabricated from metals and casting becomes available as an alternative, new flowing forms to suit the casting process are then required, which will give the designer the chance to explore forms that were not feasible for a fabricated approach.

Whether to work within the production facilities immediately available or to go 'out of house' to get something made elsewhere is the sort of decision you might face personally as well as professional designers. Similarly, given the requirements of a particular design, there will often be a choice of possible manufacturing approaches (see Choosing a manufacturing system page 159).

"How will it be made?" should be a constant question throughout your design development. Also, you should be consulting others about this question regularly. (The PDSA case study page 224, shows a student team consulting manufacturers at a number of stages.) Thirdly, and probably most importantly, do not try to conclude your design on paper – you will not discover many of the main manufacturing questions you will have to face if you do this. Your designing should progress as a constant to-and-fro between 'the drawing board and the bench' – you will almost always need to make a number of three-dimensional models as you design, some of which are to directly help with decisions about manufacturing feasibility.

Examples of manufacturing feasibility models:

- parts of a product full-size, from the correct materials to test a joining method
- colour, fabric swatches or other material samples
- fabrics laid over a framework or form to see how they 'drape'
- full scale prototypes (where feasible) for pre-production testing and production planning.

 Modelling, D&T Routes Core Book 96–102

Case Study: Food product development – Pennine Foods

Pennine Foods generate new chilled and frozen food products constantly in response to changes in the season, fashion and sales levels of existing products. Initial work is carried out in a test kitchen by chefs working from basic recipes, experimenting using trial-and-error methods.

Transferring these prototypes to volume production is liable to distortion as the processes to be used will be different, and food ingredients can react differently when used in large quantities. Other considerations also have to be taken into account such as the shelf life of a commercial product between production and consumption. Developing a new cheese sauce for a pasta recipe to be produced in volume required an initial attempt to match the chef's original and then developments to refine the taste, texture, viscosity, appearance and overall consistency. Tests have been developed to assess each of these, some of which are scientifically based and objective. Some have to be subjective such as taste tests carried out on a number of trained volunteers. As with most products both individual components (such as the sauce) and the full product must be tested, as the latter can be disliked despite a favourable reception being previously given to every part.

Current trends suggest that subjective tests will remain the final adjudicator but that improvements in electronic product definition (EPD) techniques may bring many changes. It is likely that mini, flexible manufacturing systems will be developed which allow much of the process to be carried out by simulation. Trial production will then take place on a small scale, but using volume production techniques to allow much more highly refined prototypes and precise recording of ingredients and measures. Only then will a specification be finalised for volume production.

 Electronic product definition   85

A product in the development kitchen at Pennine Foods.

Manufacturing specifications

A product's specification whether in the food or any other product sector usually starts in outline form, often as set out in a design brief. Throughout the design development process the specification is detailed further until it reaches a more or less final form ready for manufacture. At this stage, the materials and processes that have been decided upon go into the development of the original specification to make up a **manufacturing specification**. The specification is an important reflection of the two-way dialogue between designing and manufacturing. In the Psion case study on page 79 you can see how a company uses a specification to ensure that every possible decision has been weighed adequately and then recorded prior to major investment in preparations for manufacturing.

 Manufacturing specification, D&T Routes Core Book   147

Designing for cost-effective manufacture

Use this checklist repeatedly during designing to see if you can make your production more cost-effective. Ask yourself whether you can:

- reduce the number of components
- reduce the number of processes (see the PDSA case study, page 224)
- reduce the range of materials
- standardise parts to use repeatedly
- use more efficient materials (e.g. casting rather than fabricating)
- use standard sizes of readily available materials

- use standard available components (cost-effective but may inhibit ideas)
- design shapes that nest well on a sheet
- use more efficient structures (e.g. a shell instead of a frame)
- design for easy assembly
- design jigs for machining and assembly operations
- reduce the skill needed for production
- buy in ready-made components
- buy in external expertise.

Approaches to designing

Many people have tried to unravel the processes that designers use. Designers have tried to do this for themselves and some have worked with psychologists; usually with the intention of discovering what makes for success in designing, to improve their own work, or to pass the processes on to others. We do some of this here, to help you improve your designing processes.

In your previous school experience you probably met the idea of 'the design process' and perhaps had a set of steps given to you to follow. In this book (and others in the D&T series) process diagrams have been used to help you to take a sensible route through your designing that should result in high quality products.

| ▶ | **D&T Challenges Green Book** | 95 |

| ▶ | **D&T Routes Core Book** | 65 |

Diagrams and procedure lists can be useful, but they can also be misleading as designing is in fact more complex than any diagram or list can portray. Most people agree that to talk of 'the design process' is misleading for there are as many design processes as there are products being designed. One of the key characteristics of designing is that for every occasion special factors apply that make every one unique. For example, the target market may be different, the materials and technologies available may have changed, cost limits may alter and the background knowledge and skill of the designer will constantly vary. However, study of designers' ways of working in many sub-disciplines such as industrial design, fashion, architecture and food product development reveals many common factors and this book among others, tries to make these clear, so you have a hope of learning from those who have gone before. You will benefit from reading the books that designers and others have written whilst you are busy with designing and making yourself. You should always try to relate what the 'experts' say to what you are doing and how you are going about doing it.

Three golden rules will help you as you struggle to bring your designing and manufacturing up to an advanced standard:

DO read the books, listen to your teachers, study magazines, talk to professionals, visit exhibitions of work and learn from them.
DON'T believe a word of it unless it makes sense to you and relates to what you are doing!
ALWAYS question everything – don't be complacent or comfortable.

❝ *If you feel comfortable with what I'm doing you should probably fire me.*❞

Jonathan Ive, Design Director Apple Computer (International Design magazine, Jan/Feb 1997)

By this stage in your work you should be moving on from routine procedures – not working on today's project in the way you worked on the last one. You should be reflecting on the processes you used previously and considering the extent to which they apply in the present situation. You should also be challenging everything – only by doing this will your work be creative, original, appropriate and successful. This is why designers are always arguing!

The following case study will give you some insight into one successful designer's progress.

Case Study: Design and ideas — methods and instinct

This case study was written by Steven Kyffin, Royal College of Art.

"To come to a full understanding of design, the discipline and the manner in which designers (the practitioners), approach the activity is, in both cases, probably unfathomable and unusually personal. I say 'unusual' because frequently, writing about the activity of design suggests that there are one or two methods to choose from that guarantee a successful result. My anecdotal research and indeed my own experience, shows that this is plainly not the case. Here, I am considering the different approaches to, or values of, design the discipline; in the realms of educational and professional activity through my own experiences as an industrial designer: an autobiographical account of the union of design and ideas, methods and instinct.

"My journey begins as an 11 year old schoolboy and continues through a life of professional practice, to today as Course Director of Industrial Design at the Royal College of Art. This is the life of someone as they learn to look and observe, interpret and communicate ideas, through the language of making; to someone who now practices as a consultant industrial designer and a director of design education at the highest level. These two roles bring together the two complimentary, yet apparently opposing, views of the designer as artist and cultural communicator and designer as commercial engineer, problem-solver and wealth creator. I have come to believe that it is impossible to be fully one without the other. One concerns itself with ideas, conceptual notions, process and instinct, and the other with useful formula, method, technique and logical accountability.

"The conflict between logic and intuition, for that is what we are discussing, has been debated for ever, not only in design but in every other discipline. I came to experience both ends of this non-linear spectrum through secondary school, university and in my professional life through practice and education. My secondary education was taken in the late sixties and early seventies at one of the few schools in the UK which valued the parallel of learning through designing and the whole educational process. The process of problem-solving was seen by many schools to be the ideal way of structuring this process, but in my case this was not as important as what might now be termed problem-finding or just creating, looking, investigating and communicating one's ideas through making. By contrast my university education provided an understanding of the vocational process of industrial design, and of the materials and processes of manufacture in wood, metal, plastics and ceramics. I also experienced the professional world of the designer as it existed at that time. Postgraduate study at the Royal College of Art involved study and exploration of how design could make a difference to the way we made and used things. In summary, undergraduate study was about 'how' and the post graduate study was more about 'why'.

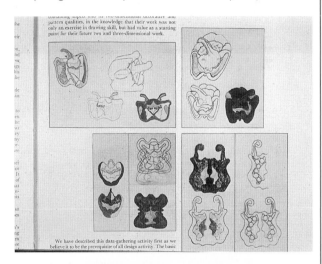

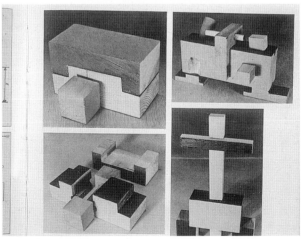

a) Work from the Pocklington school design basic course. Peppers drawing and interlocking forms.

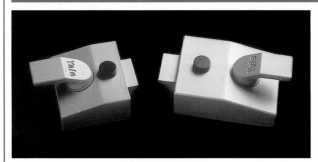

b) Commercial work for Yale.

c) Later work; a sextant

d) Later work; a waste bin.

"After a few years in London consultancies and eventually my own, I slowly began to realise that my work, although fortunately making me a lot of money, was becoming repetitive and I was losing the ability to think about and see design in the wider context. This resulted in work that became entirely limited to technical innovation. It lacked poetry or meaning, other than profit.

"A greater involvement in teaching part-time at the Royal College of Art highlighted these ideas while helping the students to develop their own views. My eyes were opened and finally I made the connection between my secondary school experiences, what I had instinctively tried to achieve at the Royal College of Art as a student and the enormous breadth of European architectural education.

"In my secondary school experience I was essentially learning through design to discover the possible and how to make decisions and connections that would enable me to act on my discoveries. I began to develop my own methodologies and processes, to rely on my intuition and instinct rather than relying on closed prescriptive methods.

"The school's objectives were:

◆ to lead the student towards a conscious and critical awareness of the ethical, emotional and aesthetic values, technical possibilities and the ability to make both valid and intellectual decisions. (This was termed **design awareness**.)
◆ to extend and improve the facility to find and bring ideas to physical fruition (**design activity**).
◆ to make conscious the experience and satisfaction of creative activity that one hopes will last into adult life.

"When considering in some detail the design experiences at the Royal College of Art, a post-graduate and in many cases now, a post-professional institution, the second objective is also central to our work. The 'finding and bringing of ideas to physical fruition'. This in the language of industrial design, now reads 'using one's creative process to find ideas and express them as object'. The aim of the Industrial Design course at the Royal College of Art is to enable designers to reposition themselves as creative people who can lead design as a discipline. A discipline that connects the disparate fragments of the present and opens the possibilities of the future rather than relying on the prescriptive methodologies of solving the problems forced upon us from the past.

"This means that primarily we are looking to work with student designers who each represent elements of the many different approaches to the design discipline, but who are not yet focused in the direction that their future work might take. We suggest that Design as an activity has ceased to be reactive, following the needs of the marketing department and providing stylistic answers to technical problems. It now needs to be strategic and proactive and co-lead the commercial process, interpret our daily lives and provide the things and systems that enliven it. Design is a rich, complex and connective activity, drawing its references from, and in turn addressing a wide range of concerns. I believe that connective structures actually widen the designer's field of vision rather than inhibit it. A greater variety and richness of ideas leads to broader human experiences through the resulting objects and proves that design has a voice and a perspective that truly contributes creatively to our future lives.

"Open encouragement to explore and interrogate one's own creative process and one's own vision for the purpose of design provides each designer with the creative foundation to build a thesis for work in the second year of the course that might propose the beginnings of a new future for Design. So, at the Royal College of Art we bring together designers from many backgrounds and disciplines to question industrial design and begin to propose a future for this connective and multidisciplinary profession both in terms of its methods and its effect on the future. We hope that they leave the College with the confidence and refined perspectives to enable them to lead design into the next century as the practitioners of tomorrow.

"Through these personal experiences I have attempted to reveal something that shows that the way we approach design (the organisation of the manufactured world) is entirely dependant on who we are and how we see the world around us, interpret and communicate what we think about it.

"In conclusion then, my vision of design in education:

- at school, design is part of the whole education process of personal growth
- at undergraduate level, design is primarily vocational training for professional practice
- at post-graduate and beyond, we have the opportunity to reassess what design is, knowing both worlds.

"But without a breadth of education inspiring the instinctive creative ability and the professional application, the designer today will risk becoming formulaic and repetitive."

Pity the poor designer!

The case study above shows that there is no one 'correct' approach to designing. Methods of designing are as varied as the products themselves and even in a field that is limited to say industrial product design, many influences come to bear on the designer.

The intentions of all the 'stakeholders' in a design will influence the process and may be reflected in the outcome. At a company level, stakeholders include all those who contribute to how a design evolves, the designers, their clients (including their product manager), marketing, finance and other responsible people. At a system-wide level, the pressures from competitive products and the demands of the final customer or user will also come to bear.

At the level of the individual product, the basic functions it has to perform will of course matter as will other considerations such as aesthetics, style, life expectancy, maintenance considerations and environmental impacts etc. Which way is the designer to turn therefore, to know how to approach a design task?

If we should attempt to categorise the approaches to designing, two contrasting poles could be identified; the intuitive approach, and the systematic. But, all designers must work both systematically and intuitively to a greater or lesser degree. The essential differences between the two approaches is that, intuitive design depends on the designer's personal perception and feed-back from the design process, in 'real-time' while designing is taking place. The systematic approach, as the name suggests is far more deliberate and methodical. This does not necessarily mean reams of calculations (though it might), but the design will be considered, sketched and generally thought-through before attempting any critical design phase.

These descriptions may seem to imply that intuitive designing is more enjoyable than the systematic approach but this need not be true. Carefully planning the approach and execution of a design can be just as exciting and rewarding as the intuitive approach, particularly when the outcome is successful and goes to plan. Conversely, intuitive design can easily get out of control, frustrating the designer, who may have to make several new attempts wasting valuable time and materials.

133

The boundary between art and design

Fine artists, painters, printmakers and sculptors, may be considered as having the greatest design freedom, involved in a largely self-assessed activity. Primarily they satisfy their own creative purposes, with other considerations coming second or not considered at all. However, they too have to obey limits such as the constraints of the materials they choose to use and some of these impose strict disciplines. For example, a painter's pigments will behave in particular ways and these differ between oil colours and types of water colour. Mastering their respective materials and techniques and working within inherent limitations impose constraints on any artist. Within these they can work intuitively.

Designers seldom have so much freedom, but they still have opportunities to apply their intuition. Designing by 'eye' or 'feel', as it is often termed, is a very satisfying way to work. The sensation that the process is just slightly out of your control allows the designer to exploit uncharacteristic opportunities, pushing the boundaries. An intermediate example of this is the ceramicist or potter, who may work directly with clay to develop new designs – a material that may collapse at any moment – making judgements about the form, strength, function etc. of the emerging artefact. The terms 'eye' and 'feel' are often code for experience. Every designer works, if only occasionally, in this way but a person with good design judgement (based on experience) evaluates each decision and outcome.

In the catering field, star chefs from famous restaurants in particular are known for their creative, artistic flair, equalled with technical knowledge about the balance of flavours, textures and nutritional value in a meal. They create their own recipes as 'one-offs' initially and then are expected to re-create them on demand. In the test kitchen where new food products for volume-production start their life, the first 'generating ideas' stage is much the same but the one-off that is developed to the level of the ideal prototype has to go through a complex further stage similar to 'production engineering' in other fields.

Fine art can also be very system-based. Mathematical principles were applied in the work of artists Klee, Kandinsky, Miro, Duchamp, Gabo and the Constructivist movement, who demonstrated a very systematic approach to art. The 'golden section', mathematical and visually perfect, has been used by artists and designer alike.

S9
Amplify L3/4, L3/7, L3/10 . . . (i.e. every third L3, starting with L3/4 . . . L3/58 by a factor F about straight lines joining their extremities.[5]
Designate areas between L3/4 and L3/7, L3/10 and L3/13 . . . (i.e. alternate areas) . . . L3/52 and L3/55 as areas A3/1, A3/2, A3/3 . . . A3/9.
S10
Amplify L3/6, L3/9, L3/12 . . . (i.e. every third L3 starting with L3/6) . . . L3/57 as determined by S8, by factor F.
Designate areas between L3/6 and L3/9, L3/12 and L3/15 . . . (i.e. alternate areas . . . L3/54 and L3/57 as areas A4/1, A4/2, A4/3 . . . A4/9.
S11
Invert the *Mirror-Image* of S9 and *Superimpose* this on S10.
Adjust all A4 numbers to read from North to South.[6]
S12
Subdivide P into 5 equal areas A5/1, A5/2, A5/3, A5/4, A5/5 by 6 straight lines L4/1, L4/2, L4/3 . . . L4/6 in D2 along intersections of lines L3.
Exchange lines L3 between areas A3 and A4 so that each area A5 contains either crests or troughts but not both.
Establish and *Apply* a system of preferential overlapping 01 within and between A3 and A4.

A painting by Jeffrey Steele with some of the program that generated it on the left. Oil on Canvas, 1967.

By contrast with the artist, the designer must consider others. Designers work to meet the views and needs of other people (for example, architects – spaces to live in, transport designers – moving people and goods etc.), but they can also *create* needs and wants.

The process of designing

Design problems are always complex, having a number of (often conflicting) objectives, many constraints and just as many possible solutions. The designer will be attempting to satisfy a client or clients, the specialised requirements of a user group, the constraints of manufacture, the limitations of equipment and material suppliers, and the demands of the market place. This inevitably makes any design an optimisation (rather than a compromise) between these pressures.

The process of designing is in some phases noisy, active, exciting and creative, in other phases it is a slow process of developing and refining a set of ideas. Drawing becomes a thinking device for the mind, drawing as you 'feel' as well as to communicate with others – intuitive and rational at one and the same time. Designers need to look, question, interpret, communicate ideas and respond imaginatively. This is more than just solving problems! It involves leading and directing a creative and innovative activity, possibly managing teams of specialists and experts, bringing together all of the contributors to a successful design conclusion.

The designer's role is one that is always responding to change and in many cases instigating change. The constantly shifting attitudes and desires of society and advances in materials and technology ensure this. The designer needs to change mode between pro-active and reactive responses as dictated by the design situation.

Systematic design

A rigorous, systematic approach to design is to be found in software engineering and computer software design. In large software design projects, involving many teams of experts, a systematic approach is essential. The project can be so large that the outcome becomes abstract to most involved. No one person has a complete overview of the task, therefore structure and organisation is essential. Each team will have a clearly defined sub-task with precise standards applied to the input and output data. Standards will also be specified for the format and language to be used for the programming task. But even within these tight constraints, the designers can apply creative skills and intuitive design to produce an elegant and beautiful solution to their programming task. The end result may not be easily compared to the aesthetic heights of the latest automotive styling from Italian design establishments, but it does compare to the best poetry and prose or graphic design.

Concurrent engineering and you

This section, bridging between detailed consideration of designing and then manufacturing, aims to help you both understand how concurrent engineering is bringing these processes closer together in industry and to apply some concurrent engineering (CE) techniques in your own work. More about CE in the industrial context can be found on page 175. The focused tasks give you lists of CE procedures from which you will have to select. It is unlikely that all of these tasks will be relevant to your projects and extremely unlikely that you could carry out all of them even if they did! Reference to the lists of tasks however, should guide you through the management of your project.

The integration of designing and manufacturing processes is extremely complicated for most companies because the development of complex industrial products requires the specialist skills of different people. However, concurrent engineering approaches have been developed to do just this, seeking to bring closer together designing and manufacturing considerations and to draw in other functional areas including marketing, finance, production engineering etc. The key feature of concurrent engineering is the grouping of personnel from different departments (or 'functional areas') into a product team which combines their expertise throughout a product's development process. In the day-to-day running of the project, these people will work together with frequent informal consultations, often in the same building but, increasingly, in separate countries with telematic links (phones/fax/computer networks/video conferencing). The whole project team will meet as often as the Project Manager considers necessary.

▶ Psion Case Study	77

Product development teams do not generally have authority in themselves to decide on (or 'confirm') the development routes the company will pursue. This is usually done with senior managers from the company at a series of stage points in the process when review meetings are held (see Milestone Planning, page 79). The working pattern might therefore look something like the diagram.

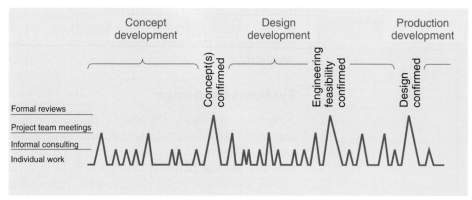

A typical pattern of product development activity.

It is important that the progress of the project is marked by this series of formal reviews as the schedule of meetings gives the team a set of targets. Also, the team knows precisely whether what they are working on is still speculative and exploratory or confirmed by the company. Reviews therefore mark the points at which decisions are 'signed-off' (with the signature of the responsible senior manager and/or client) and the company accepts corporate responsibility.

When designing and manufacturing in school you may be both designer and manufacturer but you too will have to report to others for confirmation or a 'go-ahead'. Whilst it is easier for you to work concurrently on your projects than for a company with many personnel, you might also try simulating aspects of their process to gain some of the benefits of working in a team. At the very least, you could schedule progress reviews with your teacher and your client and preparation for these with some co-students – acting as a support teams for each other. In any event you will need to spend time on some industrial product development considerations at every stage of your designing and manufacturing.

▶ Using support teams, D&T Routes Core Book	10

Generating the concept and early design ideas

To generate the first ideas for a new product, the whole project team will be very active and several initial meetings are likely to be held. This sets up the team, starts the ball rolling and gets everybody thoroughly inside the new project – it is the first really creative stage. Marketing people have a lead role at this stage as they have the 'intelligence' to feed in from the market place. Designers, typically have a critical role in both the creative thinking – generating ideas – and in being able to visualise and organise ideas on paper as they emerge. Production engineers may have ideas to contribute about production processes or materials.

Focused task: Concept development and early design ideas

While at or approaching this stage you could:

- check that a market actually exists and the market's potential
- research consumer characteristics and economic factors such as age, gender, lifestyle, social trends and employment statistics, to see how they will affect demand

- research competing products
- consider marketing strategies for your (undeveloped) product idea
- obtain and use feedback from marketing to help develop early design ideas
- create an outline specification
- generate initial ideas.

 Generating ideas, Routes Core Book   53

Design development

Once a design concept has been generated, a period of concentrated development must follow. Commonly, two or more concepts will be developed alongside each other at this stage, sometimes, depending on the scale of the project, with a different sub-team responsible for each concept. This can be seen in the Jaguar XK8 case study (page 201) with design themes labelled 'evocative ' and 'traditional' being developed in competition with each other for a time. The purpose of this is to explore the potential in a concept. It is not usually possible to know how feasible, how attractive, or how functional an initial design concept is until its limits have been explored. By no means the least important aspect of this is the gradual progress up the level of quality at which models are produced, from initial sketches and outline 'concept models' through to large scale, detailed mock-ups.

Focused task: Design development

While at or approaching this stage you could:

- start to detail your specification, prioritising needs and requirements of both the customer and manufacturer
- consider ergonomic, aesthetic and functional requirements
- check your design ideas and develop them to meet these requirements
- model your ideas

- identify and take account of some production parameters, such as the quantity of products to be manufactured
- identify and take account of some production process constraints, such as suitability and availability of resources, environmental considerations etc.
- check the likely cost implications.

Design confirmation

This phase sees the project team starting to close in on the final design, though more than one concept may still be maintained as a possibility. The team will continue to consider each design's 'manufacturability'. Advanced models will be made which amount to pre-production prototypes. Initial tests will be carried out to indicate the suitability of manufacturing processes, finalise materials specifications and confirm that the design will meet performance requirements. Marketing will be considering the sales potential of the emerging design and confirming their sales strategy. Production engineering will be exploring the details of the demands on them and starting to calculate costs and production rates. Approval at this stage means the company is committed. Further investment will be undertaken and the chosen design will go ahead to the next stage.

Focused task: Design confirmation

While at or approaching this stage you could:

- test various designs to measure their relative merits/deficiencies in both production and user terms
- calculate the resource requirements, including materials, equipment, tools and labour, that each design alternative would need
- work out usage rates and lead times for different alternatives
- work out the likely processing times needed for each key stage of production
- work out when and how often materials would need to be ordered to meet the demands of your level of production

- develop a production plan for your product
- confirm your production costs and selling price, including prime costs, production and non-production overheads
- identify the kind of quality assurance systems you would need in place to be able to provide product reliably and the quality required by customers, within budget
- identify packaging needs for your product package.

Production development

At this stage the company commits itself to the final design and moves toward manufacture. The production engineers will come to the fore to ensure that the company is equipped to produce what is intended. Training needs are determined, volumes are finalised, precise production processes determined and details of costings confirmed. This stage becomes very mathematical as amounts, rates of flow, sequences of supplies etc. are all calculated. It is common that as these details are worked out, the designers will still be involved in detail design development and modifications. A production prototype may be manufactured incorporating, and further demanding, modifications. Some of the modifications will come about because the final production processes decided on will drive changes to the designs. The PDSA case study (see page 224) illustrates this well as the Telford students adapted their design to take advantage of the new production process that their chosen manufacturer could offer. Changes to factory provision or layout will be undertaken with previous production being moved elsewhere, ceasing or tailing-off.

Focused task: Production development

While at or approaching this stage you could:

- finalise all aspects of the design of your product
- select materials that can be most easily adapted, handled and stored in the quantity required to meet your scale of production
- confirm that the materials will suit your design specification
- produce a manufacturing specification and manufacturing plan
- choose equipment and machinery that best suits the material input and rate of production you intend
- specify the use of safety equipment and health and safety procedures
- ensure that components will be produced and assembled according to your specification
- plan finishing procedures for each part.

Manufacturing

To be ready to manufacture, a considerable amount of detailed planning will have been carried out. Production managers will schedule every single process with a master plan (GANNT chart) to show the workflow. Contracts will have been drawn up and agreed with suppliers, and supply chains will have been organised that feed into the manufacturing plan. Sales will be ready to deal with the flow of new products and marketing will be starting to implement their strategy.

Focused task: Manufacturing

While at or approaching this stage you could:

- place orders for all parts or components that are being bought in
- ensure that material supplies are available in the right quantity and quality
- finalise quality assurance procedures
- ensure that all necessary tools and equipment are available
- prepare necessary jigs and fixtures
- predict needs for later stages in your process and put appropriate arrangements in hand
- continue recording design changes
- keep a commentary on your manufacturing decisions, revising your manufacturing specification as necessary.

CHAPTER FOUR **Manufacturing**

This chapter sets out to increase your understanding of contemporary approaches to manufacturing in industry and to help you relate these to your own ways of working. It will be most valuable to you if you constantly ask yourself, "What influence might this approach in industry have on my working procedures?"

The word 'manufacturing' originally meant 'made by hand' in the days when products were individually crafted even if the same product was individually made, repeatedly. We now rely almost entirely on industrial manufacturing methods, and products made in large numbers (high volume). Increasingly though, manufacturing technology will make possible individualised products with the cost-benefits of high volume production. Manufacturing methods are continually developing, to improve existing products and to develop new ones.

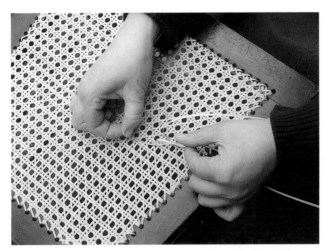

This hand-made chair was designed for hand processes and construction techniques. Hand manufacturing methods mean dependence on manipulative skills. No two chairs will be exactly the same. Is this an advantage or disadvantage?

Millions of these drinks cans are manufactured every year. Automated manufacturing methods mean little reliance on hand skills and highly uniform products.

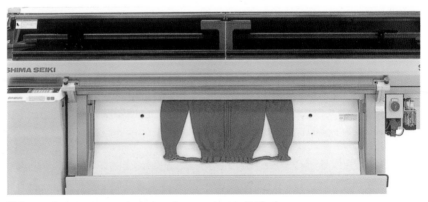

This seamless garment was designed to meet an individual customer's requirements. The manufacturing system that is being used to produce it also allows the benefits of automated repeat manufacturing.

From customer need to customer satisfaction

In chapter 2 (page 50) we explained how customer needs form one of the main driving forces behind successful manufacturing and why customers are so important. When the main product development functions, including marketing, design, production, engineering and finance are working well together, the need to satisfy customers is usually the principle motive.

Manufacturing activity must be seen as much more than the series of production processes needed to form products from raw materials. Manufacturers have to respond rapidly to the market forces that result from customer preferences, including those likely to exist in the future. They also have to maintain the production of existing products, for at least as long as these remain profitable, and to use all of their available resources to maximum effect. For example, expensive tooling developed for an 'old' product might have to be re-used in a new one to help reduce production costs and make products more saleable.

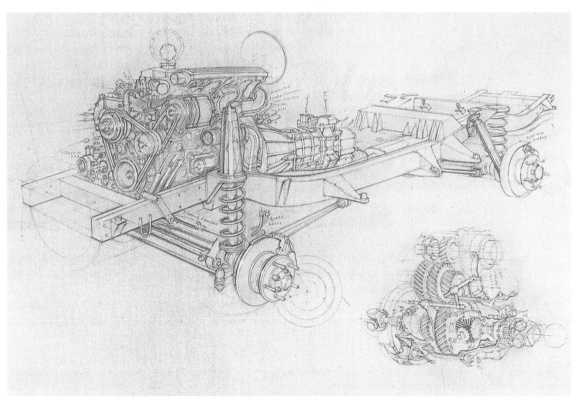

The chasis of the Land Rover Discovery was developed and used on earlier models.

At first sight this might appear contradictory. Surely brand new products deserve brand new tooling in every respect and ought not to carry vestiges of old ones or parts not specifically designed for them? In reality manufacturers also make decisions that help satisfy their own needs, especially the need to make a profit. This does not necessarily conflict with satisfying customer needs, especially if quality is maintained and savings are passed on to them in the form of reduced prices. In this section we will re-visit this idea from time to time.

Market research is used by manufacturers to help identify the kind of market that the product will need to serve. This will include such things as the size of the market as well as the product life-cycle. This information is critical in determining the manufacturing system that will be needed to provide the required scale of production – how many products will be made and over what time scale e.g. 1000 per week for a year to produce a total of 45,000. (No factory can produce consistently at target numbers for every day of the year.)

Understanding the consequences of volume variations

While volume of production influences the manufacturing methods chosen, other factors are involved and you need an understanding of these. The numbered points below state information that is shown on the following diagram.

1 Higher volumes allow savings to be made in labour costs through more efficient production methods, e.g. a high volume, off-the-peg outfit could cost less than you would pay for the material to make one yourself. This shows the high proportion of distribution costs.

2 Lower volumes may mean higher labour costs if less is produced in the same time, e.g. a tailor-made or made-to-measure suit.

3 Lower volumes often need higher levels of skill to cope with the demands of small batches, or a succession of individual products with each having different requirements to be met. Because few stages are repeated in exactly the same way the staff must be more skilled to cope with varied demands, e.g. an individual meal produced by a chef at a high quality restaurant.

4 Higher volumes may be less dependent on highly skilled staff, at least for certain stages of production, e.g. fast food served from a drive-in take-away. Because fast-food items are standardised, many of the stages can be easily repeated or made easier by more efficient methods. Overall, the staff need less skill to cope with the demand (but this does not mean they are totally un-skilled).

5 Higher volumes allow more efficient production through narrowing the variety of work tasks, e.g. fast-food production often depends upon very specialised staff who will concentrate on a few tasks.

6 Lower volumes often demand that a wide range of tasks is expected of personnel, e.g. the chef may be preparing a variety of dishes for customers in a restaurant, all at the same time.

7 Lower volumes have meant that products can be more individual and unique.

8 Higher volumes usually mean that the design of components is more standardised to simplify production.

9 Higher volumes generally rely on the use of more specialised tools and equipment, e.g. production-line equipment used to assemble a modern mass-produced motor car.

10 Lower volumes require more general equipment to be used flexibly, often in the hands of the highly skilled craftsperson, e.g. the hand tools used to make an item of furniture.

Focused task: Volumes of production

For this task you need to refer to at least two of the following case studies. A group choosing different ones to study could then compare notes in a discussion afterwards.

- McLaren F1 door hinge page 198
- Jaguar XK8 page 201
- The Handihaler page 212
- Neocreole cooking pot page 126
- PDSA page 224
- Frank Walsh page 214
- Petits Filous, Frubes page 68

1 Read through all of the text titled 'Understanding the consequences of volume variations'. Locate each of the numbered statements onto the continuum diagram given opposite.

2 For each of your selected case studies identify on the continuum diagram:
  - the volume of production
  - the implications for each of the categories shown.

You could draw up your own table to show the comparisons between the products.

Volumes of production

One-Off (job/custom) Production ◄──────────────────────────────► Mass Production

| Job | □ | Batch flow | □ | Line flow | □ | Continuous flow | □ | Automated continuous flow |

Consequences of volume variations

One-Off (job/custom)	Parameter	Mass Production
High	Labour costs	Low
High	Labour skills	Low
Broad	Work tasks	Narrow
One off	Product design	Standard
Low	Capital costs	High
Low	Efficiency	High
High	Product cost	Low
General	Tools	Specialised

In this diagram some of the results of variations in volumes of production are shown as arrows representing continuous change across the spectrum (or continuum).

Case Study: The Decorative Tile Works, Ironbridge, Shropshire

The Decorative Tile Works Limited (DTW) is a company licensed by the Ironbridge Gorge Museum to use the site previously occupied by the Craven Dunhill tile factory. This factory was in the past one of the world's largest producers of decorative ceramic tiles. The DTW company is now a much smaller operation and produces tiles in a range of production volumes.

Original Victorian tile making machinery at the Decorative Tile Works.

The standard tiles are produced by the many thousand, pressed in an automated machine that converts blended clay powder into accurately pressed 154 mm square 'green' (unfired) tiles which are absorbent and strong enough to be handled, in preparation for their initial 'biscuit' firing and then glazing and final firing. The company has a range of traditional colours and patterns available within their range, based on the standard format. This means that a standard production process is followed for much of the time with some additional expense incurred to broaden customer appeal, but only at the glazing stage.

At a second production level, the standard tiles are given added value through smaller 'batch' processes. Some tiles are hand pressed using a Victorian power press capable of producing only one at a time but able to produce consistent quality and repeatability. This press uses a range of different moulds including complex raised patterns. Alternatively the company use skilled artists to apply decoration by hand to the top of the standard tiles to give greater individuality but at greater cost. Further alternatives at a similar cost level see standard tiles taken from the first 'biscuit' firing for decoration with hand applied screen printing, using up to thirty screens to apply colour and pattern and others decorated with slip (liquid clay) and areas flooded with oxide glazes – again by hand. These tiles can cost up to £30 each to produce when the cost of the basic clay in the tile is about 20p, the rest of the cost coming from the production process, especially the cost of highly skilled labour.

At a higher cost level still, the majority of the company's work is based on even more labour intensive one-off pieces being restored or specially manufactured to individual order. These individual commissions involve producing designs for customers as one-off or small batches of hand decorated and finished tiles and mouldings. The customers may be individuals or architects working on the restoration of old buildings or requiring replicas of traditional designs. These products are costed on a commission basis and can cost many thousands of pounds due to the complexity of the requests, but they all stem from the same basic product – pressed clay powder – though resulting in widely different final products.

Applying tile decoration by hand.

Focused task: Volumes of production: furniture

See the following case studies:

- Domida Design page 190
- Home Pac Ltd page 194
- Simon Turner page 197
- Asda cafeteria furniture page 220

You could also refer to the case study in the *D&T Routes Resistant Materials* book (page 18) where students describe a workstation furniture design project.

Read each one and note down the following key points:

- Who are the customers for each type of product?
- What are their needs and expectations from the product?

- How does the product meet these needs and expectations?
- In what ways are the manufacturing methods matched to meeting the customers needs?

The volume of production, or number of similar items being produced, will have consequences for such things as costs, skills required of the workforce, work practices, the way products are designed, and the tools and equipment needed to make them.

Manufacturing systems

A manufacturing system will involve a production **process** as a response to **inputs**, such as materials, resources, people, money, information etc; and result in **outputs**, such as new and improved products, satisfied customers as well as possibly unwanted waste products. The system of production chosen will be the one that best suits the type of product and volume of production required.

Different production systems can be described in the following four categories:

- **job (or custom) production** – where a single item may be needed, such as a custom-made bicycle for an Olympic Games competitor, or an oil rig. This system is suitable for producing individual items often to a particular customer's requirements but at high unit cost.
- **batch production** – where larger quantities are sold, probably repeatedly over a period of time such as 1000 specialist loaves of bread made in a few hours daily in a bakery, for sale in local shops (look for 'batch loaves' in your local bakery). This manufacturing system can include elements of both line and job production. There are some economies of scale because of standardisation within batches. Batches can be increased or decreased according to demand.
- **line production** – where products which sell in high volumes move continuously along a production or assembly line with processes being carried out or parts being added in sequence. Examples include motor cars and sliced bread. This form of production is so named because the factory floor layout, including the positioning of machinery and people, is in the form of a line of processes in the necessary order. Significant economies of scale are achieved and unit costs drop dramatically.
- **flow or continuous production** – where very high volumes of a product are sold on an ongoing basis, production is continuous (often for 24 hours a day) over a long period. On these production or assembly lines very high cost specialist equipment using automated control systems keeps production rates extremely high, bringing unit costs very low indeed. Examples include the production of photographic film, sheet glass and car tyres.

Line and flow production systems typically require high levels of **capital investment**. However, they benefit from 'economies of scale' – economic advantage from the impact of the fixed costs (investment in machinery etc.) becoming a smaller proportion of total costs, the more of the product that is produced. This is what is most commonly referred to as **mass production** which has been responsible for the enormous increase in individually owned goods in the 'developed' countries. Unit prices – the price of each item – are brought down to the point where many people can afford them. The relationship between the number of items bought and the unit cost is very close.

Continuous production is used in the so-called **process industries** for the manufacture of engine oils, detergents, cosmetics, household cleaners and other low-complexity products such as pre-formed components and sections, e.g. nails, screws and sheet MDF used by you in school or college. This type of manufacture is characterised by relatively few processes and highly efficient automated production, where continuous quantities of goods flow from the production line.

This photographic film was produced in miles of continuous length before cutting into 24 exposure length for the camera.

▶ **Manufacturing as a system, D&T Routes Core Book**   118

▶ **Methods of production, D&T Routes Core Book**   120

The aim of manufacturing is to add value to raw materials by turning them into useful items or services that can be sold to other organisations, businesses or customers. The aim of almost every manufacturer is also to make money. In school this financial aspect of your designing and manufacturing might seem less important. You probably do not need to make a profit from your D&T activity and may be looking more towards completing your course of study successfully in the time you have available. But your capacity to plan and carry out your manufacturing, while bearing in mind principles of industrial practice, will greatly influence the success of your product. You will also need to start by being clear about the volume, or number of identical products, that is envisaged so that the success of a model or prototype made in school can be clearly judged in terms of its suitability for production beyond this stage.

Key stages of production in manufacturing

The variety of different manufactured products available to us is very great. In the UK the Confederation of British Industry (CBI) groups them into Manufacturing Sectors, including chemical and pharmaceutical; engineering, steel and allied industries; food; paper, printing and publishing; textiles and clothing. (See The Business of Manufacturing, in all *D&T Routes Focus Area Books*).

Within these sectors a great variety of different manufacturing systems exists. Different kinds of manufactured goods require different approaches to production organisation. For example, the final manufacture of high volume motor cars takes place in an assembly plant where large numbers of pre-manufactured parts will be added to each car, or unit, as it passes along a moving assembly line. However, a custom-made item of jewellery, where no two products are exactly the same, will need a different approach with parts being individually formed and joined at a bench as the product develops. Although these differences can seem great, e.g. for food products compared with those for steel, their key stages of production will all be in common:

1 **material preparation**, or making materials ready to be worked with
2 **processing**, or carrying out forming, cutting and joining processes on the materials
3 **assembly**, or putting different prepared parts of a product together
4 **finishing**, or applying finishing treatments to parts or completed products
5 **packaging**, as necessary to ensure that products arrive at their destination in good condition.

Stages of production: 1 Material preparation

Whatever product is to be manufactured it will be important to choose appropriate materials before processing into products. The particular structure or character of a material, such as deciding which flour to make a dough from or what steel to make the blade of an ice skate from, may mean that certain materials are an obvious choice. But there are other important factors to take into consideration. A few materials, such as sand or pebbles, can be used as they are found in their natural state. But even they require some preparation to have taken place before using them in manufacture. When large quantities are required this preparation may involve a particular manufacturing system, variously known as **process production,** or **continuous production**, to ensure that the materials are prepared for manufacturing into products.

 Continuous production of MDF, D&T Routes Core Book 121

Selecting a material will therefore take account not only of its inherent properties, such as physical, mechanical, chemical, thermal, electrical, acoustic and optical, but also of properties that result from their preparation for manufacturing. The development of efficient manufacturing systems, especially this century, has placed increased emphasis on using materials that make the flow of products through the factory smooth and uninterrupted. For example, this is why large pieces of wood are ground into small pieces and recombined to make chipboard – which is homogenous, reliable in its properties and produced to standard sizes. Therefore decisions are made, even before materials are ordered, that will ensure their optimum preparation for the production processes needed.

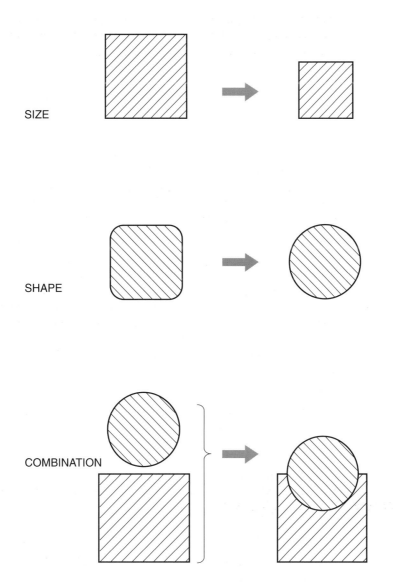

SIZE

SHAPE

COMBINATION

Manufacturing involves changing the size, shape or combination of materials.

Case Study: British Aerospace Airbus

British Aerospace Airbus specialise in the design and manufacture of wings for the highly successful Airbus family of aircraft. Aircraft manufacture involves the design, reproduction and assembly of many different parts including wings, engines, undercarriage and fuselage. The design work is shared amongst the partners of the Airbus Consortium, (Aeropatile, Daimler Benz, Aerospace, British Aerospace, and CASA), located in different parts of Europe. Aircraft manufacture uses parts made all around the world.

Materials selection at BAe

Aircraft construction and operation makes particular demands upon materials. Generally materials should be light in weight providing at the same time high strength and stiffness. The latter are necessary to reduce deflection and bending during flight which might compromise performance. It would be disconcerting for passengers if the cabin floor were to bend and twist, although this would not necessarily be unsafe. Indices of specific strength and specific stiffness are used to compare candidate materials – those from which a realistic choice could be made – at the design stage. These comprise a measure of the maximum load and minimum displacement respectively for a given unit of mass for a material.

Case Study: British Aerospace Airbus *continued*

The specific strength and stiffness of a material is determined from a standard measure from a tensile strength test which is performed on the material. Materials for aircraft construction must also be durable, offering high resistance to degradation, in order to withstand corrosion and fatigue.

Resistance to degradation, D&T Routes Resistant Materials Book | 43

But materials selection must also take account of the manufacturing processes used during initial processing and so, before acceptance, materials have to be quality checked on arrival at the factory. Some decisions are taken even before this stage. For example, metals that have been pre-formed into sections using such methods as rolling, extruding, forging and casting may already possess different kinds of inherent defects. These can be detrimental to performance and are therefore normally eliminated before manufacturing begins.

Inspecting holes on part of an A330 wing from a fatigue test specimen.

Focused task: Materials preparation

- Identify three different products which have been manufactured from contrasting materials.
- What material preparation would be needed in each case?
- Evaluate the suitability of each material in terms of
  a) its performance in this product
  b) the volume of production involved.

During one of your projects carry out an audit on materials available to you in school/college and consider:

1 How was each prepared before arrival in school/college?
2 How does their preparation influence their properties?
3 How is their suitability for your product influenced, bearing in mind also the volume of production you intend to use?

Stages of production: 2 Processing

Organisational systems for manufacturing have profoundly altered methods of processing, especially during this century. Since early times the benefits of being able to repeat processes efficiently have been appreciated, but it was during the 20th century that production methods developed more scientifically.

The 1908 model T Ford

In 1908 Henry Ford set out to make the simplest car ever, the model T Ford. To produce his car as cheaply as he wanted to, Ford knew he had to change the way that cars were built which meant changing the way that workers worked. As he redesigned his factories to turn out model Ts he was influenced by the efficiency expert, Frederick Taylor. Taylor is quoted as saying: "Hardly a workman can be found who doesn't devote his time to studying just how slowly he can work". When Taylor was first brought in he issued stopwatches and timed the workers' every move. As a result of his observations he was able to reorganise some work to increase efficiency by as much as 300%.

Ford broke tasks down into simple repeated sequences for each worker.

This first step in improving production through scientific management involved dividing production into simple repetitive steps, for example, a wheel was no longer made in its entirety by a trained wheelwright. Enormous gains in productivity were achieved by dividing wheel production into more than 100 different stages, each to be carried out by different men at different machines. But Ford's real breakthrough came with the invention of the moving assembly line. With this innovation he was able to combine scientific management and ordering of processes with a quite new concept. Prior to 1913 men built each car 'from the frame up' on stationary wooden frames. Each part was brought to the vehicle from its stock-pile and added, and then each worker waited for the one in front to complete his operation. Ford's inspiration was 'instead of moving the men past the car why not move the car past the men?'.

The assembly line allowed parts to be delivered to exactly the right point by conveyor and the workers connected them to form assembled products which gradually moved towards the factory exit.

Henry Ford was soon able to produce model Ts so efficiently that coal, iron, sand and rubber entered his factories at one end and 2,500 model Ts per day streamed out of the other. But he also encountered difficulties in keeping his staff who found the work boring, repetitive and too slavishly demanding in terms of the output expected of them. Ford countered this problem by paying the workers the highest wages in America to keep them. Many of them became car owners at a time when this was a considerable luxury.

Although car production has developed greatly since the model T, the methods now used by all car manufacturers owe much to the pioneering methods brought in by Henry Ford.

Processing methods influencing product design

Product design is always influenced, to some extent, by the manufacturing methods available or chosen. New materials and new manufacturing processes often lead to major changes in manufactured goods. For example, at one time bearings were either bushed or constructed using ball races which needed constant lubrication. The introduction of sintered products and later, the use of polymers, removed the need for oiling and greasing, reducing maintenance requirements, and changing the shape of many commonly used appliances.

Appliances such as these food mixers changed as a result of new manufacturing processes.

In school there will be occasions when the manufacturing processes you use affect the way you must design the product, e.g. the way that vacuum-formed components need rounded corners and tapered sides to facilitate removal from their former. Irrespective of whether this is the best design for the vacuum-formed component, these features must be present to achieve an output from the mould. Sometimes the nature of the manufacturing process so dominates the design of a product that the final form would otherwise be inconceivable.

The design of these bakers' trays owes much to the injection moulding process that produced them.

Processing and work flow

In a simple system raw materials enter the factory at one end and finished goods leave at the other, suitably packaged. In this way the manufacturer adds value to raw material by turning it into a product that a customer wishes to purchase.

When products are manufactured in quantity the production stages must also be carefully organised to provide the required outputs (products and satisfied customers) to the quality standards that have been set. This order, or work flow, also influences the amount of time taken and therefore the cost of producing finished products.

FLOW PROCESS CHART			
☑ Present method ☐ Proposed method			
Subject: _Part flow and inspection_			
Chart begins: _Last machining operation in dept._			
Chart ends: _Tote box after final inspection_			

Symbols	Description	Distance moved/ft.	Time involved
○⇨□D▽	Injection moulding operation		
○⇨□D▽	Stack in wire baskets		
○⇨□D▽	Conveyor to wash		
○⇨□D▽	Wash		
○⇨□D▽	Conveyor to inspection		
○⇨□D▽	Inspector		
○⇨□D▽	Load in tote box		
○⇨□D▽	Wait for truck		
○⇨□D▽	Truck to flash removal		
○⇨□D▽	Wait to synchronize		
○⇨□D▽	Remove flashing		
○⇨□D▽	Conveyor to wash		
○⇨□D▽	Wash		
○⇨□D▽	Conveyor to inspection		
○⇨□D▽	Inspection		
○⇨□D▽	Stack in tote box		

FLOW PROCESS CHART			
☐ Present method ☑ Proposed method			
Subject: _Part flow and inspection_			
Chart begins: _Last machining operation in dept._			
Chart ends: _Tote box after final inspection_			

Symbols	Description	Distance moved/ft.	Time involved
○⇨□D▽	Injection moulding		
○⇨□D▽	Operator stack in wire baskets		
○⇨□D▽	Wait for truck		
○⇨□D▽	Truck to GRWD flash removal		
○⇨□D▽	Wait to synchronize		
○⇨□D▽	Remove flashing		
○⇨□D▽	Conveyor to wash		
○⇨□D▽	Wash		
○⇨□D▽	Conveyor to inspect		
○⇨□D▽	Inspection		
○⇨□D▽	Stack in tote box		
○⇨□D▽			
○⇨□D▽			
○⇨□D▽			
○⇨□D▽			
○⇨□D▽			

This flow process chart has been used to identify the most appropriate sequence of operations for the product intended.

Flow process charts are often used by production engineers to develop manufacturing systems for new parts or to study and improve existing systems. Answers to the following questions will be sought:

- Is each operation necessary?
- Can several operations be combined?
- Is the order of operations correct?
- Can operations and inspections be simplified?
- Are all transportations necessary?
- Can storages and delays be eliminated?
- Is there a better way to organise the entire process?

Focused task: Planning an efficient work flow in school/college

The work flow chosen by you on your project will influence the success of your product. This means more than just carefully planning the use of your time.

As an integral part of your current D&T assignment, prepare a work flow analysis to plan your manufacturing.

- Identify each stage required to manufacture your product.
- Organise your production processes to identify the flow which gives the most efficient production in terms of processing time, quality of product and safe working practice.
- Use work process symbols to create more than one alternative method and compare each to identify the best.

Stages of production: 3 Assembly

Few products are made from a single part or component. A common pencil sharpener will be made from at least three assembled parts while a large product, such as a cross-channel ferry, may require hundreds of thousands, weighing many tons in total. Both products require the careful use of assembly processes.

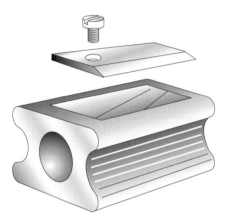

A pencil sharpener is assembled from at least three parts.

Assembly methods have been used throughout civilisation and early examples included sewing and gluing. A great variety of joining/assembly methods now exist to aid the manufacture of products. These methods can be divided into two categories:

- **Bonding**, where parts are encouraged to join as a result of either atomic closeness or through the presence of a sticky substance such as glue.
- **Mechanical** fastening where mechanical force such as a seam, tight or interference fit, or mechanical fastener such as a rivet (permanent fastener) or screw (temporary fastener).

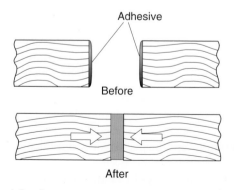

a) Bonding.

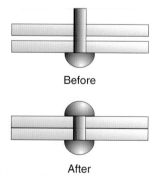

b) Mechanical fastening.

Assembly of any volume of products in a manufacturing industry usually utilises control systems, being more or less automated as necessary to reach the required quality and productivity targets. The extent to which these systems are used also depends heavily on how financially secure the company is, and how much investment they can afford. More advanced, automated methods have generally been built on the pioneering work of Henry Ford's moving assembly line, which is now used to assemble a huge variety of products from computer circuit boards to the humble sandwich.

Choosing an assembly method

When choosing the best assembly methods for a product you will need to consider the required performance of the product as well as availability and ease with which particular processes can be carried out.

Case Study: Assembly methods at British Aerospace Airbus

Careful control of manufacturing methods is essential to achieve high quality aircraft wings for the Airbus family of aircraft. It is very important to be able to specify the total stress that will eventually be present in the total aircraft structure when in flight. This total stress comprises the sum of the built-in stresses that result from manufacture (e.g. through assembly of the parts), and those resulting from cyclic loads due to stresses in flight (such as wing loading during bad weather conditions). The principles used in selecting the most appropriate assembly methods include:

I Attention to detail

Design and manufacturing must take account of the combined effect of the manufacturing methods used. Whichever manufacturing process is selected it will result in stress build-up of some kind. This is acceptable provided it does not exceed specified levels (e.g. the sum of stresses in all parts of the aircraft and the cyclic loads experienced in flight). For example, drilling a hole in a component results in some stresses building up at the edge of the hole that has been made. It may be preferable to close the hole afterwards or to avoid stress concentrations caused by **changes in geometry** (the shape or form of the part) which can lead to overrall increase in the total maximum stress.

2 Accuracy of fit

Bolted and riveted joints, as well as individual parts, must fit in ways which reduce, rather than increase, stress-concentration. This requires subtle forms of accuracy, i.e. neither too tight nor too loose.

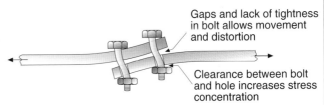

Gaps and lack of tightness in bolt allows movement and distortion

Clearance between bolt and hole increases stress concentration

The inaccuracies in this joint will lead to stress build-up.

3 Sequencing of production

The order in which parts are assembled greatly affects their integrity, or ability to carry out the functions intended for them. It is important that parts are not forced into positions or shapes for which they were not designed, causing them to become unduly pre-stressed.

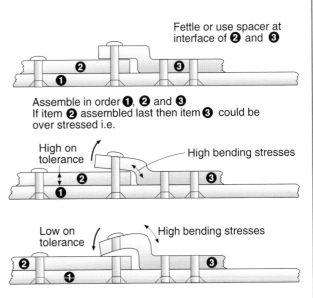

Fettle or use spacer at interface of ❷ and ❸

Assemble in order ❶, ❷ and ❸
If item ❷ assembled last then item ❸ could be over stressed i.e.

High on tolerance — High bending stresses

Low on tolerance — High bending stresses

This production sequence helps ensure that parts are not forced into positions that might lead to stress.

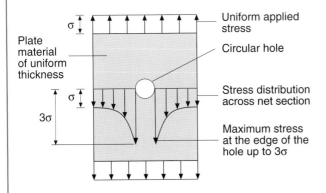

Plate material of uniform thickness

Uniform applied stress

Circular hole

Stress distribution across net section

Maximum stress at the edge of the hole up to 3σ

How a hole drilled in a plate can cause stress

The holes in this plate introduce changes in geometry and produce a concentration of stress when the plate is loaded.

4 Joining and fitting

Generally a joint must carry out its joining function, avoiding any tendency to develop stress-concentrations. It is normal to completely fill holes designed for fasteners using interference fit fasteners which are employed to reduce the degree of stress concentrations.

5 The finish that can be achieved

This will result from the materials used and the finish they come with and also the assembly techniques used. An example of the latter is heat processes such as welding which can discolour and distort.

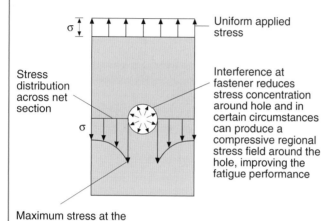

This interference fit fastener is designed to reduce the degree of stress concentration.

The surface finish on this aircraft wing could easily be destroyed during assembly unless it is well protected and no assembly method spoils it.

Focused task: Choosing a method of assembly

Produce several joints of the kinds you might use for your product. This is valuable practice and will allow you to design methods to test their strength. An idea for a strength test is shown and you could use this, or develop your own alternative. Make a record of your findings and use this to guide your future choice of assembly methods. Remember not to go to this trouble if suitable information is available on a database.

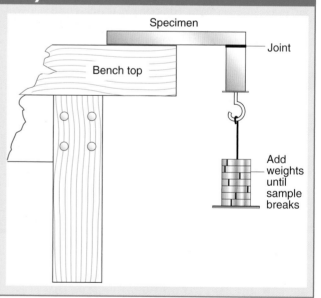

Test the strength of your joints using a method similar to this one.

Stages of production: 4 Finishing

Most manufactured products have a surface finish which has either been specifically applied (perhaps to improve appearance), or results from processing methods such as being covered with rivet heads. A finish may be intended to improve the appearance of a product or to protect the material from the environment, such as the extreme effect of moisture on exposed mild steel (rust) or the more gradual oxidation of the surface of exposed aluminium. The capacity of a material to resist change in this way is termed its **resistance to degradation**. There are also likely to be other reasons for a finish to be applied such as reducing friction to aid the aerodynamics of a wing.

Steel and aluminium have different levels of resistance to degradation.

Finishes can be classified into the following:

Conversion finishes

A product can be encouraged to develop an improved surface finish through modifying, or converting an existing one, as in the case of anodising aluminium. This is referred to as a conversion finish.

These drink cans are coated using an off-set litho printing process.

The finish of these anodised products results from a thickened oxide layer, encouraged by electrolysis, which has been dyed to make it decorative. Because it is the natural finish of aluminium it is very durable.

Surface coatings

When a product is covered with a layer of a second material that adheres to the base material it is referred to as surface coated. Included in this class of finish are paint, varnish, enamel and lacquer. Sometimes ceramic and metallic materials are also encouraged to form coatings on the surface of products. Such finishes are applied by brushing, dipping, rolling, spraying and printing.

Plastic-coated steel for factory wall cladding in production at British Steel's plant in Turkey.

Surfaces resulting from materials production and preparation

Process production carried out by process industries producing relatively non-complex products including basic materials such as sheets of steel, plywood, aluminium etc. control the form of the material (thickness, consistency etc.) and also the finish on an item. If a further finish is to be applied in manufacturing or assembly, it may be important to check the quality of materials on arrival at the factory before any further work is done. Materials containing defects may have to be rejected before processing begins to avoid the presence of hidden defects in finished components.

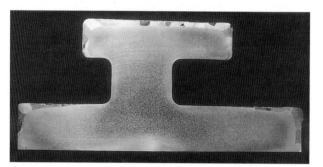

The section through an extrusion of aluminium alloy shows the presence of coarse grain at external corners and on the upper surface.

In the case of aircraft wing production, finishing progresses through the following stages:

1 Existing defects are located and eliminated, e.g. by machining out, avoiding defective zones, machining of dead or undetectable areas.
2 Post manufacturing inspection is carried out to reveal further defects that may have occurred due to production processes, leading to further removal/finishing procedures.
3 Final finishing.

Increasingly, modern production methods require finishes to be pre-applied to bulk materials during initial processing, prior to arrival at the factory.

Focused task: Materials finishes

Identify six examples of products and analyse the surface finish of each.

Use the following to help guide your analysis and make comparisons.

- What kind of base material has been used?
- Is the finish a surface coating or a conversion?
- Is there any evidence of a surface that results from the process production of the basic material?
- Would a finish have been applied to this material before manufacturing the product or after?

- If after, what might be the advantage of this?
- What methods have been used to create the finish?

Present your work as a well-designed illustrated sheet annotated with a clear analysis of the chosen products.

Stages of production: 5 Packaging

The concluding part of the manufacturing process is packaging and subsequent transportation of the products to the customer. Despite the variety of products that result from the manufacturing industry, such as household fluids handled in bulk, to one-off capital goods like power generators, some common principles apply.

Products are packaged to:

- protect the product and avoid damage/waste (e.g. polystyrene foam pads around electrical items)
- preserve contents (e.g. to retain the flavour of food)
- hold sales units together (e.g. a dozen eggs)
- enable efficient handling (e.g. stacks of small appliances on pallets)
- present the products to customers (e.g. CD sleeves)
- add value (e.g. cosmetics).

Using additional floor space to store quantities of a product is expensive as it incurs more rent, so a company will aim to have goods into transit as soon as possible – which is one more consideration for production planning – as the flow of goods out of a factory must be geared closely to the rate of production. Also, faultless records are required to keep track of the flow of products, their type (if variants are produced) and their destination, for which information technology is well suited. The logistics of the whole supply chain from raw materials through components and sub-assemblies to final product can be monitored and controlled using electronic product definition (EPD) techniques (see page 85).

 Wincanton distribution and Britvic, D&T Routes Control Products   91

Companies aim to at least partly package products as early in the production process as possible for their protection. Very delicate items such as chromium-plated surfaces may be coated with a film before supply to an assembly line, remaining in place until the product's end-user removes it. Many assembly lines for small products transfer units on protective slave-boards or other carriers for this reason and the advent of shrink-wrap plastics films keeps the quantity of packaging down, whilst providing total protection. As with all aspects of a product's manufacture, the packaging materials and methods are part of the manufacturing specification and are subject to quality assurance procedures. Storage and despatch are important ancillary areas of employment in manufacturing as their efficiency is as critical to the company's success as any other process.

 Dyson vacuum-cleaners, D&T Routes Resistant Materials book   89–90

Clearly, different products will have quite different demands and in considering your own products you will have to identify these. To do this the following criteria should be considered:

- packaging materials cost
- time, labour and processes involved
- packaging labour costs
- value added to the product (if applicable)
- product visibility or labelling requirements
- atmosphere control (humidity, temperature, sterility etc.)
- transportation methods
- durability requirements
- legislation, codes of practice or standards requirements
- promotional requirements (branding, advertising etc.).

Some packages are products in their own right such as pump dispensers for liquids, and add considerable value to the base-product. Some of these are first-class examples of highly developed, well-detailed product design and many industrial and graphic designers are employed specifically in this field.

▶ *Wind-eze case study, D&T Routes Graphic Products book*   **50**

Husqvarna sewing machines being packaged for transit.

Focused task: Packaging

- Identify a familiar package which has three roles: protecting a product in manufacture; holding a set number of items together and presenting the product to end-users.
- Redesign it to package a significantly different number of products, or related by-products with enough originality to create a new market niche.

- Present your work as a well-designed sheet of annotated sketches.

(An example of this is *Polo mints* which started as a tubular pack, spawned a tube of 'holes' and then went to a dispenser of mini ring-mints.)

A historical note: Packaging

" *Clarence Crane . . . invented Life Savers (American sweets like Polos) in 1911, punching them out on a pharmacist friend's pill-making machine, but they were a flop because the mints quickly went stale inside their paper wrappers and tended to absorb the flavour of the glue with which the wrappers were sealed. Only after a New York businessman bought the company and began wrapping the mints in tin foil did Life Savers take off – and take off they did. In just over a decade his initial investment of $1500 in the company had become worth $3300 million.*"

© Bill Bryson 1994. Extracted from Made in America by Bill Bryson, published by BlackSwan, a division of Transworld Publishers Ltd. All rights reserved.

Focused task: Changes in manufacturing methods

For this task you will need to refer to the following **case-studies**:

- The model 'T' Ford page 148
- H J Heinz page 165–66
- Golden West Foods page 167–70
- Shima Seiki and total knit page 183–86

You should:

1 Read through the tasks below.
2 Read through the case studies to get a feel for them.
3 Go back to the tasks and return to each case study to complete them.

Focused task: Changes in manufacturing methods *continued*

TASK 1: The way products are manufactured is changing. Read the following statement and look for evidence in the four case-studies to confirm or contradict it.

> *Manufacturing started from a craft base in which the worker played a key role. The introduction of scientific management by Taylor devalued this role. 'In fact, Henry Ford is reputed to have said that his ideal worker would be slightly mentally retarded. Automated machinery required less operator skills and the continuous production lines necessitated operators who were able to perform single tasks ad infinitum. Ford demonstrated that enormous profits could be made from taking the skills out of the hands of the workforce. Many companies looked set for all factories to be equipped with robotics with no human workers, but the course of history since Ford's time has changed this view. The aim of a modern machine designer and factory owner is to draw upon the best of technology, coupled with optimising the use of the skill of the workers. One of the most important, flexible and economical, assets of any company is its workforce.''*

TASK 2: Write a brief analysis of changing trends in manufacturing since the turn of the century, based on the case studies that you have read.

Choosing a manufacturing system

How and why is a particular manufacturing system chosen? A manufacturing system will be tailored to the volume of production that is intended but the cost of developing a new product and setting up the manufacturing system required, including plant, factory layout and personnel, can be very great. Decisions concerning the particular system chosen will therefore be taken at a high level in the company.

In school, a one-off (or custom made) item will need to use materials, tools and equipment that are available or which can be resourced without undue difficulty. The manufacturing facilities in your school D&T rooms will be unlike that required for high volume manufacture in industry, but they may resemble those in small companies such as modelmakers or small batch workshops. Ironically though, they may look more similar to up-to-date cell based plants, where equipment is grouped in a small area to enable flexible manufacturing approaches.

▶ **Flexible manufacturing**   **174**

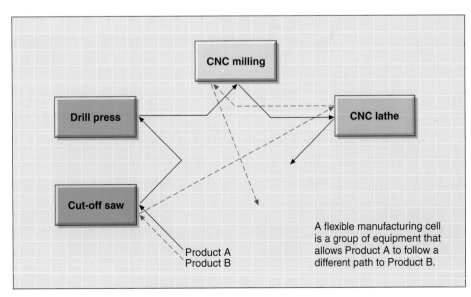

A flexible manufacturing cell is a group of equipment that allows Product A to follow a different path to Product B.

Cells give flexibility because they allow economic change-overs in production sequences for different products.

Industries are normally preparing for new products on a continual basis, even when existing products are doing very well. This is because existing consumer demand generally tails-off over time, possibly because of competing products from other companies. It is therefore increasingly difficult for a company to remain profitable without new product development. Many industries find sudden breaks or changes in production difficult to achieve due to the investment required. New manufacturing systems therefore need careful phasing-in via long-term planning and may overlap with or even incorporate older ones, making the process seem more like evolution than revolution. However there is constant pressure to reduce the time-to-market of new products and the most successful industries will be those which can produce the right product, in the right quantity, at the right time.

Renewing plant and factory layout

It is unusual for a manufacturer to start with an empty plant and sufficient capital to invest in new machinery to equip the plant totally for a new product, though this is starting to be increasingly common with, for example, car plants. In most instances plant, machinery and a trained workforce already exist. The factory owner needs to maximise the use of existing equipment and trained manpower at the same time as setting up for the manufacturing of new product lines.

The production constraints that might be faced by a manufacturer include:

- the size of the retained labour force and their skills
- the number of suitable workers available on a sub-contract basis
- availability and cost of materials and their transportation
- the ability to receive deliveries of materials on time and thus reduce potential losses resulting from holding up manufacturing processes
- technology, plant and machinery available to carry out the necessary processes
- health and safety issues, particularly if the manufacturing process is likely to produce toxic or hazardous by-products
- quality standards and the ability of the factory to meet the required standards including tolerances, finishes and performance requirements.

Which manufacturing system?
Reasons for choosing a particular manufacturing system in industry include:

- the level of demand by customers predicted for the product
- the nature of the product, e.g. whether it is based in food or steel engineering
- the location of the market, e.g. whether local, regional, national, European or global
- the intended scale of production, or turnover of finished products, which will determine the level of investment possible, e.g. for a costly automated production line.

Why new manufacturing technologies develop
Companies develop new technologies in order to continuously improve existing products. A range of issues will be considered in the development of these new manufacturing technologies. These will be of benefit to the company but often will benefit the consumer as well.

Developing manufacturing technologies.

Industry interests	Consumer interests
Control over processes to deliver the precise product required, on time	Immediate availability of products
Quality – consistency and continuous improvement	High quality products
Performance and functionality	Products that work well
Reduced processing	Desire for more 'natural' products (particularly food products)
Environmental benefits – reduced environmental impact; meeting requirements of legislation and industry standards	Demands for reduced environmental impacts
	Protection through legislation
Reduction in manufacturing costs	Cheaper products
'Added value' products	Better 'value for money'

Focused task: Developing manufacturing technologies

For this task you need to refer to the following case studies:

- The story of the McLaren F1 door hinge (e.g. requirements to match processes to quality required), page 198.
- The Handihaler, page 212.
- Domida Design (e.g. tips on plant layout and different processing zones), page 190.
- PDSA (e.g. ways in which designing for manufacture can be considered in school), page 224.

See also the 'Manufacturing to high specifications' section of this chapter.

You should:
1 Read through the task below.
2 Read through the case studies to get a feel for them.
3 Decide how you will present your assignment – as an essay, a chart or another way.
4 Go back to the task and return to each case study to complete the task.

Task
1 For each of the items in the table above, identify examples in the case studies.
2 For each example, explain:
   a) the benefits to the company
   b) the benefits to the customers.

Costs and prices

Total product-costs are a serious consideration amounting to far more than just the cost of materials to make a prototype or one-off, such as might be made in school. To remain profitable, manufacturers must take great care to calculate accurately their total costs and set a suitable product price. Setting the selling price means allowing for direct costs, indirect costs and a realistic profit. Even when the **cost** of developing and producing a product is calculated thoroughly, setting the **price** may still be a difficult decision. Too high a price may reduce sales below a profitable level, while too low a price will not allow the product to be profitable even if large numbers are sold. Prices are determined as much by competition and what the market will bear as by production costs.

You will need to estimate the expected costs involved in your product well in advance, as well as to consider the factors involved in setting a price. Only in this way will it be possible to determine how well your product might perform in the market place.

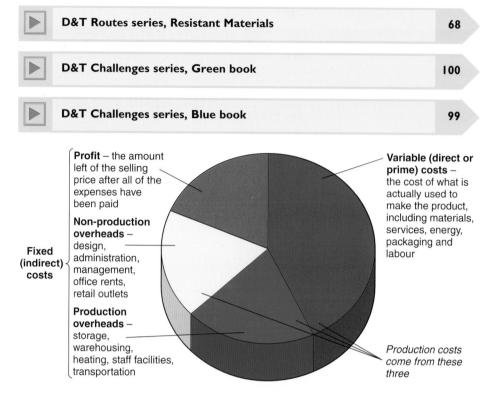

A company will see the best price as the one that generates the maximum profit, not necessarily the one that sells the most products.

What is in a price?

The total cost of a product has to include **overheads** consisting of marketing, selling and distribution costs, company administration costs, interest payable on loans required to purchase the materials, plant and machinery, and research and development costs. It is common for the actual cost of production to account for only 50 to 65% of the total price of a product. Marketing and selling costs are often in the region of 15–20% of the selling price. Products such as trainers, perfumes, cars and CDs all have a much higher **mark-up** for marketing, selling, distribution and research and development.

Variable and fixed costs

Companies often separate the money put into a product between **fixed costs** and **variable costs**. **Fixed costs** (or **indirect costs**) stay more or less the same no matter how many products are made. The fixed costs include purchasing or renting property, tools, machinery, furniture, staff training and set-up expenditure. Non-production employees such as sales, design and accountancy staff are also often included in these fixed costs. Whilst these costs stay relatively constant no matter how many products are produced, it is clearly important to note the relationship between fixed costs and the number of items produced as a proportion of these costs must be added to each product's price.

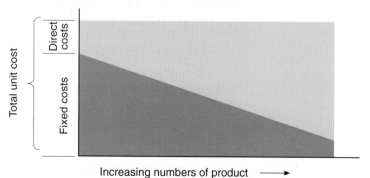

The relationship between fixed and variable costs.

Variable costs (or **direct costs**) are directly related to the number of products being made. These include the costs of materials, tools and labour each of which will have to increase if production rises (unless efficiency gains are made). The variable costs are therefore approximately proportional to the number of products being made. When you are manufacturing your own products you should include estimates of all these costs, not only the materials you purchase. Your time, lighting, heating, machinery, tools, equipment and building rent and rates all need to be considered (and perhaps, the cost of consultancy advice!).

Profit

A company must aim to make a profit and will often refer to a **gross profit** or gross profit margin. This is a simple equation calculated by deducting the cost of the products sold from the revenue (income from sales). The total gross profit is usually called the **operating profit** of a company, but the company does not gain all of this profit for itself. Tax will be deducted from the gross profit, leaving what is called **net profit**. Net profits are used to pay dividends to shareholders, bonuses to employees based on company performance, and for reinvestment, in new machinery, developing new products, improving existing production methods etc.

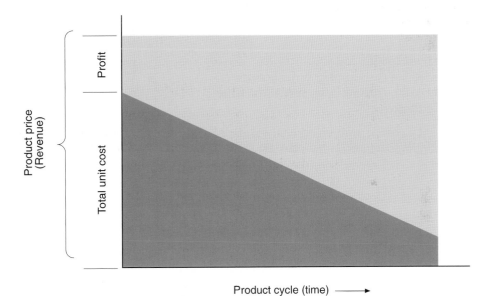

Profit margin and product cycle.

Whilst it is logical to assume that a new product will arise from a perceived customer need, manufacturers also need to maximise their existing production potential and profit margins. Most manufacturers prefer to carry their fixed costs over a range of products. This is sometimes achieved by the creation of new fashion trends and thus customer demand by the advertising industry. It can be said that through advertising some products have changed from consumer driven production to manufacturer led production as in the case of many new cult toys.

Price, cost and value

Products are often defined as having a **product value**, a **product price** and a **product cost**.

The product value is always perceived by the manufacturer as being less than the product price because he/she has invested money in the new product and would rather have the income from the finished product than a stock of products. The potential purchaser would rather have the product than the money and perceives the product value as being greater than the product price.

To ensure a maximum return on investment the manufacturer needs to cost every stage of production to ensure that the product price is higher than the sum of the costs involved in manufacture, which will include all the inputs such as raw materials, processes, manpower, tools and machinery that are required. There is no direct connection between the product cost and the product price. They are independent variables. If a product is very popular, yet limited in supply, the manufacturer will be in a position to charge a higher price than might otherwise be expected, or to add a significant **mark-up**. This is known as the price the market will bear.

Focused task: Calculating product-costs and price

For this task you will need to be familiar with the following case studies:

- Handihaler page 212.
- Frank Walsh page 214.
- Ukettle page 209.
- PDSA page 224.

To help you understand them, consider how the costing and pricing issues referred to above would feature in the situations presented in each case study. For example:

- What are tooling costs?
- Are tooling costs fixed or variable costs?
- Why did the tooling costs nearly wreck the UKettle project?

Carry out a costing and pricing analysis of a product that you are designing (or have designed).

Use the following questions to help develop your design.

- Does your solution really need so much new work?
- Is there a simpler solution?
- Has somebody already thought of it?
- If you were trying to make a living out of this product what price would you charge?
- Could different manufacturing methods help you reduce your costs?
- If so, what proportion of these savings would you pass on to the customer?
- What might be the effect of competition on your pricing decisions?

Present your answers in the form of a well-designed sheet of illustrated notes.

Systems and control in manufacturing

Manufacturers now deploy systems thinking and control applications in many different ways throughout their company but perhaps the most obvious impact has been on improvements to high volume production methods. Systems must ensure an efficient and cost-effective manufacturing operation and will typically include linked mechanical, electrical, electronic and pneumatic control systems to process materials through the factory. Computerised control applications may also be used to schedule the production runs, manage the arrival of materials and other inputs to the factory **just in time** so that its outputs, in the form of finished products, arrive at their next destination at the right time, in the right amounts.

Some reasons for using control systems in manufacturing are:

- repeatability – carrying out the same function in exactly the same way, time after time
- accurate control of complex processes, removing the possibility of human error
- quality control – working to tighter tolerances and higher levels of accuracy
- to automate systems for tedious, repetitive tasks
- increasing the speed of the process and productivity
- safety protection, including working in hostile environments
- reducing and handling waste material
- controlling continuous processes
- reducing maintenance and repair times through the use of warning and safety systems.

You will find control systems used in:

- production and assembly lines, for materials handling and processing
- cutting, folding, fastening, joining operations
- batch, mass and (particularly) continuous production.

 Home Pac Ltd. case study   194

Systems and control, product development and manufacture

Systems and control are also essential for the development of some kinds of product, such as high volume foods, where complex measurements or performance data may be needed in order to programme machinery for production runs. A control sample will be processed first, usually involving accurate measurement through the use of strategically placed sensors, and the resulting performance recorded. In the case of food products this will be essential to ensure that new products are heated to the correct temperature and for the correct time, for health and safety reasons, and also that each food item looks and tastes as it should when it reaches the consumer. The behaviour of a new food product during high volume processing is impossible to predict without such testing. The resulting data allows control systems on the production line to manage large amounts of material to the required quality standards, ensuring that every individual product is correctly and safely processed.

Case Study: Product development at H J Heinz

When a new food product is developed at Heinz, the chefs make a variety of trial samples using slightly different recipes, perhaps varying the flavouring or one ingredient. They also run trials to simulate the manufacturing process with some cans filled to the correct level and others overfilled with either the sauce or the garnish (the lumpy bits!). One product in each trial is put into a special can containing a sensor at one end which uses a thermocouple to monitor temperatures.

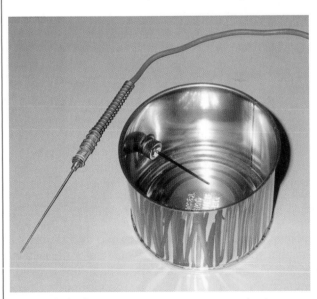

A can with the Datatrace in-can temperature monitoring device.

All the trial products then pass through a simulation of the cooking/sterilising procedure in order to:

- time how long the product takes to get to the required 'processing value' (equivalent to 8 minutes at 121°C)
- to simulate the worst scenario: overfilled cans; too much garnish in the tin.

As the cans move through the process the sensor sends information which is logged on a computer (data-logging):

- time/temperature data
- target temperature
- time taken through each stage of the process
- time taken to process the food to the correct and safe temperature.

The system can be adjusted as it is happening to make sure that the right information is obtained. From the data the length of cooking time is established, optimum conditions, rate of heating/cooking and the tolerances (amount allowed over or under that which is recommended) that can be used in the manufacturing process.

 Tolerancing   170

Case Study: **Product development at H J Heinz** *continued*

During the manufacturing process, a few cans are data-logged using a temperature monitoring device which passes through the complete process in order to record what has happened. Every product is different and needs a different time to cook. The process has to be kept within tolerances; for example, some products can take an extra 20 minutes to pass through the process and still be acceptable whereas others, such as those with a high proportion of milk powder, will burn after two extra minutes. The information gained from the data log is used to adjust the manufacturing process.

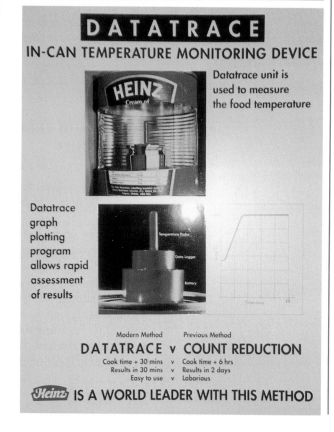

DATATRACE
IN-CAN TEMPERATURE MONITORING DEVICE

Datatrace unit is used to measure the food temperature

Datatrace graph plotting program allows rapid assessment of results

Modern Method		Previous Method
DATATRACE	**v**	**COUNT REDUCTION**
Cook time + 30 mins	v	Cook time + 6 hrs
Results in 30 mins	v	Results in 2 days
Easy to use	v	Laborious

Heinz **IS A WORLD LEADER WITH THIS METHOD**

Systems and control to aid production

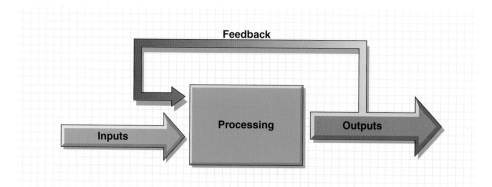

Feedback

Inputs → Processing → Outputs

A feedback control system.

A system involves inputs, processing, outputs and feedback. At a fundamental level these are all at work during most kinds of production activity. Some companies avoid reliance on sophisticated control systems because workers may be able to control processes more reliably through observation and manual sequencing of processes.

An example of this irreplaceable human component was provided by a factory manufacturing bath tubs. The plan was that raw material would enter the factory at one end, leaving the factory at the other end in the shape of bath tubs with no human intervention, the manufacturing being controlled by robotic systems. So that each tub would be moulded correctly, it was necessary for it to be lubricated by coating with oil in such a way that the press tool would exert its pressure evenly. It was found, after numerous attempts, however, that it was quite impossible to achieve an accurately dispersed coating of oil by machine. A human worker with a simple paint brush could apply the oil quickly and more accurately. He had the advantage of sight and the ability to respond to what he saw.

Even with high volume production some processes are still better done by hand.

With few exceptions, though, it has been usual for control systems to manage higher rates of production keeping worker intervention to a minimum. The information handling demands of this kind of production, including controlling quantity and consistency of quality, would be impossible to meet by other methods. Increasing sophistication in tools and machinery is now also influencing lower volume production methods. In some cases, such as with total garment knitting, flexible manufacturing systems can provide an individual item with many of the cost advantages of high volume production methods.

 Shima Seiki Case-study **183**

Case Study: **Golden West Foods Ltd**

Golden West Foods was established in 1977 in partnership with McDonald's restaurants to produce hamburger buns, soft drinks, tomato ketchup, ice-cream toppings and milk-shake flavourings. At Hemel Hempstead they have a purpose built, automated bakery manufacturing up to 36 000 McDonald's hamburger buns per hour for the UK and European markets. The product range includes, Regular, Big Mac, Quarter Pounder, McChicken buns and muffins. The million 'made to order' buns and muffins produced each day have to be of a guaranteed size, consistency, quality and flavour. Each bun takes up to two hours to produce on fully automated production lines operating in totally hygienic surroundings.

Systems and control at Golden West Foods

The day's requirements are scheduled on computer. Computers also control the mixing temperature and fermentation of the flour, yeast and water which makes up the liquid 'brew' that eventually becomes the familiar bun or a muffin. A range of sensors including load cells provide the feedback information for the computer to process. The main operations providing inputs to the computer are:

◆ measurement and temperature control of liquids
◆ weighing – ingredients and mixes
◆ baking – temperature and timings
◆ specific gravity readings.

Using systems and control to reduce environmental impact

Golden West's first priority is operational efficiency, but it also has systems and control procedures in place to reduce the environmental impact of its processing operations. Originally built in 1982 the automated plant at Hemel Hempstead reduces energy consumption and uses raw materials more efficiently, for example heat exchangers are used for heat recovery. The volume of food waste is reduced during production by the system known in the food industry as 'cleaning in place' or C.I.P.

The Processing Operations

Processing Operation 1: Flour brew

The 300 tonnes of flour used each week to make the buns is tested and checked for protein, water absorption, starch damage, colour and moisture. The flour 'brew' consists of a mix of 40% flour with water and yeast. It ferments in a large stainless steel vessel for two hours during which time the brew heats up considerably. When the fermentation process is completed the brew is transferred automatically through a heat exchanger to bring the temperature down to a range of 6–10°C. This unique method gives the bun its strength, resiliency and flavour.

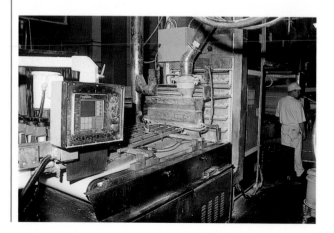

Processing Operation 2: Mixing

A batch of dough weighing 608 kg is made every 20 minutes. Flour, chilled water, oil and brew are added to the mixer automatically and monitored using computer based control systems acting on information provided by a range of sensors and input transducers. Other ingredients are added to the mix by hand. The mixing takes place for about 8 minutes using a motor-driven mechanical stirring system. Mixing time and temperature control (in a range from 20–25°C) are critical to the manufacturing operation as mistakes made at this stage are impossible to rectify.

Processing Operation 3: Dividing and Panning

The dough moves from the mixer to a mechanical dough pump and then onto the dough divider which cuts the dough into pieces of an exact weight. After a short period in a holding device called a Pan-O-Mat the round dough pieces are then flattened out using mechanical fingers made of a strong but flexible plastic before being moved into the baking pans. This part of the process operates at speeds between 520 and 560 dough pieces per minute. The speed of the line is controlled by a computer acting on information feedback from a series of electronic reflective opto-switches.

Processing Operation 4: Proofing

The filled baking pans automatically pass along mechanically driven conveyor systems to the final prover. There they rotate slowly for a period of 55 minutes in a temperature of 38°C and a relative humidity of 95%. This provides the ideal conditions for the yeast to interact with the proteins in the flour, developing the gluten which gives the bun elasticity and resiliency and produces the gas to give the bun volume. Four hydraulic motors operate in series to provide an 'endless chain' drive system that is over 1000 metres long. The chain is kept in correct tension using pneumatic pistons reacting to feedback information from sensors in the system.

Processing Operation 5: Baking

The baking pans are automatically moved from the final prover into the oven. If sesame seeds have to be applied to the top surface of the bun, this is done on the way to the oven. The buns are moistened with a fine liquid spray, the seeds are dispensed from metal 'sifter' trays with wire mesh templates set into the bottom surface which control the seed distribution according to the shape, size and type of bun being produced. The trays are shaken by pneumatic actuators controlled by computers.

The gas-fired ovens have six temperature zones each of which can be individually controlled. The temperature of the oven is in the region 250°C and the buns take between eight and nine and a half minutes to travel through.

Processing Operation 6: De-panning and cooling

When the cooked buns leave the oven they pass through the de-panner where they are gently lifted onto the cooling conveyor system by rubber suction cups operated by a pneumatic control system. The empty baking pan returns on a separate conveyor system to the Pan-O-Mat. The buns move on the cooling conveyor system for about thirty minutes before they reach the slicing and packing machines by which time their internal temperature has dropped to 25–29°C.

Processing Operation 7: Slicing and packing

At the slicing and packing machines the buns are inspected for quality, and grouped into batches of thirty automatically, using position sensors to control a mechanical holding system. The buns are then passed through a metal detector, vacuum sealed in polythene, date coded and automatically fed into bun trays, which are stacked before being transported to the delivery vehicles.

Quality assurance systems

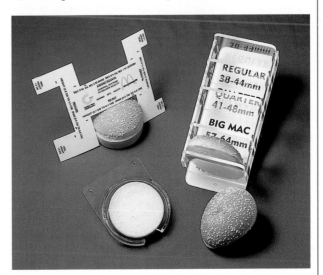

The quality control gauge used for checking the dimensions of the finished burger bun.

Regular quality checks are made by the line operators at critical control points in the manufacturing process. Quality control supervisors make regular quality inspections and spot-checks on the manufacturing process. As part of the quality control system, their laboratory measures the resiliency of a sample of buns from each batch produced. The finished buns are compressed using a mechanical device controlled by electronics and monitored by a computer system. The machine compresses the bun to half of its allowable height, and to pass the test it must recover by 83% or more. This is an example of a 'go/no go' test. If the bun recovers within the specified range the computer will issue a 'go' signal. If the bun fails the test operators are alerted and the manufacturing processes adjusted accordingly. The laboratory also tests the toasting performance of a batch of buns throughout their expected shelf life.

Final Inspection

To meet production parameters the final qualitative and quantitative inspections will involve: measuring the colour, height and diameter and determining the 'bake out' weight of the bun, the quality and position of the slice or slices and the seeding quality.

Recording results: 'Bun scoring'

Production staff assisted by the quality assurance team carry out a 'bun score' every week. This displays the findings for all the production staff to see. There are a complete set of design specifications and criteria that the finished buns must satisfy. They are:

◆ overall quality of complete bun
◆ crown
◆ heels
◆ texture
◆ toasting
◆ laboratory tests (purity etc.)
◆ quality of seeding (if appropriate).

Focused tasks: Manufacturing control systems

1 Having read through this case study use a simple flow diagram to describe the manufacturing process. You should be able to suggest where the critical control points are and what quality checks are needed at each of the operational stages in the system.

2 Produce a reasoned list of the advantages of using control systems in the manufacturing processes to:
● Golden West Foods
● McDonald's restaurants
● McDonald's customers.

3 To understand the control systems described in this case study you could use systems electronics, other kits and possibly a computer with an interface and control program, to model all or part of the production process.

Tolerancing

In the *D&T Routes Resistant Materials* book we explore the place of tolerancing and its relation to the quality of certain kinds of manufactured products, namely those with parts requiring high levels of accuracy.

| ▶ | Case studies: H. J. Heinz | 165 |
| ▶ | Shima Seiki | 183 |

When we use the word **tolerance** we are really defining how much variation from a precise standard can be allowed, or tolerated, before the product becomes unworkable or fails. Obviously, we might prefer there to be no variation, or **zero tolerance**, but in reality few products need to be made to such standards. Because there is a cost implication to the production of very accurate components or products it is usual for tolerances to be set within an acceptable range rather than to zero. An exception here might be the distance allowed between two tracks inside a micro-chip but very few products need this level of accuracy. An engineering part may have to be accurate to a few microns bigger or smaller than the specification of a product, a tolerance of, for example ±10 microns (10 microns over or under the recommendation). Some pieces of a rabbit hutch may be accurate enough if made to a tolerance of ±50 mm! Accuracy and how well parts fit together are often crucial if the product is to work as intended however, excess accuracy inflates costs. Tolerances are specified for many different manufactured products to keep accuracy adequate and costs to a minimum. Examples include the processing of paper (thickness or surface finish), textiles (the tension in knitted yarn) and food (the required heating and temperature times).

Tolerancing is the process carried out by engineers to set allowable tolerances for a component or product. A tolerance will usually be defined at the design stage for manufactured products. Acceptable variation, or non-conformance, to tolerance may also be permitted or tolerances may be subsequently redefined in the light of a product's performance in service.

The wings of this Airbus A330 have been specified by BAe engineers for fatigue and damage tolerance.

Maintaining tolerances

When a complex product, such as a passenger aircraft, is designed its required performance in service is first carefully analysed. This includes consideration of the customers who will use it, the typical distances that it will be flying when in service, the anticipated inspection and maintenance schedule for the aircraft and its intended life-span. Aircraft commonly experience **cyclic fatigue loads**, or stress in repeated flights, and certain components may begin to experience wear before the end of their intended life. The owners, or operators of the aircraft depend on regular inspections to be able to detect the first signs of wear or damage. The important point here is that the extent of wear or damage must *never* reach product failure level during intervals between inspections, as this could result in an accident during flight.

This kind of tolerancing is therefore based on a specification, worked out beforehand by designers, which allows for an acceptable level of wear or deterioration during spells of flight between inspections. Too great a level of wear would lead to product failure and must at all costs be avoided. But *some* wear can be tolerated, provided it is small and gradual enough to allow inspection and maintenance to keep the plane airworthy at all times. This type of tolerancing also makes demands upon the materials and manufacturing methods used.

Tolerancing and materials selection

A required tolerance, identified at product design stage, may help with materials selection but this requires understanding of the performance characteristics of materials.

▶ **Materials selection of BAe** 147

The specific strength of a material can also be determined from its **Young's Modulus**, a standard measure of tensile strength which is based upon scientific testing. Materials for aircraft construction must also be durable, offering **high resistance to degradation**, in order to withstand corrosion and fatigue.

Tolerancing and manufacturing methods

Careful control of manufacturing methods is essential to achieve the specified quality for a manufactured product. Where products comprise mainly resistant materials, such as in cars, ships and aircraft, control will probably extend to certain levels of detail, accuracy of fit, the sequencing of production and methods of joining and fitting and the required finishing processes. Maintenance and reliability of the work demands that regular checks will be made, both during production and service. Production quality control checks will be made against pre-determined **tolerance standards** for dimensions and fit. Components that fall outside tolerance level (**non-conforming** ones) may either be scrapped or, if allowed will be accepted **against a concession**.

The manufacturing processes used during initial processing may also fundamentally influence the way that a product performs in service. For example, metals that have been pre-formed using such methods as rolling, extruding, forging and casting may already possess different kinds of inherent defects. If these will be detrimental to performance they must be eliminated before manufacturing begins or it may be that an alternative material, using a different initial processing method, must be found.

Meeting structural requirements, including working within tolerance standards can be critical.

Tolerance, quality and product life

Tolerances are often defined within a product specification and will be used to help quantify certain quality requirements. They may also be used beyond the production stages of manufacturing and allow the performance of products to be monitored during service, or to provide helpful information needed to extend their useful life.

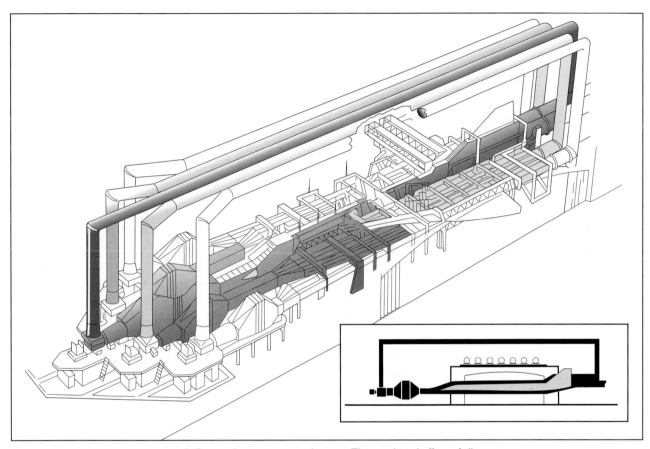

A Concorde prototype under test. The combined effect of all manufacturing processes and cyclic loading is simulated by subjecting a full size structure to loading, including checks for crack-initiation.

Tolerance, quality assurance and quality control

Tolerancing information will be used throughout the company quality assurance programme. It will be used to influence design decisions taken before products come into existence, the work practices expected of the workforce during manufacture (including checks for quality at many different stages of production), and as the inspection and maintenance schedule requires, while products are in service. Manufacturers intend to achieve a product of a set quality, and guarantee this quality when despatching the product to customers by conforming to BS 5750/ISO 9000, the UK/International standards for quality management systems.

Focused task: Tolerancing your product

- Identify the main features of your product which require a set tolerance, or margin, within which measurable parts should conform.
- Use tolerancing as a method of being more quantitative about aspects of your design and manufacturing specifications.

- Check your own work against the tolerances you have set for yourself and record your success at relevant points in your design portfolio.
- Are tolerances more helpful when products are to be manufactured in higher volumes, rather than one-offs? If so, why?

Flexible manufacturing technology

The term **flexible manufacturing technology** (FMT), describes a condition or aim, rather than a particular set-up. FMT draws attention to work practices which will be helpful (and should be encouraged) rather than inefficient and unhelpful (to be avoided) in the interests of better designing and manufacturing. To understand this idea more easily try imagining what in-flexible manufacturing might look like if you saw it. This may sound a strange idea but, in fact, all designing and manufacturing has this potential.

At the heart of all successful volume manufacturing is the process of breaking down and organising individual stages to make volume-gains in speed and output. Efficient manufacturing relies upon this, demanding the smoothest possible flow of work and avoidance of hold-ups. But it is all too easy for this rather idealistic model to slip into chaos, especially if such higher volume methods are not well synchronised with each other or if a breakdown in communication should occur between different personnel or departments.

Often such breakdowns or inefficiencies are present without anyone realising it. But, in today's world of global markets and intense international competition, even the smallest inefficiencies can affect the market share that a company will eventually gain, influencing the time to market of new or existing products, and therefore competitiveness of manufacturing response to customer needs.

More recently designers and manufacturers have come to realise that they themselves pose the greatest potential for production chaos or product success, and that the product performance may be decided before even the first piece of raw material enters the factory gates, or the production areas on the shop floor have been created. Traditional ways of working, where designers designed with little or no consideration for manufacturing consequences have caused products (and whole companies) to fail before a single customer is satisfied. The orthodox basis of designing and (then) manufacturing is now being called into question.

It is simply not good enough any more to design new products without simultaneously designing their manufacture. Taking this idea further it is probably now true to say that manufacturers would prefer to trial-manufacture new products before they have been designed. This may seem a strange idea: how can something be manufactured before it has even been designed? But just think of some advantages if it could – if all production and user consequences of a new product were known from the earliest or most tentative design stages – designers could create products that needed little or no further improvement.

Traditionally, bringing a promising new product to the market has been made difficult through failure to consider key manufacturing concerns until near the end of the development cycle. When investigation of the manufacturing processes come after the detail designing we can expect serious difficulties to occur. These can become so serious that products fail to reach the production stage and may be dropped altogether.

| ▶ | **Concurrent engineering and you** | **135** |

Traditional manufacturing

For many years the traditional approach to designing and manufacturing new products has followed a step-by-step process: the concept is developed before the detailing of the design takes place, followed by putting the new product into manufacture. Testing and evaluation of an idea has been carried out on prototypes made before the production item could be available by modelling the design in 3D from detail drawings. This step-by-step, or **consecutive engineering** approach can take a long time and is therefore costly in employing people and requiring companies to invest a lot of money in the manufacture and testing of a series of models up to production prototype stage. With a large product such as a new motor car, this sequence is very expensive and time consuming.

As can be seen from the diagram below, some activities in the process of bringing a new product to the market do not take place until near the end of the development cycle, well after the design has been confirmed.

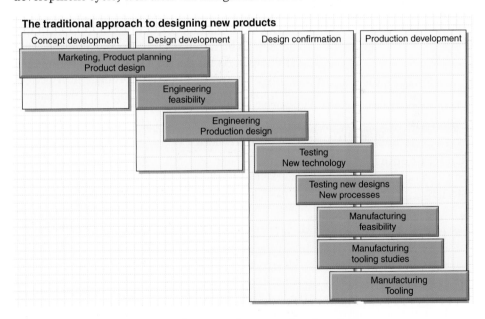

The traditional approach to designing new products

Concurrent engineering and manufacturing

When concurrent methods are adopted the step-by-step, or **sequential model**, is replaced by one where stages run parallel or overlap. This avoids many of the pitfalls of the traditional approach because the manufacturing outcome is known before the design is finalised.

❝ *Concurrent Engineering is an integrated approach to new product introduction. Using multi-functional teams or task forces, it ensures that research, design, development, manufacturing, purchasing and supply and marketing all work in parallel from the concept through to the final launch of the product into the market place.* ❞

Simultaneous Engineering, DTI 1994.

The diagram of concurrent engineering (CE) below shows for comparison, parallel rather than sequential product development and how these activities are planned to run concurrently and overlap.

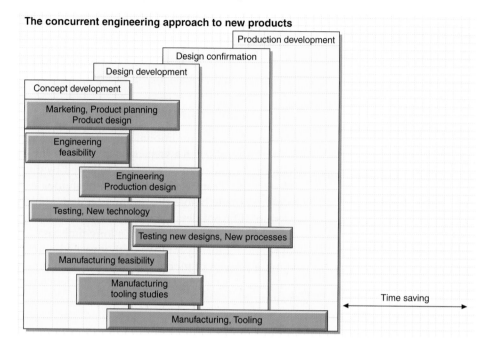

The concurrent engineering approach to new products

Here it can be seen that investigation into many aspects of the design are started much earlier in the development process. Computer technology in the form of CAD with simulation of materials and production processes enables design concepts to be tested without the need for manufacturing the prototype in the early stages. As the design nears its final form new technologies, such as rapid prototyping, can be utilised to produce near perfect replicas of the product for functional testing and that it is right for the market.

Focused task: Understanding and applying concurrent engineering approaches

Understanding

For this task you need to refer to the following case studies:

- McLaren – the F1 Sports car door hinge page 198. Assess concurrent versus consecutive engineering in the designing of the hinge, support strut and mountings.
- Jaguar XK8 page 201. Look out for simultaneous engineering teams. Were they working as well as the company hoped? What does the company aim for in future?
- ASDA page 220. Why did designs have to be modified for standard timber sections? What was the effect here?
- PDSA page 224. How was it possible to consider manufacturing issues at an early or very early stage with this product?

Applying

To adopt a concurrent engineering approach you will need to consider the manufacturing implications of your design ideas at *every* stage from your initial ideas, rather than only in the closing stages. You could show evidence of your concurrent thinking using notes and sketches as your ideas develop. In particular remember to draw conclusions and identify courses of action that result from this.

The following questions may help you to structure your concurrent approach.

- How is ease of manufacture a feature of this idea?
- How would users be affected by the likely manufacturing processes?
- What are the likely cost-implications of your manufacture?
- How might manufacturing change your view of its design?

Quick Response manufacturing

There has been an increasing trend towards manufacturing products more quickly and in the exact quantities needed to meet customer demand. Productivity in traditional manufacturing was measured only in terms of the turning of raw materials into finished products and not always in response to the levels of demand for them. It was common practice therefore for factories to have large stockpiles of finished goods, even where there was no ready market for them.

More recently there has been a move towards the measurement of productivity in cash-flow terms. Measuring factory output in this way has led to **just in time (JIT)** delivery of raw materials and normally, to the absence of stockpiles of finished goods. Prior to JIT, companies needed to stockpile components to ensure that the production was not held-up due to a lack of suitable parts. Making sure that there were sufficient parts to complete a production run was a major planning exercise. Buffer stock, as it was called, took up space all round the factory, and was expensive to store, handle and purchase. Travel light was the new message – order materials etc. in frequent, just-enough, quantities, just in time for processing.

Whilst JIT deliveries can improve efficiency, it is vital that components arrive on time as any delay in processing can be extremely costly. JIT requires therefore good supplier relationships, more careful planning and accurate time estimates for each stage of manufacture.

 Lead time, D&T Routes Core book 127

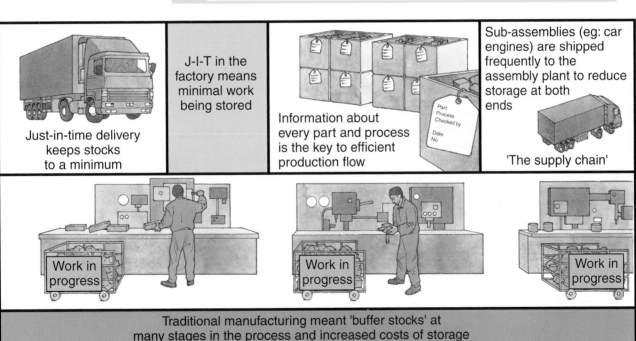

Just-in-time delivery keeps stocks to a minimum

J-I-T in the factory means minimal work being stored

Information about every part and process is the key to efficient production flow

Part Process Checked by Date No

Sub-assemblies (eg: car engines) are shipped frequently to the assembly plant to reduce storage at both ends

'The supply chain'

Work in progress

Work in progress

Work in progress

Traditional manufacturing meant 'buffer stocks' at many stages in the process and increased costs of storage

As manufacturers refined quality control and improved the study of the scheduling of raw materials and components to ensure adequate quantities of finished products, factory layouts changed to avoid unnecessary delays in the stages of the production process. These studies were known as **manufacturing resource planning** and **material resource planning** or **MRP**. Manufacturers would draw up a master plan to schedule deliveries in terms of all the resources needed to produce the product. MRP is, therefore, an inventory management and control tool. The aim of a good MRP system is having the right materials, in the right quantities, in the right place, at the right time.

These resource plans include the ordering and purchasing of materials and components, the processing capacity of the factory, maintenance of tools and equipment, labour capacity, finished product storage and distribution. The advent of computers engendered a wide range of software packages able to offer the manufacturer MRP. This is now often known as MRP2.

Responding to customer demand

The needs of customers are continuously changing as fashions come and go or as improved products are expected. Increasingly it is those manufacturers who respond quickly enough whose products sell and who gain the market share needed to thrive. Where traditional manufacturing methods sometimes led to delays of weeks or months before the arrival at the shops of new stocks, today's turn-around times for certain products are more commonly measured in days. This is particularly true in the clothing, or apparel, industries where fashion is usually highly volatile. Both over and under-production of goods have to be avoided and a production-on-demand approach adopted as far as possible. New design and tooling for garments may become redundant within months as fashion changes demand the latest styles, and keeping up with this demand requires an approach to manufacturing which can respond to change at very short notice.

Quick response may mean using sales information about what is actually sold in the store during a particular week and using this to order new supplies to arrive within as few as four working days. The pace of quick response is increasing and merchandise in some shops is now expected to be supplied every other day based on what actually sold at store level.

This approach places enormous demands on manufacturers to supply on a right-first-time basis, where there is minimum delay or hold-up in production. The entire process, or chain, from raw material production, through manufacturing and into retailing is evolving to meet these demands.

 Marks and Spencer case study   **83**

Reducing manufacturing lead times

The **lead time** for manufacturing a product is defined as 'the time that must be allowed between the decision to build a product and completing it'. Reducing this increases manufacturers' flexibility to respond to fluctuating customer demand.

The drive to reduce lead times will therefore influence most levels of company activity, including long-term planning, forecasting, scheduling of new products and management systems. In this section we look at certain improved manufacturing systems and methods of production. These centre on ways of reducing the waiting time between procedures during design and production, often through the use of more sophisticated manufacturing machinery and equipment. Three examples of this follow.

Rapid prototyping
Increasingly, in the interests of quickness and reliability, products are modelled and prototyped direct from designer's CAD drawings. Using the CAD files passed direct into CNC machinery for this stage may be preferable to hand-crafting due to the accuracy and convenience that such systems usually offer.

This body form is being cut from a solid block of foam by a special milling machine, using data from a CAD drawing.

A model may provide important manufacturing information, such as tooling needs, as well as information needed by the designer. Increasingly sophisticated methods are being developed to allow improved models to be created for designers and manufacturers. They help shorten lead times needed for new products by revealing difficulties or problems at an early stage, so avoiding unnecessary delays later.

Stereolithography

Stereolithography (SL) is a process which further expands the benefits to designers and manufacturers of realistic models and working prototypes. Data is taken from the company's CAD/CAM system to build prototypes of components by scanning an argon laser across a vat of liquid resin. The CAD/CAM data drives the laser which acts like pen, 'drawing' outlines of the component onto the resin, curing it as it goes. Where the laser touches the resin this solidifies, building up the component into a 3D solid form exactly to the CAD drawing, contour-by-contour. The effect is to 'print' a 3D, real-world version of the prototype out of the computer in a relatively soft material.

Stereolithography creates a precise resin replica of the product, but its potential goes much further than this, allowing tools and finished trial-components also to be created. While the cured resin itself has insufficient resistant properties to work as a prototype it can be converted into an identical metal product by using it as a former for casting.

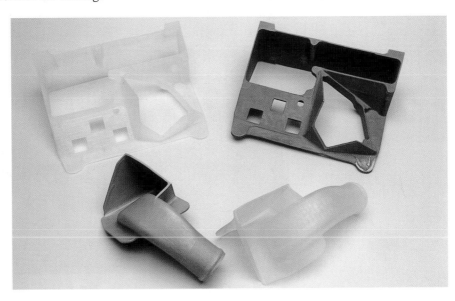

Metal aircraft components and the original resin stereo-lithography models.

Resin models dip-coated in ceramic slurry.

When metal castings are required the SL model is first dipped into a ceramic slurry, giving it an even coating. At the metal foundry, the ceramic coated model is then heated to burn away the resin and to harden its ceramic skin. The empty ceramic shell can then be filled with liquid metal which, when it solidifies, takes on the exact form of the SL model, saving the time that would have been needed to produce a finished product.

Burning away the resin.

The benefits of SL can be summarised as:

- saving time by avoiding the need for a full mock-up before a prototype
- helping trial and prove sub-assemblies before final manufacture
- allowing trial-fits of components being designed to improve or replace existing ones
- avoiding the expense of hand/machine-crafting methods for one-off's and small quantities.

Quick change injection moulding techniques

Injection moulding allows large numbers of plastic components to be made quickly, but the cost of making moulds can be prohibitive. Injecting the polymers into cavities at high speeds and the pressures in this process requires that the tool be made of hard steel. Machining the cavity in the original blank is therefore expensive and time-consuming. The margin for error is small and mistakes are costly. A typical cost for a tool that might produce a component the size of a lunchbox is £10 000–£20 000. To recover this cost, manufacturers have to be sure of selling large numbers, running into tens of thousands, of the item being moulded. But quick response manufacturing tends to demand smaller and more varied production quantities than this, so encouraging the development of new quick response injection moulding techniques.

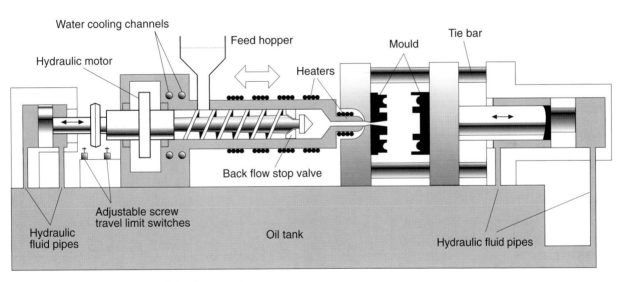

Injection moulding.

Reducing both waiting time between processes and tooling costs in this field has recently centred on the use of materials that might previously have been restricted to prototyping. Although easier to form into mould-shapes or inserts, their strength and durability was in question. But they are proving suitable for the production of quantities from tens to the mid-thousands and their deployment therefore contributes to quick response needs in this particular field. Some quick-change tooling systems, such as using kits of 'inserts' to modify existing moulds rather than making entirely new ones, have also helped to reduce setting-up times.

This kind of quick response exploits the properties of some resistant materials, creating moulds more quickly and at lower cost for lower volumes. Some of the key properties of materials for mould manufacture are shown overleaf.

Materials and 'Quick Response' mould construction.

Material	Fabrication method	Pattern	Quantity	Complexity index	Thermal conductivity	Surface finish	Correlation	Comments
Plaster	Casting	✓	10	2	Extremely low	Poor	0.2	Needs a supporting frame to take clamp force of moulding machine.
Epoxy resins	Casting/ machining	✓	50	6	Very low	Can be good	0.3	Enclosing metal frame may be necessary which will increase life or enable higher pressures to be used.
Low melt point alloys	Casting	✓	25	5	Low	Usually poor	0.4	
	Hobbing	✓	100	5	Low	As good as	0.4	Hydraulic press and extremely robust master required.
	Spraying	✓	100	5	Low	pattern	0.4	Spray equipment required and sprayed shell needs to be backed with something, eg more alloy or concrete.
Zinc alloy	Casting/ machining	✓	1000s	10	Fair	As required	0.8	Generally known as Kirksite.
	Spraying	✓	100s	5	Fair	As required	0.6	Has normally been used reinforced with reinforced concrete. Used for large moulds, eg car boots.
Aluminium	Casting	✓	1000s	10	High	As required	0.85	
alloys	Machining	No	1000s	10				
Steel	Machining	No	1000s	10	Standard	As required	0.95	
Diecast tool	Existing	No	As required	10	Standard	–	0.9	May require modification to suit moulding machine, but if existing possibly quickest way of obtaining mouldings.

Reproduced with permission from *Eureka on campus*, 1992, Findlay Publications

Quick response in the knitting industry

Industrial knitting methods have changed dramatically in recent years. This industry illustrates, perhaps more dramatically than any other, the trend towards achieving shorter manufacturing lead times and therefore quicker design and manufacturing response. For this reason a more extended case study follows.

Case Study: Shima Seiki and total-knit

Knitting presents some remarkable possibilities for computer-aided design and manufacture. You may have experience in school of outputting CAD drawings to a plotter, vinyl cutter, tool path of a lathe or milling machine and you may have discovered that your output could be stitched as in computer-aided embroidery or knitting.

Outputs to machines which convert continuous lengths of yarn into knitted products, such as woollens and other garments, are now commonplace. Converging technologies in this area now allow whole, seamless garments to be produced from complex designs that have been created on screen or with the assistance of virtual reality modelling techniques. It is now possible to display a simulation of a proposed garment on a virtual-version of an individual customer on-screen, which means that we will soon be able to purchase individually designed clothes made precisely to our own unique body dimensions, with the same cost-benefits as mass produced items.

Some underlying principles of knit

Knitted textiles are formed from a continuous length of thread which has been made into loops, or stitches, linked to one another.

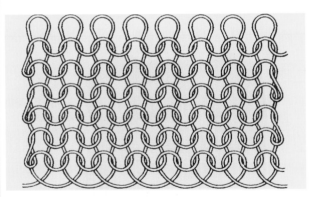

This diagram shows a series of uniform stitches all going in the same direction, known as single bed or 'jersey' fabric.

Many thousands of loops, knitted together, may be needed to give a finished garment the special feel and look that we expect of knitwear. Because hand-knitting is very labour-intensive, we usually now rely on machines to carry out the process for us. Since the first knitting machine, a stocking frame invented by William Lee in 1589 (note the date!), there have been many improvements and a great variety of machines developed for use by the knitting industry.

Volume knitting production

Traditionally, high volume production has relied upon **cut-and-sew blanket knitting** and **shape knitting**. This is gradually being replaced by **WholeGarment knitting**. Blanket knitting is the production of rolls of knitted fabric which are then cut to shape and sewn together to make the product. In shape knitting the individual components of products are knitted to shape, so avoiding waste. Whole garment knitting allows whole products to be created in one piece, without having to rely on blankets or shapes.

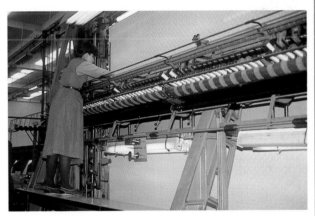

A blanket knitting machine.

Shape knit components.

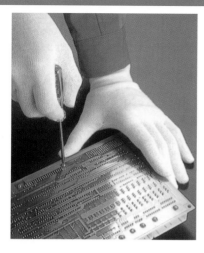

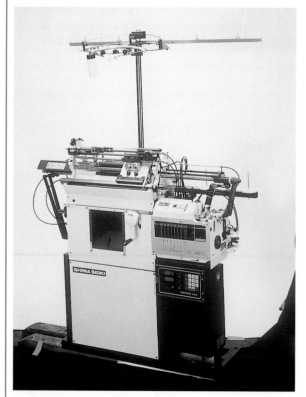

WholeGarment knits

The development of 3D knitting technology

'WholeGarment' technology was first developed from seamless glove making. A glove is quite a complex shape, consisting of six adjoining tubes, one for each finger, the thumb and the wrist. While a single tube is not especially difficult to knit, manufacturers have always compromised glove manufacture by knitting each tube separately and then stitching them together to form the final glove. Shima Seiki were the first company to challenge conventional glove making by investing in the development of new machinery to knit the entire glove structure in one piece. Because the glove machine led to new methods that allowed the knitting of the whole item, requiring no sewing or joining of individual parts, new and improved products are now possible.

In 1965 the Japanese Shima Seiki Manufacturing Company invented a machine that could knit a complete glove without any seams.

This seat in this car is covered by a seamless knitted structure, an improved product which fits the seat like a glove.

Knitting and CAD/CAM

Computer controlled knitting machines use CAD/CAM to knit complex products in minutes, direct from the designer's concept drawing. This includes the selection of stitch pattern, colours, and the shape and design of the final product to very precise limits. Manufacturers are able to respond more quickly because the process provides information concerning the viability of new designs before any work is begun. This can include such things as lead times, yarn requirements, the cost of materials and the total cost of processing a new product in the quantity required.

Reduced waiting time between stages is also achieved through:

1. **computerised,** instead of mechanical, **control** of each stroke and stitch-row
2. **digital stitch control,** which makes sure that each loop in every row is the same
3. **compound needles,** which make loops easier to form
4. **four-bed technology,** which allows more loops to be managed at any one time during manufacture.

1 Computerised control providing variable stroke length

A variable stroke motor was developed allowing very precise stroke-control by computer. The 'step-less' AC servo motor drives a super-lightweight carriage by means of a high-tech toothed belt, replacing the traditional chain drive.

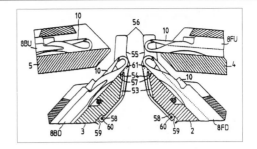

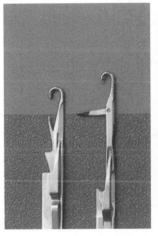
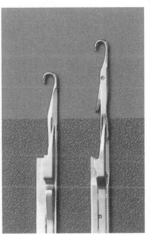

The compound needle reduces the tendency to snag and requires a smaller amount of movement to be activated.

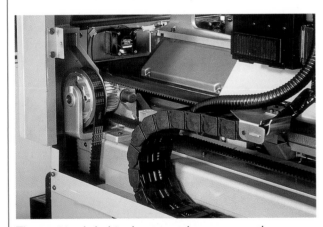

The precision belt drive has many advantages over the traditional chain drive, including increased sensitivity to control and precise stroke length.

2 Mechanical control through the Shima Seiki compound needle

Conventional latch needles are not conductive to tight knitting, particularly at the 'selvages', or edge of the garment. Also, the mechanical hinge of a latch needle required greater movement within the knitting head. A new concept was developed to make the needle slide more easily through the loops created in the knitting and to use less movement. The solution required high precision tooling of the new needle which uses a slider instead of a latch.

3 Improved control through four-bed technology

The improved compound needle allowed more needles to be managed at any one time by the knitting head of the Shima Seiki machine. The extra needles are essential to provide complex shapes such as structured tubular fabrics.

Complex knit forms require a larger number of needles to manage increases and reductions in the number of loops being managed at any one time.

4 Systems and control through DSCS

The digital stitch control system (DSCS) regulates every loop in the knitted structure. Digital checking of each one makes sure it is the same when connected to its neighbour. DSCS is a good example of a feedback or closed-loop control system. This can be represented using a systems diagram showing the input, processing and output stages.

In DSCS the yarn feed and tension is automatically adjusted allowing knitting with continuously stable loop length. In systems not making use of DSCS, even those using computer control, the garments produced can lack uniformity and have irregular dimensions. This is due to changes in temperature, humidity, dyeing and tension strength. The DSCS monitors any changes in these conditions and makes adjustments automatically. Every garment produced will conform to the specification with a tolerance of within ±1%.

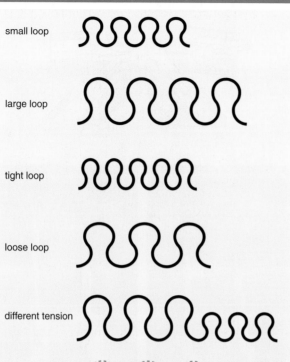

small loop

large loop

tight loop

loose loop

different tension

loop affected by humidity

intended

actual

Each of these loops is different. In a perfect knitted structure their differences must be eliminated.

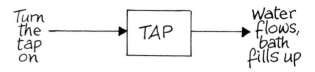

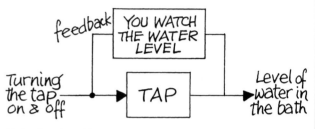

a) In a system a process produces the required outputs in response to the inputs it receives. This system has no feedback – once it has been started it will continue without taking any account of what is actually happening to the output. This type of system is known as an open-loop control system.

b) In this closed-loop system, information is fed back from the output. This information is used to monitor or control the system. This is used to keep the output at the required level or to make sure it is doing what was intended.

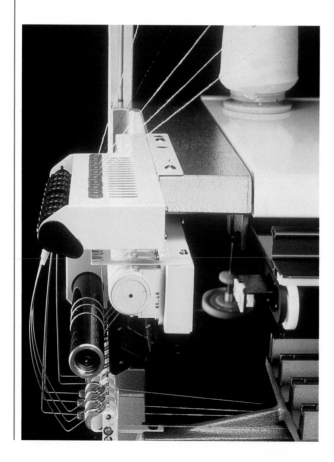

Case Study: Quick Response manufacturing and you: the Hungry Crocodile

Chris Sunderland, a GNVQ Advanced Manufacturing student at George Ward School in Wiltshire, identified a need for a novelty pencil case that would be used by children of primary school age. Concept development and early design activity suggested the pencil case might be formed in the shape of a reptile which contained the pencils in a zip-up tummy. Market research confirmed the market potential for such an idea and a crocodile design was soon developed.

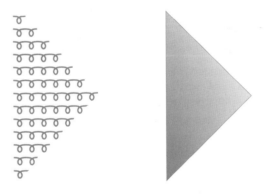

Flechage knitting or short stroke knitting
(Fleche = arrow)

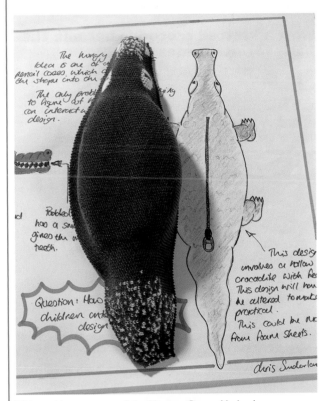

This rapid prototype of the Hungry Crocodile body was provided by a manufacturer while Chris was still working at design development stage.

Children-consumers for this product required a friendly, soft but durable product which could be manufactured in a variety of colours and designs. The product would need to be manufactured in high-volumes but able to be customised to the needs of individual owners. A high quality, regular, seamless shape was envisaged. What kind of material would be most suitable? How could such a shape be made in high volumes?

Early consideration was given to thin plastics and other flexible materials but the special tactile properties of knitted material were considered ideal. An early problem was how to create such a complex shape using conventional knitting techniques which are limited by production process constraints.

The traditional method of creating a three dimensional knitted shape, where triangular zones of stitches known as flechage (arrow) knitting are used, was considered too complex and difficult to control.

Basque berry knitted by the Flechage method

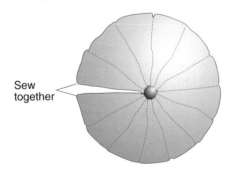

Sew together

Creating a simple 3D shape, such as this beret, would have been difficult and time consuming.

As Chris wanted to create a 3D, seamless shape for the crocodile body his early research into knitting did not confirm its suitability. However a contact was made with a company specialising in the use of 3D knitting machines and the feasibility of a knitted shape was explored using quick response manufacturing techniques. The manufacturer was optimistic from the outset and even claimed that "no shape is now too complex to knit in one piece, even an exact replica of a banana skin!" The early prototypes that were produced of the crocodile body form, allowed Chris to develop design confirmation for his concept drawings.

187

Case Study: Quick Response manufacturing and you: the Hungry Crocodile *continued*

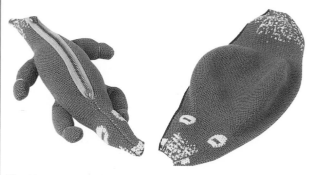

The Hungry Crocodile stores pencils in the central compartment, or zip-up tummy.

This proposal for a full size knitted canoe is considered feasible. Once knitted, the structure would be impregnated with polyester resin to make it rigid.

The crocodile prototype helped to provide the design confirmation needed by Chris for the pencil case. Total-knit could provide a high volume manufactured product, capable of being developed for individual customers, yet providing the cost-benefits of mass production. It was also possible to calculate exact resource requirements, usage rates, lead times, production costs and a selling price using information from the manufacturer which was downloaded from the knit software.

How a knitted crocodile became the basis for other ideas

The company that produced the hungry crocodile prototype did so to assist a student in school. Valuable time was set aside to carry this out, including more than one day of the use of expensive equipment. But as a result of this work other uses for the hungry crocodile form are being considered. One idea is the production of knitted canoe reinforcement using glass fibres instead of woollen yarn.

Focused task: Quick Response Manufacturing

❝ Flexible manufacturing, requiring increasingly quick response to customer wants and purchasing decisions, has become the driving force behind the successful manufacturing operation. A commitment to QR will have implications for all involved in manufacturing the products, including the skills of the workforce, their work practices and the plant, equipment and manufacturing methods that they require.'

Choosing one or more of the questions below, present a short written and illustrated account of flexible manufacturing.

Refer to the case studies in this book to help illustrate your account.

1   How are production methods changing in the areas of prototyping, plastics moulding and knitting to enable reduced lead times and production that is more responsive to the individual customer?
2   What kinds of new machinery are being developed and how do they achieve a quicker response than previous processing methods?

3   In what ways have control systems been used to develop improved machinery which can provide quicker response times?
4   In flexible manufacturing a company will often produce a wide range of products using the same tools and equipment. How do the examples in this section make this more achievable?
5   Do you think that flexible manufacturing might lead to more highly trained and motivated workers? If so, why?
6   Whilst it is not important for a workforce to be recruited with the exact skills necessary, it is increasingly important that workers are able to adapt and learn new skills as required. What do you understand by this statement, in relation to flexible manufacturing?
7   Group technology, or cell layout, is now a common manufacturing system. Products are first classified into a limited number of groups with similar sub-process sequences. A product layout is then installed for each group. How might this kind of factory layout assist flexible manufacturing?

CHAPTER FIVE Case studies

Contents

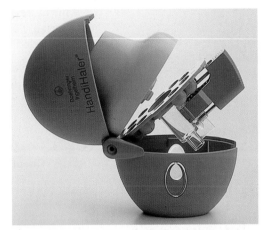

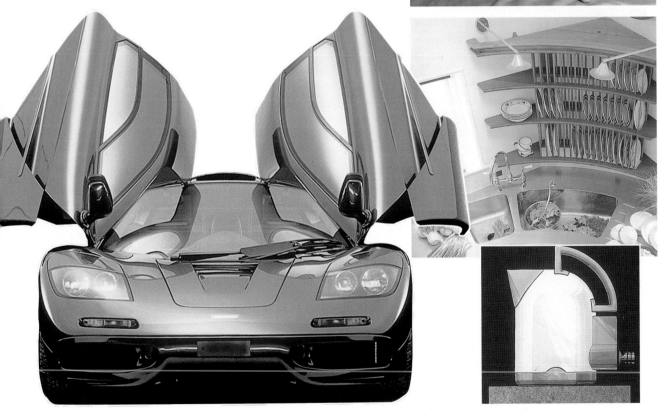

Furniture design and manufacture

- One-off design and manufacture – luxury fitted kitchens from Domida Designs.
- Home Pac Furniture (Lancelot) – high volume manufacture of flat-pack furniture,
- Simon Turner – a furniture maker who makes extensive use of scrap and discarded materials,

These three case studies illustrate some of the issues related to manufacturing products in different volumes, to different levels of quality and for different types of customer.

 Chapter 2 From customer need to customer satisfaction   50

Focused task: Customers' wants, quality and volumes of production

Read through the three furniture design and manufacture case studies and make notes about the following points relating them to the volume of production, the level of quality of the product, the needs and aspirations of the customers and the cost and price of the products:

- the manufacturing processes used including the use of automated processes

- labour, material and distribution costs
- skills of the workforce including specialised skills and multi-skilling
- quality assurance and quality control procedures
- the individuality of the product
- the use of standardised components
- the use of specialised tools and equipment.

Domida Design: Designing and manufacturing one-offs

Domida Design is a small firm in Bruton, Somerset, which produces kitchen furniture, designed by Johnny Grey. Most of the furniture is designed and manufactured as one-off pieces. Often, the pieces are part of a complete set of kitchen furnishings designed and made for an individual client, and a piece may take up to five weeks to make. The manufacturing team works closely to the designer's concept drawings to ensure that the final product looks and performs as both the designer and client expect.

Johnny Grey (who was trained in architectural design) has been called 'the creator of the unfitted kitchen'. He believes in the kitchen as the heart of the home, the centre of activity and in kitchens as multi-purpose spaces which must be fully functional both as kitchens and as comfortable, social areas.

Production

Levels of production are determined mostly by individual client demand. Some units may be a variation on a previous design, but they are still built as one-offs. This is a 'up-market' niche where the emphasis is on exclusivity and quality.

Even though Domida Design are mainly involved in the production of one-off products, because they are often producing sets of units batch-production of parts may well be involved. (For example, multiple-use fittings include brass hinges and specially designed and made components, like handles.) Much of the strength of the construction depends on designing for strength and wear and tear, accurate joint-making and forming and the strength of the materials. Some units are very heavy.

Pieces for a kitchen are manufactured in parallel, with each team member taking responsibility for particular units. However, when there are processes that involve lots of sections that are similar in some way, one member of the team will do the job for everyone.

Domida Design have three main workshop areas:

- An assembly area where the parts of the units are put together. Here, mainly familiar hand-held tools are used, many of them power-tools.
- A processing area where the sawn timber is stacked. Here there are bigger machines, but not unlike those in school or college: tenoning and mortising machines; a linisher/sander; a planer/thicknesser; a large bandsaw; a cross-cut saw; a saw-bench (with travelling table to support and move the timber) and a spindle moulder.

Case studies

◆ A finishing shop where veneers are pressed in a large, flat-bed machine and cut and taped. The copying machine is also here. A separate area of this shop is used for spraying and drying. The spraying area is ventilated by huge, wall-mounted filters, to protect the workforce and to ensure that only clean air goes out of the building.

Throughout the workshops, ducting carries sawdust to sealed sacks, keeping the work environment dust-free and safe.

Quality control

Domida Design specialise in quality products which meet the specific desires and needs of particular users. The products are designed and made to last. Their work is carefully controlled for quality throughout designing and manufacturing. Much of the quality assurance comes through the specialist skills and understanding of the experienced workforce – through touching, handling, working, assessing the visual qualities of pieces and constantly checking the work in progress. More QA comes through working closely as a team who take great pride in what they produce: many quality control measures are systematically built-in to the processes involved. For example, very accurate measuring is critical throughout the designing and manufacturing of these products. Because the kitchens are built for individual clients, the site measurements are crucial. A member of the team takes all measurements on-site and a detailed scale site-plan is produced. If building work is to take place, it is critical that the builders follow the plans accurately. Anything built even fractionally out of line can cause huge problems later when fitting the finished kitchen pieces on-site. Consequently there is frequent liaison between the builders (and they may be in another country), the workshops, and any outside specialist-makers involved. Quality of interpersonal communication skills is therefore also crucial.

The designs for the kitchen pieces are translated into detailed scale drawings. Not only must each piece be drawn-up accurately but accuracy regarding all the pieces fitting together and into the site is also critical. If the design is for something like an island unit, the plan view is drawn out, full-size, like a pattern which must be correct in every detail as the unit will then be built on top of it.

Domida Design also use a range of mechanised systems for ensuring that batch or repeat processes are exactly the same and for ensuring that one-off processes are exactly accurate.

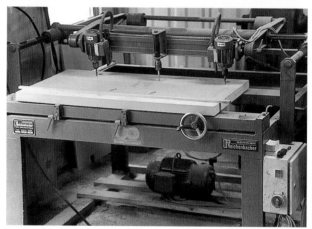

A copy router.

Clamping a curved door in a former.

Materials

Domida Design mainly work with woods though granite or marble may also be used for worksurfaces. They use some metals, for example, a steel beam to support a very heavy work-surface or brass for decorative work. Wrought-iron work is completed by an outside specialist, as is wood-turning for legs of units, and so forth. These specialists work to the plans provided by Domida Design. They complete their work in parallel with the units being manufactured. These specialists must work very accurately, or their sections will not fit the main body of the product.

The woods that are used are mainly MDF, plywood, flexi-ply and quality European hardwoods, such as oak, cherry and maple. The ways in which traditional and new materials and processes of working are combined contribute towards making the Domida Design products special. Another reason for being particularly careful with taking measurements is, of course, related to the cost and availability of the quality woods. Even at this top end of the furnishings market, cost of materials, labour processes and undue wastage have to be considered in designing for manufacture. However, conversely, generosity in material use is often a feature of 'couture' design of this nature.

Conclusions from this case study

This case study shows that one-off designing and manufacturing can be competitive if a niche market is found and appropriate materials and processes are used. Also that the design and manufacture of one-offs can include batch production, and forms and processes repeated in subsequent designs.

A similar example would be from the made-to-measure or couture end of the clothing industry. But neither of these are very dissimilar to your own situation in school or college. Key features would include:

- planning, and constantly thinking ahead
- accuracy and highly developed skills in measuring, fitting and making
- careful selection, quality, and generosity, of materials used
- creativity
- good interpersonal and team-working skills
- familiarity with historical and contemporary designing and making processes
- empathy with the context in which the products will be used and the clients using them.

But perhaps, most strongly, a real belief in quality – so that quality runs through every vein of how the company operates and everything it produces. Only then will the client perceive value for money when the products are expensive.

These products have a aura of quality and yet simplicity, that sets them apart whilst enfolding them within their setting. And they function very, very well.

Some things to think about in your own work

- Where does responsibility for quality stop?
- Is the designer-maker of a one-off product more directly responsible for the quality of their work than the designers and makers of mass-produced products?
- How can quality be assured throughout the work you do? Where does your responsibility start and stop? What lessons can you personally learn from this case study?
- How do your finished products relate to your original ideas? If they are dissimilar, why, and are there good enough reasons?
- Consider the balance between labour, material, overhead costs, the intended market value, intended product life and maintenance of your products. Look at the appropriate sections in the Designing chapter and consider how Domida Design have achieved this balance for their products.
- Do you use jigs and formers enough, e.g. setting stops to control the accuracy of repeat processes?

- Is there a difference between needs and wants? Why do some people feel that paying a high price for quality products, especially one-off products, is worthwhile? Would these kitchen products fill needs or wants anywhere in the world? If not, why not?
- Domida Design use a mixture of hand and machine processes – why does this suit the products they make? What balance can you achieve in your manufacturing? Where can you use machine processes? What are the advantages of doing so? Where would hand processes suit your needs better?

Home Pac Ltd: High volume production of flat-pack furniture

The use of systems and control at Home Pac Ltd

Home Pac use processes based on the extensive use of control systems to ensure an efficient and cost effective manufacturing operation. A range of mechanical, electrical, electronic and pneumatic systems and sub-systems are linked together to process the materials through the factory. A computerised system is used to schedule production runs. The system identifies the critical path of each operation and routes panels through the factory with each section receiving work lists that are sequenced to enable packing dates to be met for each customer's order.

The Processing Operations

Process operation 1: Sawing the panels

The panels that make up each unit of furniture are cut to the required length and width using a new sawing machine controlled by a dedicated computer running pre-programmed software. The software sends cutting instructions that give detailed dimensions and the cutting order, as several panels are produced from each large piece of laminated chipboard.

Home Pac Ltd, established in 1973 is a high volume batch producer of 'flat-pack' self assembly furniture, their customers are mainly mail-order catalogues and well known high Street retailers such as Argos and Woolworth's. The company produces a range of bedroom, kitchen, office and audio-visual storage furniture from laminated chipboard and knock down fittings that are bought in as standardised components. The manufacturing site is located in Hertfordshire to the north of London and the finished goods are sent to a distribution warehouse for onward delivery to customers all over the country. Some furniture is sold to directly through Lancelot Furniture which is a trading arm of Home Pac Ltd.

Station 1   Cutting square

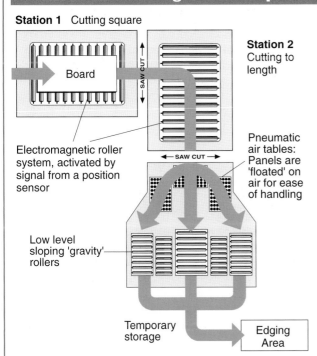

Station 2
Cutting to
length

Electromagnetic roller
system, activated by
signal from a position
sensor

Pneumatic
air tables:
Panels are
'floated' on
air for ease
of handling

Low level
sloping 'gravity'
rollers

Temporary
storage

Edging
Area

The diagram illustrates the main sub-systems that come
together to make up the sawing process.

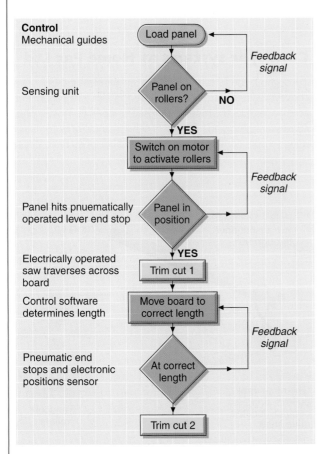

This flowchart describes part of the sawing operation and the
control devices and sensors used during each stage of the
operation.

Processing Operation 2: Edging the sawn panels

The ends of the panels that will be seen have to be edged
using a plastic edging strip that matches or contrasts with the
face veneer of the panel. The edging is applied to the panels
automatically as they pass through the 'edging unit'. The
adhesive used to stick the edging is applied hot and pressure
rollers hold the edge in place until the adhesive sets. This
process is used to edge the panels. Two parallel sides are
edged in the first part of the unit. The panel is then passed
onto the second part of the unit where the two other edges
are applied. The final two sections of the edging unit trim off
any surplus edging strip.

The edging unit is a complex system that is made up of
several sub-systems:

Inner stack   Individual panels are fed from a stack into the
machine by way of a motorised roller system. The height of
the stack is pre-set by software on a dedicated computer. The
height of the stack is continually monitored by an electronic
system which sends a feedback signal to the computer. As
long as the stack is below the sensors the rollers continue to
operate. Once the correct height has been reached a signal is
sent to the computer which switches off the motors on the
roller system. A signal is then sent to electrically controlled
pneumatic arms which close the barriers to the inner stack
and start the process of lining up.

Lining up   Electro-mechanical booms or bars are activated
by pneumatic power lines to straighten the stack vertically and
horizontally so that the individual panels can be accurately fed
into the edging sections. This is a critical system, errors here
can mean a large amount of panel wastage.

Feeding the edging strip   Edging strip is stored on large
spools to one side of the production line. The feed
mechanism is electrically operated and the speed of operation
is determined by several factors such as the heat of the
adhesive and the position of the panel. For the feed
mechanism to operate, two conditions must be met: a panel
has to be in place and the adhesive has to be at the right
working temperature.

Heater Units   Electric heaters soften the heat sensitive
polymer adhesive to 107°C and electronic sensors continually
monitor the temperature. An ON/OFF feedback temperature
control system is used. A display provides the machine
operators with a visual record of temperature; if there is a
system failure an audible and visual alarm is activated.

Applying the adhesive   Pneumatically operated
mechanical spreaders apply the hot glue to the sides of the
panel as it is fed from the heater units.

Pressure devices   Mechanically controlled clamps hold the
edging strips in place until the adhesive cools down and sets
hard.

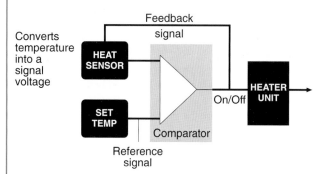

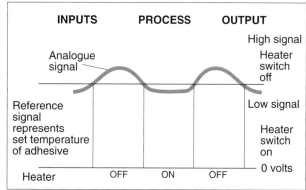

This block diagram shows the operation of the heater unit.

Electro-mechanical counters
These record the progress of panels through the unit.

Processing Operation 3: Drilling the fixing holes
All the holes required in a panel for fixing hinges, handles, shelves and so on are drilled simultaneously in multi-tooled drilling stations; this is an example of a one stop operation. The drill bits are motor driven and operate under the control of a dedicated computer running pre-programmed software which determines the positioning (using x- and y-axis co-ordinates) and the depth of hole (z-axis) and the sequence of the drilling operations.

The panels are fed into the machine manually but electronic position sensors operate pneumatically controlled end-stops. Once the board is in the correct position, pneumatically driven clamps hold the panel in place for the duration of the drilling operations.

Processing Operation 4: Packing the knock down (KD) fittings
Each piece of flat pack furniture includes a range of KD fittings to enable the customer to assemble the piece of furniture. Home Pac have an automated system for packing the smaller assembly items such as nails and screws. The items are difficult to handle and it is time consuming and costly to count out the required numbers of each item. The items are packed by weight, a rotating drum contains the items to be weighed. The number of items and their total weight has been calculated and the information or data stored in the processor. As the drum rotates it also vibrates to separate out the individual items and a pneumatically controlled arm diverts a stream of items into a weight sensing holding device. Once

the correct weight is in the holding device a feedback signal is sent to the processor controlling the diverter arm so that no more nails etc. are allowed to pass in. The required number of items are passed along the conveyor and off the weight sensor. Once the weight is removed a feedback signal is sent to the processor to divert the arm once more and so repeat the cycle.

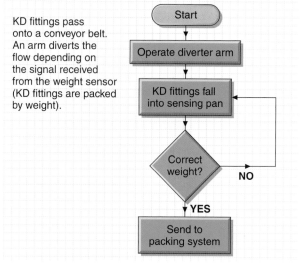

Packing the KD fittings.

Conveyor systems at Home Pac Ltd

Throughout the factory a combination of roller and belt conveyor systems are used to move the furniture panels and accessories. Electric motors are used to operate most of the conveyor systems and control is either manual or automatic, using sensors combined with mechanical or pneumatic stops.

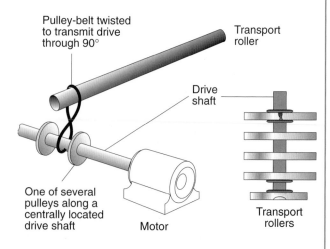

A schematic diagram showing a typical arrangement of part of the conveyor system – the pulley belt drive system.

Focused task: Manufacturing control systems

1 What are the advantages to Home Pac and their customers of making extensive use of control systems in the manufacturing processes? Are there any disadvantages?

2 To understand the control systems described in this case study, you could use systems electronics, pneumatics, mechanisms and other kits to assemble a model of all or parts of this process. Use block and systems diagrams to help design the systems.

Simon Turner: Furniture designer and maker

Simon Turner trained as a D&T teacher and now also works as a freelance furniture designer-maker; fitted kitchens are one of his specialities.

"Almost everything in my home has been stolen, borrowed or donated," says Simon who finds a use for the things that other people throw away. Old sink strainers, discarded steel work-surfaces from office canteens and rusty scaffolding have all found their way into Simon's designs.

Simon has combined his furniture making skills with these discarded and re-claimed materials to develop a style somewhere between Shaker and industrial chic. This style is warmer and more user-friendly that some of the more hard-edged industrial recycling that is becoming fashionable. This is because he is making things for a family home rather than the warehouse and loft conversions which adapt more naturally to furniture made of steel and aluminium.

"I try things out in my own home, to see if they work before suggesting them commercially. It's a house full of prototypes."

Simon used some old aluminium catering work surfaces and counters from the college where he teaches, to make the doors for his kitchen units. The aluminium was cut using a jigsaw and then set into softwood frames. The carcasses of the units he constructed from MDF. For the doors on the wall units he inset aluminium sink strainers, polished to a sparkling shine with a buffing wheel, into softwood panels.

In a small kitchen, space is at a premium. Instead of a conventional drawer for cutlery, Simon used food storage units from the self-service counter of his college canteen fitted into a narrow vertical gap between the sink and the stove. A platewarmer becomes a light source and a place to hang utensils. Light is thrown up onto the ceiling and through the holes. Rubbish goes into an aluminium flour bin, also taken from the college, which was set onto casters and is just the right size for black bin liners.

"The kitchen work surfaces were given to me by a school who were getting rid of the old teak tops in their science laboratories. I cut-away around the sink, and routed in grooves for the water to run away."

A complete kitchen like Simon's would cost a client around £1500 to £2000.

A kitchen table is one of Simon's latest experiments; it is made from birch-faced plywood with wooden legs and industrial glass bricks set into the centre. It adds light to the room because a light can be shone up through the glass. A table like this costs about £400.

Fitted wardrobes using scaffolding for the shelving uprights, another speciality, cost around £1000 for an 8 ft by 8 ft set.

When Simon is working on a commission, he draws up the designs first and then sees what he can source second-hand. He looks in skips and visits reclamation yards and sites where renovations are taking place. Items used in Simon's designs can come from as far afield as France where he makes a habit of checking out *brocantes* (second-hand furniture shops). Each finished item is unique.

'It was decided that our first product would be a Super Sports Car to end all supercars – a unique and advanced vehicle that would be usable, fast and safe. But, above all, the F1 would be a pure driver's car.'

Gordon Murray, technical director, McLaren Cars

Talking about his initial briefing to the new company's team:

'It had to be a driver's car, which immediately ruled out offset controls and poor visibility. I told them about the three seats. . .'

Designer Peter Stevens (an RCA graduate) and Gordon Murray assessing the tape drawing of the F1 design.

Front view of an F1. Three seats, carbon fibre advanced composite monocoque and body, BMW 6 litre V12 engine. Price when production of the final, 100th car was finished in June 1998, £634 500.

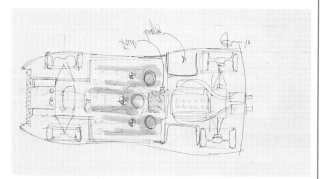

The concept of a central 'single seater' driving position and passengers on either side was fundamental – an early sketch.

The McLaren F1 doors

The McLaren F1 has a unique driving position, with the driver's seat centrally placed ahead of the two passenger seats. This unique configuration has led to a number of design needs for many features of the car. Not least of these is the design of the doors and the door furniture, their fixtures and fittings. The driver needs to get to the central driving position across the space in front of one of the two passenger seats. This means they have to enter the car backwards, sit on one of the structural 'tunnels' either side of the driver's seat, swing their legs into the central footwell and lower themselves into the drivers seat, all in one unobstructed movement.

To enable as comfortable and straightforward access as possible, the door aperture had to be very long, from the front towards the rear of the car, and extend into the roof section. This prevented the need for drivers to have to bend their legs or crouch too much. The F1 is a very expensive car and the first point of contact for the customer is the door so it must be user-friendly and give the right impressions of high quality.

A long door could cause problems in use. If it was hinged in the conventional way it would protrude a long way from the car when open, so the driver would have difficulties in car parks finding a space wide enough to open the door. It would also be awkward for the driver to reach the door to open or close it from the driving position. If it was hinged to open vertically and pivot forward, or open vertically in the 'gull wing' style there would still be problems reaching the door from the central driving position and it would be difficult to open it in a garage without it hitting the ceiling. Although

Above all, the door must be user friendly and give an impression of high quality.

the door itself is very light at just 5 kg, when all the fittings, furniture, speakers and glass are fitted it is over 25 kg. This puts tremendous stress on the hinge, the mountings and the strut used to assist the opening of the door.

A 'buck' of the cockpit was made to enable design ideas to be developed.

The dihedral door and the hinge problem

Ultimately the door was designed to open out, up, forward and over the car in one smooth action – the 'dihedral door' as it is now called. This solved all the problems of space, access, operation, weather and sound sealing and 'shut gaps' but now caused enormous problems for the engineers designing the hinges, the strut and its mountings. The car door has to move through different planes when opening and closing so normal hinges could not be used – rose joints had to be designed into the hinges. The mounting points for the hinges on the body and on the door are a long way apart. One is on the top of the front wing, the other is toward the centre of the roof. The hinges are a feature on the car and can be seen on the outside whereas most car door hinges are hidden from view.

The hinges, on the wing and the roof are 1.5 m from the door latch.

Whatever design was adopted it was obvious that the unique characteristics of the hinges would cause them to be expensive to produce. The hinge and door latch positions dictated the design of the body because the hinges and the body surfaces had to match up and be of sufficient strength. Traditionally, the door latch has always been on the door and the striking pin on the body. On the F1 this would not be possible so the opposite was adopted with the latch on the body. This, along with the latch being 1.5 m away from the hinges, made it extremely difficult to draw the shape of the hinges and the body at their mounting points. All of the design drawings were done manually and took over six months. Just showing what they would be like and understanding how they would move made it necessary to create drawings of the hinge from many different angles (auxiliary elevations).

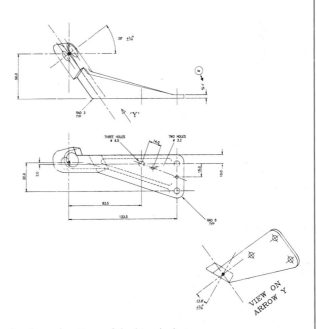

Auxiliary elevations of the hinge's design.

The effort that was put into designing and making the doors and hinges, and therefore the development costs, were disproportionate to many other apparently more important features of the car.

From design to prototype

Once the hinges had been designed on paper a prototype had to be produced to mount a door in the buck to test its operation. McLaren Cars found it very difficult to find a company that would produce the one-off hinge prototypes. They needed to be machined out of very high quality solid aluminium alloy and have the rose joints mounted in them. Finally a company was found that would do the work but a single prototype hinge cost £10 000!

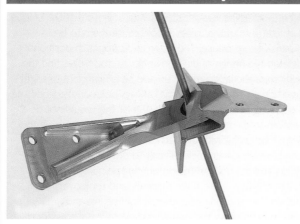

A prototype hinge (machined).

The prototype was produced and testing went ahead. The design proved to be very successful but a method of production had to be found that reduced the cost of the part when the car was in production. Three alternatives were considered and tried:

◆ fabrication – welding flat shapes to machined parts
◆ sand casting
◆ investment casting.

Fabricating the hinges was the most straightforward way and the cheapest, but in practice it was found that the jigs used to hold the parts while welding were not strong or accurate enough and there was a lot of variation in the accuracy of the hinges. A decision was taken very early on in production that this variation in accuracy and quality would not do and an alternative method would have to be used.

Sand casting was the next obvious choice but it was felt that because of the quality of finish required, as the hinges were seen on the outside of the car, this would not do and it was decided to have the hinges investment cast in high grade aluminium alloy. Using this method, all the design criteria were met. The accuracy, quality, performance and cost were all acceptable and this is the method that has continued in production.

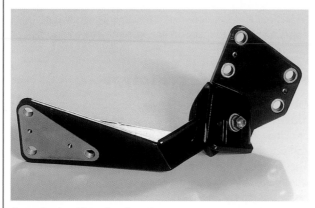

A production hinge (cast).

Designing the support strut and mountings

The design of the support strut and its mountings ran concurrently with the design of the hinges. It needed to be as unobtrusive as possible when the door was open, and out of sight when the door was closed. The movement and consequent locus (path followed) of the strut was even more complex than that of the door hinges. This meant that rose joints again had to be used in the mounting points for the struts.

Once the design of the hinges had been resolved the testing of the strut could take place. It was found that the strut raised the door very well but when the door came to the end of its movement the force from the strut made it 'thwack' unpleasantly against the stops and the door vibrated for a few seconds. To prevent this occurring a hydraulic damper had to be incorporated into the strut. This dual function strut would cause the door to lift and then slow the action as it neared the end of its travel to prevent the sudden, vibrating stop. A large gas strut manufacturing company that makes hundreds of thousands of struts for mass produced cars went to a great deal of trouble to ensure McLaren Cars had the exact component they needed.

The hinge and door strut in situ.

The strut also had to hold the door in the closed position. This involved the strut moving fractionally past its pivot point just before it reached its parked position so it was not trying to lift the door open. However once the door latch is released, moving the door a few millimetres causes the strut to be taken back beyond its pivot point starting it to lift the door.

Once the function and performance of the strut had been resolved the interior trim had to be designed to allow for its movement and at the same time hide as much of it as possible. This involved hours of opening and closing the door with a plasticine lining and gradually scraping away the lining until the strut no longer marked it.

McLaren: The story of the F1 sports car door hinge *continued*

Was it all worth it?

As the designers pointed out, the effort put into the design of the door, its hinges and support strut was totally disproportionate to the effort that went into the design of the whole car. However, it was felt that customers paying a great deal to have the fastest road car in the world would expect the door action to work perfectly every time they got in and out.

Another aspect also emerged in discussion. When building such a special car, every element of customer satisfaction is important. The complex design of the hinge and strut created a very special mechanism which looked superb and was extremely satisfying to use as the door slipped smoothly and quietly through a complex set of movements coming to rest in its open position smoothly, solidly and safely. As passengers meeting the car for the first time watched the new driver draw the door closed they could admire the complexity, efficiency and beauty of the mechanism controlling it. Drivers of cars like this want to share their pleasure!

Focused task: Customer satisfaction

- How could McLaren have avoided the need for so complex a hinge system?
- At what stage in their design process did it become unavoidable?
- Why didn't they adopt a design that would avoid the need for such a complex hinge?
- No mass produced car has such a hinge. At what stage in their design process would this be avoided?

- Does high quality functionality give aesthetic satisfaction?
- Can you identify an engineering mechanism that you feel is beautiful, or aesthetically satisfying?

A part, such as a novel hinge, rather than a whole product could be a valid project for you.

Jaguar XK8: The development of a car interior

Background

Jaguar decided in 1991 that it needed to renew the 15 year old XJ-S coupe and convertible. The XJ-S had been sold in far higher quantities than its predecessor the E-Type, but it had not caught people's imagination in the same way.

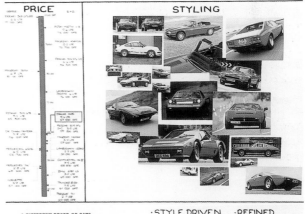

These 'product definition boards' show the position of the cars against their competition in the market, and the words which characterised them.

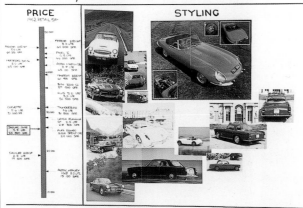

Customers were showing a lack of interest even though it had become a design classic. The XJ-S replacement programme started off with a small budget. As a result of this the design brief was based on keeping the floor pan, cabin and doors of the XJ-S and just changing the nose and tail. However, the brief had to be revised as initial sketches showed that this did not provide scope to change the design significantly enough to attract new customers and make a profitable business case. The aim of the new car was to regenerate the soul of Jaguar – i.e. to have an emotional appeal to Jaguar devotees. It also had to be competitive with other cars that would be of interest to their prospective customers with a similar character and refinement.

The design brief

The team looked back at what was said in the press about predecessors, what was liked and disliked, and projected this to current and future market trends. The interior design team were then given a very open design brief. They worked very closely with the exterior design team so that the design themes for the interior and exterior were compatible. The teams were given some constraints in the form of hard points, as they knew that the floor pan of the existing XJ-S would be used. It had to stow two full-sized golf bags and have a sufficiently long fuel range. The brief was deliberately left open in order to give the management a variety of initial concepts to choose from.

The preliminary 2D sketches were based on five strategies:

◆ Traditional, making use of Jaguar's heritage – saloon derived, wood and leather.
◆ Evolutionary, taking the existing car and developing a more contemporary and competitive product.
◆ Progressive, remodelling the best from their heritage to be appropriate for the future, making use of new technologies and a 'spinal' theme, with a strong centre console.
◆ Avant-garde, emphasis on innovation in form and style.
◆ Radical, innovative in use of latest technologies, redefining Jaguar's image.

Design development and modelling techniques

The development of the exterior and interior of the car was undertaken in parallel and themes for both overlapped to ensure that there would be a suitable match in interior and exterior proposals.

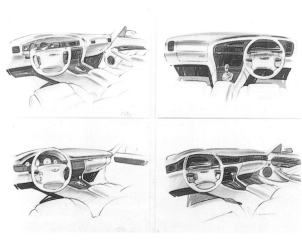

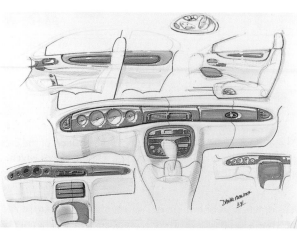

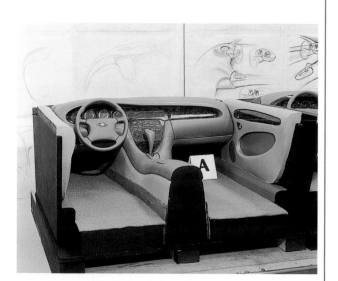

Initial styling sketches on the traditional theme.

Four full size exterior models and five half scale interior models were shown to management at the same review in order to get a direction in which to progress. The managers had difficulties in understanding the designs, as the half size interior clay models did not suggest the right proportions so they could not give a clear direction. It was therefore decided that there would be a second management review with a choice of two full size clay models. The styling team decided to develop the progressive spinal theme/cockpit concept with the occupants sitting low beside a high centre console, as this was considered the strongest theme out of the five models. The stylists went back to their sketchpads to develop two new themes. One was again 'traditional' and based on existing proposals for a saloon car interior, the other was described as 'evocative', inspired by a combination of aircraft cockpits and Jaguar's heritage. It incorporated traditional luxury with a multitude of dials, mounted in a linear aeroplane-wing shaped swoop of wood on the dashboard together with controls grouped in the centre console.

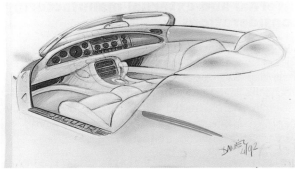

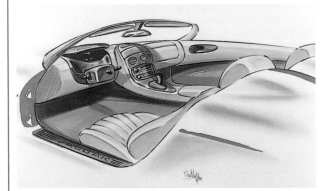

Time was ticking away and to meet important deadlines a decision between the two sketches had to be made. Three comparative sketches were then produced which showed identical perspective views of the progressive, traditional and evocative themes. On the basis of a review of these sketches,

the Jaguar management chose to progress the 'evocative' aircraft theme into full size clay. The rationale for this decision was based on:

◆ the best match to exteriors currently under development
◆ the desired sports image
◆ being sufficiently different from the competition
◆ being sufficiently different from the previous sports interior to warrant the investment
◆ the inherent values of the Jaguar management.

The designer responsible for the chosen theme developed the idea as a tape drawing, using transparent film so that package and feasibility CAD data could be used as underlays. Tape drawings for fascia, door and console, internal front elevation and plan view were developed with help from a team of engineers and ergonomists. The information was then transferred from the tape drawing onto a clay model, the designers and modellers developing and refining the theme together. During this same period parallel activities were taking place in exterior design with sketches, models, clinics etc. and CAD systems servicing the stylist with the hard points or fixed requirements which had to be taken into consideration. Much of the package already existed on the CAD system. This included the floor pan, suspension, power train, wheel base and engine heights; many of the legislative requirements such as light angles and vision heights and ergonomic data for different countries. This all went together to provide the outline structure which the designer had to work with. At regular intervals the clay was digitised so that surface points could be transferred to engineers to check feasibility on the CAD system.

This is an 'iterative' process, that is the ideas are reiterated, again and again, further refinements coming in at each stage, involving a close interaction between team members with backgrounds in different company functions including styling and engineering. After about six weeks of intensive development and refinement, the interior clay themes were finished to a presentation standard. This involved using paint and real veneers and models of parts. It was then presented at the Theme Decision management review, together with the exterior models that were developed in parallel.

Finished 'evocative' theme model for management review at the Theme Decision gateway on the timing plan.

At this point the 'evocative' theme was chosen by Jaguar management to be developed into production. The information used to make this choice included:

◆ market research data about current customers and competitors' customers
◆ market research data from a design clinic where the clay proposal was compared with competitor cars
◆ the feasibility of the designs.

Jaguar was looking for a younger, sportier image without putting off the traditional customers. Jaguar is constantly updating its customer research with questionnaires sent out to owners of competitor cars as well as their own asking what they like and dislike about the cars and what they want from their car. The data constantly kept the design team up-to-date and if important changes came to light, the design was changed. For example, two late alterations in design which were required by the customers were:

◆ the incorporation of a height adjustment system into the driver's seat – it was found that a significant number of prospective drivers were women
◆ a pop-out cup holder was incorporated into the elbow rest and storage box lid – this was a feature considered desirable by US customers.

Feasibility

Completed whole-interior model.

After approval was obtained, the aesthetics and feasibility needed to be further refined; the complete interior was then developed and reviewed as a whole. At specific intervals the clay was scanned and the digital data obtained was transferred to the designers responsible for the whole package to check hard points and legislation, and to the Engineering department and suppliers to check tooling requirements, materials properties and costs. The data is also used by the CAD smoothing function within the styling department which smooths out any slight irregularities in the clay model. The CAD operator then uses the digitised data, the design intent and feasibility information to produce a surface model for each component. This information is again sent to Engineering and suppliers to be checked. In cases

where modification is required they will be done on the clay first if they are likely to affect the style's integrity, or on the CAD system if not. After a feasible design for each component is achieved, this is transferred to the CNC machining department. They write cutting sequences for a CNC machine to mill the surface. The milled items are assembled into a stack model for review. If modifications are necessary these are done on CAD, CNC milled and again reviewed until the project team is satisfied. This part design is then released to Engineering and suppliers for the preparation of prototype and production tooling. Within one year from initial sketches the final design was frozen, the styling development taking approximately 20% of the total development time.

Prototype phase

During this phase the design team's role changes into supporting the engineering and manufacturing activities. If modifications to the released part design are necessary, the designer will give an expert opinion. Prototypes of the car interior and exterior together are now constructed to investigate fit and finish, materials properties, assembly methods and dynamic properties – a 38 month development phase where several types of prototype are used. These were initially built on a dedicated track, simulating the normal production line assembly practices. Eight months before production, prototype assembly was moved over into the main production facility.

Internal and external manufacturing considerations

Customer requirements and materials

The colour and trim section of the styling department started to develop design themes for colour and surface finishes around this time. These were based on trends in industry and fashion that were projected to the time of production for the specific group of customers identified. Different materials were tried out on interior trim bucks (models).

The fascia board which frames the instrument panel is the focus of the whole dashboard design. Alternative models were completed, using different colour and trim themes including brushed aluminium, carbon fibre and other synthetic finishes and burr-walnut veneer. They were used in market research clinics of full size clay models which showed that customers wanted natural materials and that tactile qualities were important, e.g. deep leather seats. The results of the clinic were used to decide the final colour and trim options.

Jaguar XK8: The development of a car interior *continued*

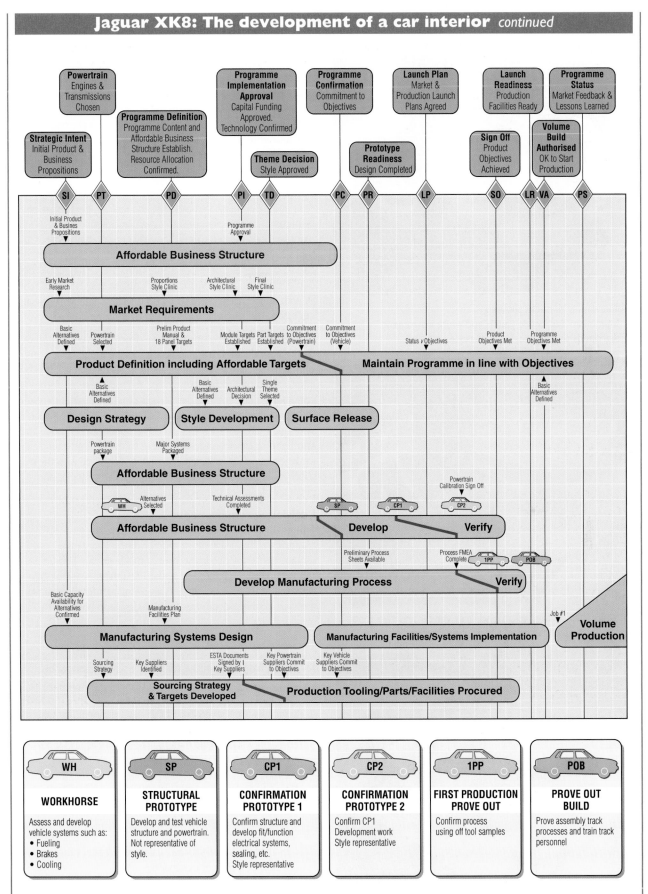

World Class Product Development Process. The time-chart of the entire process with an explanation of different prototypes and their purpose.

Colour and trim bucks showing
a) aluminium dashboard panels and white instrument backgrounds to give sporty appearance.

b) white instrument background, grey veneer and two tone grey trim to give traditional and sophisticated appearance.

c) two tone coffee trim and walnut veneer specially designed to suit the US market.

Many different materials are used in the same interior. Expanded vinyl composite on the fascia, leather on the seats, injection moulded parts for switches and radio controls, and wood veneer for the instrument panel. The gloss and grain for these natural and synthetic materials need to be in harmony. Master samples of the required gloss and grain are issued to suppliers who produce samples of production and prototype parts. These are then checked to ensure quality and consistency across all components.

In addition all materials have to be tested for heat and light resistance, durability, flammability, and specific performance requirements. For example, all Jaguar woodwork is manufactured in-house using specially grown khaya walnut or bird's-eye maple veneers. The panel in front of the passenger had to be specially developed to ensure the air bag could be deployed through the wood. This is not as easy or predictable as with plastic. Each piece of wood is unique so they will not necessarily behave in the same way every time.

Jaguars are driven in many countries from the oven-hot mid-day temperatures in the middle east to the arctic conditions of northern Canada. The materials that were selected for the interior trim had to be able to pass tests at these extreme conditions. The temperature on top of a fascia panel exposed to bright sunlight can rise to 140°C, which means that only synthetic materials such as vinyl composites can be used. They also need to be dimensionally stable to avoid large gaps between panels in different conditions. Together with their suppliers, Jaguar develops new materials, technologies and processes to meet these difficult demands.

Legislative requirements

The new car had to be able to be sold in more than 60 countries without significant modifications. Legislative requirements, for occupant front and side impact and visibility, can vary between countries. Jaguar used their expertise to ensure that these requirements were taken into account from the start of the programme, to avoid late and costly modifications.

Two requirements specifically affect interior development:

1 **Head impact**   In the case of a crash, passenger head and body damage needs to be avoided. Tests are done on CAD and later confirmed with a 3D model. The test simulates the movement of the head during a frontal impact. If any part of the interior is contacted, it needs to conform with specific material requirements and forms, e.g. the radius on corners must not be smaller than 3.2 mm.

2 **Forward vision**   Adequate forward vision for different sizes of people is again tested by simulation. An area of four degrees downward, from a horizontal line through the eye, needs to be unobstructed. This means that the design of the under-bonnet package will affect the position of the front occupants.

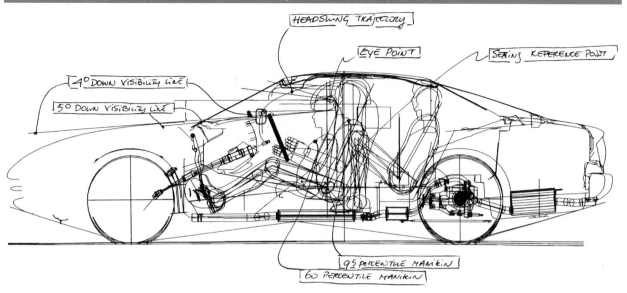

CAD printout to illustrate forward vision considerations.

Compromises in design development

The development phase that followed design theme approval was again an iterative process involving balancing decisions between style integrity, ergonomic requirements, marketing input, engineering and manufacturing needs, and last but not least, cost considerations. Constraints also came from using the XJ floor pan such as difficulties in placing switches because of the high, deep sill which is needed to maintain torsional rigidity for the convertible. The frames of the seats are carried over from the XJ-S and remodelled to give a sportier shape and the coverings were developed in conjunction with the manufacturers. Height-adjustable seats were added because of marketing (customer) and ergonomic input. Team work was essential at this stage to meet all criteria and maintain the style integrity.

The role of teams

Developing a style through to production is very much a team-focused activity. Several teams are involved in this.

Ergonomic assessment model to evaluate gear lever to radio-cassette clearance.

The **design team** consists of designer, modeller, feasibility engineers, ergonomists and colour and trim experts. They interact closely and continuously to achieve a design that is attractive and feasible. This team is supported by package engineers, component engineers and suppliers.

From the minute the stylist starts there have to be engineering, ergonomics, feasibility and manufacturing checks of individual components as they are designed. This is to ensure that the least possible number of changes is necessary when the design is released to engineering. This saves time and other resources as well as preventing changes which would compromise the style. It is also an advantage when the manufacturing department is committed to the project as then they, and the engineers, are all motivated to find ways to make the design work. Suppliers are also included in the team at a fairly early stage to start looking at the feasibility of the components required.

Simultaneous Engineering teams consist of representatives from component engineering, manufacturing engineering, purchasing, service, finance experts and supplier representatives. The team is tasked to ensure that components and systems are feasible and follows the development phase through into production.

The Programme team is a high level team that manages and co-ordinates the programme. It consists of management representatives of each functional area involved in the programme: styling; component engineering; timing; marketing; the programme office and purchasing.

Important lessons learned

The XK8 was developed in a record time with state-of-the-art technology and soon proved to be a very successful product with a long waiting list. Nevertheless Jaguar identified the following issues as needing further improvement.

◆ Feasibility checking needs to start earlier in the process and run in parallel with the design. When the design is frozen for production it must be thoroughly checked for feasibility. On-going checks from the start make production time shorter, keep the cost of changes lower and the integrity of the design intact.

◆ Teams should be resourced earlier with the right people. The location of team members is also important, people who are physically a team located on the same site work better together.

◆ The use of Computer Aided Engineering (CAE) was limited by the technology available. With the increasing availability of affordable technology with improved capabilities, a shorter development time and higher quality product should be possible.

◆ It is important that design proposals are communicated through an appropriate medium to any group. For example, the half-size scale model was not a form which communicated well to senior management.

A clipping from the Times newspaper, June 1997 (after the XK8 was in production).

Jaguar's expanded workstation network can make better cars

Supercar goes on the server

AN IT project worth £6.25 million is creating a collaborative environment for Jaguar's 1,000 design engineers in the Midlands.

The luxury car manufacturer has added 50 Silicon Graphics workstations and 13 new desktop servers to its network. There are now more than 150 Silicon Graphics seats at the company's engineering centre, which will give its employees all the computing tools they need to do their job interactively.

Roger Staines, Jaguar technical services manager, says: "We are heading towards a position where we can exploit collaborative engineering to work together with colleagues and suppliers around the globe."

The latest acquisition will vastly reduce the amount of machine-sharing time and generate a massive leap in data-sharing. Howard Rippiner, Silicon Graphics marketing manager says: "Visualisation is a key technology that can create significant competitive advantage. SiliconWorks solutions provide the tools for analysing products as 3-D models. These models can be rotated, taken apart, the colours changed and so on. Teleconferencing facilities now mean engineers can discuss them without having to be together."

The systems allow the rapid sharing of design information, which means fewer physical prototypes have to be made and better products come to market faster and for less money.

The technology also enhances effective design, Rippiner says. "Airbags can be designed to be safer. Also you can minimise a car's weight for a given strength through this technology. Metal can be taken out without reducing a car's strength, and if the weight is reduced fuel consumption is more economical."

GAVIN HADLAND

Source: Gavin Hadland © The Times Newspaper Ltd, 2nd July 1997

Bill Smith was a British entrepreneur who studied design in England before going to manage restaurants and cafes in Europe and the United States of America. When in the USA he noticed that electric kettles are not widely used or available and realised that there was potentially, a massive gap in the market. He decided that a kettle for the US needed more flair than the standard British kettles which, he felt, would not appeal to the American market. However, he called his company 'Great British Kettles' (GBK) because the British connection seemed to add a little glamour!

Polymer Solutions Inc. (PSI) is a joint venture between a large developer and manufacturer of engineering plastics and a large design consultancy. A six month contract was agreed between Bill Smith and PSI for the kettle design. The designer at PSI was Scott Stropkay who was given four weeks to complete the concept and design work.

The design challenge

The only features in the design brief were that the kettle should make a design statement and should hold one and a half US quarts of water (1.7 litres). The real challenge was the lack of time available – the kettle was to be launched at a trade show just over six months later.

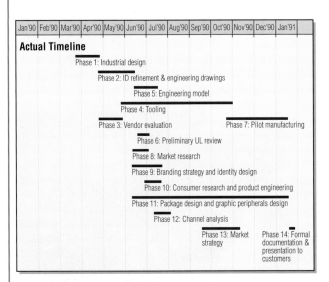

The schedule for the development of the Ukettle.

The development process

The first step was deciding how the various parts could be assembled in a cost-effective way. The first fundamental choice was whether the kettle should be:

◆ a shallow vessel, sealed to the body of the kettle with the heating element in-between, or
◆ a large one-piece vessel with a hole for the element.

The latter was chosen as the most reliable assembly.

The next step involved producing a range of sketches and 3D studies of 'what one and a half quarts looks like'. Models were created using foam which took about two and a half weeks. They wanted the design of the kettle to look different from anything else currently available and yet still communicate intuitively that it was an electric kettle.

Two months into the design work a mechanical engineer, Dave Privitera joined the project team. Considering the amount of complex engineering work required this was later than it should have been.

Designing for disassembly

Design for disassembly (DFD) became popular in the early 1990s in ecologically conscious green design circles. The principle is that materials such as plastics that are assembled into a complex product, should be easily separated for recycling, which also makes repair and maintenance of the products easier. (This is also a key feature of the very successful Dyson Dual Cyclone vacuum-cleaner, see *Routes Resistant Materials*, page 89.)

DFD was to be considered in the design of the kettle as it was felt that it would give a competitive edge to the product. PSI believed at the time that by the year 2000 legislation in the United States would require manufacturers to be responsible for the disposal of their materials and products. It was also felt that ecologically aware consumers would pay 10 to 15% extra for environmentally friendly products.

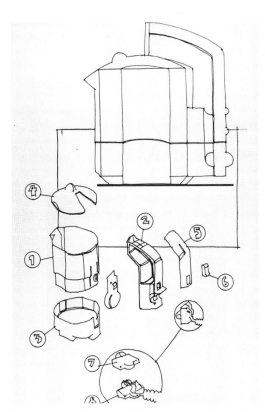

This diagram shows how the different parts of the kettle could be assembled in the most cost-effective way.

Because of this, three weeks into the kettle project, DFD was added to the product requirements. DFD implied snap-together parts which could be disassembled easily. This was, however, difficult to achieve, especially when tolerances had to be very tight to prevent leaks. The designers were concerned that if screws were not used, the product would not be strong enough and might easily be pulled apart, perhaps by a child. However, at the same time if they used screws, they would be criticised as the plastic used in the product would be more difficult to re-cycle. Given the timescale it was not possible to produce an optimum solution, so they decided to design two screw slots where the handle/lid attaches to the vessel – just in case!

Sorting out the details

Having decided on the basic concept and what would make up the kettle, the design team were then able to consider other aspects of the design:

◆ function
◆ ergonomics
◆ aesthetics/styling
◆ design for disassembly
◆ engineering aspects such as suitability for moulding.

1 The handle

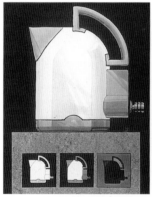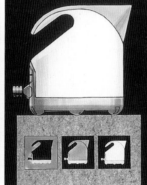

The feature of the UKettle which immediately catches the consumer's eye is its unusual handle. Scott explains "We did lots of versions of the handle. We tried it on the top, on the side, and at the back of the kettle. We knew it had to feel right, but we couldn't get people to pick one version or the other – it depended on what they were doing with the kettle. When you have a full, heavy kettle, it feels more balanced if you can pick it up from the top. But when you want to pour, its easier to grasp the handle from lower down, from the back. It also prevents you from burning your hand as steam escapes during the pour. So that's how we came up with the big arching design."

A lot of time was spent on the design of the handle. It was the main point of contact with the consumer so they wanted to get it just right.

A new type of material was used for the handle which was softer and provided more grip, however, when the prototype was built there was a problem with the big arching handle: it flexed too much. It had to be strengthened with a vertical wall under the top of the kettle and more ribs inside the hollow handle itself. The screw slots became useful at this time!

2 The plug and cord

A very large plug, nestled under the handle, and a heavy coiled cord were other striking features of the design. The intention was to make a statement about the plug – to make it obvious that it was an electrical product. Although some people questioned the cost involved it was argued that this would add to the perceived value of the product.

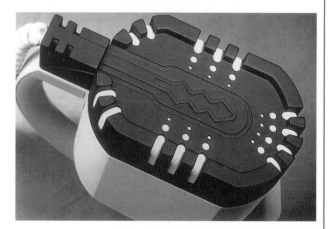

3 The base and bottom plate

In the middle of the base the designers drew an outline of the heating element. A series of holes was built into the bottom of the kettle to represent bubbling, boiling water. "It's like tennis shoes" the designers argued, "so much attention nowadays is given to the bottoms of the shoes because the design of the soles influences the purchasing decisions – not because anyone will see them when you're wearing the shoes."

Alternative design ideas.

4 The switch

One key feature of the kettle was a switch with a steam sensor to automatically shut off the kettle when the water boiled – this is something that everyone now expects on an electric kettle.

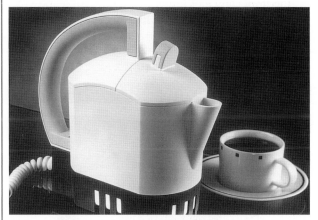

Reaching the goal – the finished product. After little more than four weeks of day-and-night design work which generated dozens of drawings and models, the kettle was born.

The next steps

At this point the UKettle only existed as a design concept model. To get the kettle ready for the trade show eight months later, PSI had to totally 'engineer' the product and send part drawings to the toolmaker. An engineering prototype is normally the first requirement – a hand-built model which tests aspects of the design which cannot be tested, even on a computer. For example, whether the kettle is going to be reliably water-tight. However, because of lack of time PSI were forced to send unchecked drawings to its toolmaker. This led to some problems and, with hindsight, this decision proved to be unwise. With seven parts and six moulds, the kettle was very complex. Each mould was made of several parts – even the smallest error in one of the parts could affect the entire product. The toolmaker began to produce the tools.

In the meantime PSI was able to make the engineering prototype, discovered a number of faults and contacted the toolmaker, who had already cut the tools. They were informed that changing the tools would cause several months delay and cost an extra $1000 (£700). However, the toolmaker did agree to give priority to the order. Even at this stage it was still uncertain whether the handle would need the two screws.

Colour, packaging and name

Bill Smith wanted the kettle's packaging to be eye-catching and colourful. However, the designers argued that white with black accents would suit the market they were aiming at. Consumer focus groups had already suggested that white was the favourite, with red and black coming second.

Deciding what to put on the packaging was simple. The kettle was a US marketing dream: British-owned, energy saving, new, designed for disassembly – there were so many good things from the consumer angle. After weighing many alternatives, it was decided that UKettle would be the most appealing name for the product.

Using focus groups

Two focus groups were organised. One liked the kettle and the other did not! The group that didn't consisted of older people with more traditional views. The group that liked the kettle were younger professionals. However, when the kettle was put next to alternatives both groups were excited by the product.

Next steps

In September 1990, three to four months before the launch at the trade show, an feature on the Ukettle appeared in a leading journal, *Business Week*. This provided excellent publicity but made claims about the DFD qualities of the kettle which perhaps would not be met. Also the kettle was not yet ready! Fortunately Great British Kettles had had the good sense to alter the claims about the 'greenness' of the kettle on the packaging. It read 'Responsibly designed for material reuse'.

In the meantime there were a lot of logistical details to cover. For example, there were negotiations with the switch and cord manufacturers to follow up, materials issues such as colour and texture to discuss and so on. In addition there were new problems for discussion such as how to protect the kettle inside the packaging.

What happened to the UKettle?

Patience and dedication finally paid off. The UKettle made the housewares show in Chicago in January 1991 and was a tremendous success. The exhibit booth had to be staffed around the clock by every person available, as representatives from stores far and near placed their orders. The Museum of Modern Art considered adopting the kettle for their collection and within a year it had been recognised in several design publications.

However, production of the UKettle did not meet consumer demand, essentially because of cash flow problems. The kettle cost nearly twice as much per unit to produce as had been expected. Part of this cost consisted of per-unit payments to the toolmaker. Some cost overruns were due to inexperience. GBK was unable to keep up with the payments so the moulder stopped delivering the product and, without further consultation, sold the tools to another company. This company made some cost-reduction changes and began to manufacture the kettle outside the US. Some of the legal issues are still to be resolved.

Source: The Design Management Institute, 29 Temple Place, Boston, Massachusetts 02111–1350; Telephone: (617) 338 6380; Fax: (617) 338 6570; Email: dmistaff@dmi.org; Web site: www.dmi.org

Focused task: Ukettle case study

Make a balanced assessment of lessons that can be learned from this case study. Make both positive and negative comments about each of these:

- design features
- features that, given the benefit of hindsight, were not so successful
- quality assurance and control
- marketing

- meeting customer needs
- the importance of design in product development and sales
- the importance of design, manufacturing and marketing working together. (See concurrent engineering page 135.)

The Handihaler: Better design and lower costs

When the major German pharmaceutical group Boehringer wanted a new asthma inhaler, it turned to Bristol-based designers, Kinneir Dufort. The radical result has improved the delivery of asthma treatment and considerably cut costs. It has also led to other companies having to re-design their inhalers leading to benefits for all asthma sufferers.

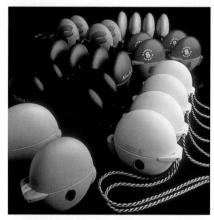
c) Different graphic treatments.

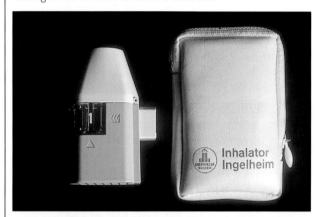
a) The preceding product.

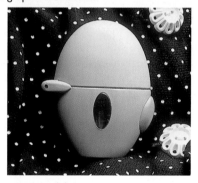
d) Demonstration models.

b) A 'pebble' concept model in foam.

In the summer of 1994 a series of freak storms combined with very poor air quality in the London area caused an asthma outbreak of epidemic proportions. The wave of stories about besieged hospital wards focused attention on the fact that asthma is the only treatable chronic condition in the western world that is growing in prevalence. In the UK, one in 20 adults suffer and in children it is nearly three times as common.

The outbreak also highlighted the short-comings of the asthma inhaler. In general, good design is not associated with health-care products despite the benefits it could offer. On

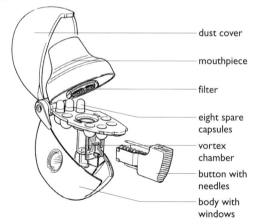

- dust cover
- mouthpiece
- filter
- eight spare capsules
- vortex chamber
- button with needles
- body with windows

the rare occasions when well-considered design, skilled engineering, perceptive marketing and far-sighted management are brought together to reconsider one of these

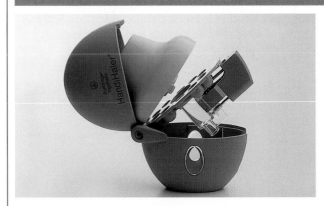

The final product.

products, the end-result can be like light breaking into a dark room.

There are numerous inhalers and patented methods of efficient drug delivery. In Europe alone, more than 30 inhaler development projects have been undertaken. It is unlikely that any of the resulting products will match the new Boehringer Ingelheim device for its sensitivity to the needs of its users and its manufacturer. The inhaler developed at a cost of £2 million, sets new standards in ease-of-use, compactness, ergonomics, robustness and user-friendliness. Switching to the Handihaler has also halved the manufacturing unit cost and has to led to increased sales.

Asthma is treated with either oral or inhaled drugs. The inhaled medicines are produced in a variety of forms: blister packs, aerosols or capsules of powder. Generally, the pharmaceutical company markets the devices needed to deliver the drugs they make. Asthma inhalers are often provided free with the drugs so the dispensers need to be cheap to produce. As a result, inhalers have tended to be rather shoddy plastic devices.

Boehringer Ingelheim produce their anti-asthma drug in powder form. In their inhalers a small capsule is punctured to release the drug which is then inhaled – they do not use propellants. This has the advantage over aerosols that the patient does not have to co-ordinate pressing a canister with inhalation. The operation needs to be as simple as possible as the patient may be disorientated by the asthma attack.

The company carried out market research to determine what users felt was wrong with current inhalers. Ergonomic deficiencies and aesthetic short-comings were high on the list

of complaints. The design brief for the new inhaler had one critical feature – it should involve no redesign of the vortex channel through which the drug would be inhaled. This was to avoid the need for extensive approval trials. The brief also included these demands:

◆ ease of handling and simplicity of use
◆ control of 'taken' and remaining capsules
◆ enough capsules for one day's treatment
◆ should be suitable for patients including children, bronchitis sufferers and the elderly
◆ style should be consumer-orientated
◆ should reduce production costs
◆ two models – one to hold six capsules and one to hold twelve.

The four design companies who were issued with the brief had three weeks to respond with design proposals! One of the key features of the successful design presented by Kinneir Dufort was the idea of air-tightness. By sealing the inhalation chamber inside a shell when not in use, the need for a separate zip-up pouch was removed and the design kept the inhaler free from dust. This immediately cut out a significant cost. The new design is also compact, easy to use and attractive.

Less than one month after the go-ahead, Ross Kinneir had four prototypes ready. A team of physicists, biochemists, marketing experts and engineers was assembled with as project manager, John Barnes, their UK marketing director. The industrial design was contracted out by the project manager.

'My estimation was that the pharmaceutical expertise – the business of delivering medicine correctly – was excellent at the company. But the capacity for designing the means was not so. Design had been R&D (Research and Development) led, not consumer led. It wasn't unusual for commercial people to head project teams but my background was in marketing. That was the difference. Nevertheless I wanted the scientists to be highly integrated into the team; and they were, from the start.

The entire project team met each month. Some of these meetings considered detail design issues such as the hinges, the ribs inside the capsule holders and the various snap-fits which ensure than the lid, mouthpiece and deck are opened in the correct order. These require very precise engineering. The gelatine capsules are sensitive to the atmosphere and the ribs had to be put through temperature and humidity cycles to check their effectiveness.

An injection moulding company in Plymouth, Algram, used the CAD files produced by Kinneir Dufort to produce near-finished prototypes that could be market-tested with asthma sufferers. The information obtained from these tests was fed into the final design stage.

The development of this new inhaler has been achieved in half the normal time and production costs have been reduced by over 50%.'

Focused task: Handihaler case study

Against a list of the original design criteria explain how the Handihaler meets each of them. What features of the Handihaler make it innovative?

Consider the following aspects of this case study:

- the advantages of the new product to
  a) users
  b) the company
- the advantages of using a team to produce the new designs
- the role of the Project Manager
- how both development time and production costs were reduced
- the difference between R&D-led and consumer-led design? What might be the differences in the product designed by these two different approaches?

Now take another existing design which you feel has serious deficiencies and using annotated sketches, suggest some ways of improving it.

 Technology push and market pull 65

Frank Walsh: Celebrating the centenary of the British Embassy in Ethiopia

This case study is about an independent designer, Frank Walsh, who is mostly engaged in one-off designing for unique situations; it describes just one project in his portfolio. These designs always involve teamwork and often, batch production. You will see that this sort of designing is very creative but also requires a very systematic approach, partly because both design and production work are very intensive, to very short time-scales, and involve a lot of considerations that other kinds of designers do not usually have to take into account.

Focused task: design and manufacture in different cultures

In reading this case study consider:

- How did the opportunity for design arise?
- How did the wider project team operate and how did Frank's role fit within that of the wider team?
- Why is it that a big country like Ethiopia has a shortage of adults with the skills required by this project?
- What sort of attitudes, skills and abilities do the Ethiopians have which a wealthier country might not have?
- What are the gains and/or losses for both the Ethiopian and the UK people involved in this project?
- Are the designs, production processes and materials used appropriate within the context? Would this way of doing things be equally appropriate in a wealthy economy?

Frank Walsh

Frank Walsh is an independent theatre and film-set designer who trained in 3D/Furniture Design at Hornsey College of Art and in Architectural Design at the Royal College of Art. He then entered the British film industry.

Addis Ababa is a fast-growing city where visible wealth and some of the most extreme poverty in the world exist side by side.

Celebrating the centenary of the British Embassy in Ethiopia

In 1996 the British Embassy in Addis Ababa, the capital of Ethiopia celebrated their centenary. As the climax of the year's celebrations they decided to hold a spectacular evening event in Meskal Square, Addis Ababa on 28 November 1996. This huge square in the centre of the city is one of the largest in the world and has stepped terraces around part of it.

Meskal Square, Addis Ababa, Ethiopia.

This was to be a unique event, nothing quite like it had been planned in Ethiopia for many, many years. There was to be a huge firework display (many Ethiopians had never seen fireworks), the massed band of the Royal Marines (flown out specially) a performance by the young people of the Ethiopian Circus Jari, and a dance-drama performance by one hundred Addis Ababa street children. Street children were also to act as ushers, working alongside the police.

The street children of Ethiopia desperately need a voice: the Street Symphony Project helped them to find one.

WALK ALONG ANY STREET IN ADDIS ABABA AND YOU WILL DISCOVER AN OVERWHELMING NUMBER OF STREET CHILDREN.

TODAY IN ETHIOPIA THERE ARE WELL OVER HALF A MILLION YOUNG PEOPLE LIVING OR WORKING ON THE STREETS.

REVILED AND WRITTEN OFF BY LARGE SECTIONS OF THEIR COMMUNITY, STREET CHILDREN SURVIVE BY DOING ODD JOBS, BEGGING AND SEEKING OUT FOOD AND SHELTER AS BEST THEY CAN.

IN A LAND OF CHRONIC UNEMPLOYMENT AND BADLY-OVERCROWDED SCHOOLS THESE NEGLECTED YOUNG PEOPLE FACE A BLEAK FUTURE.

IT IS REMARKABLE THAT SO FEW HAVE - AS YET - DRIFTED INTO CRIME

THE STREET SYMPHONY DEVELOPMENT PROJECT

The street children of Ethiopia desperately need a voice

THE PLIGHT OF THESE STREET CHILDREN OF ETHIOPIA HAS NOT YET REACHED THAT TRAGIC POINT OF NO RETURN THAT IS THE EXPERIENCE OF SO MANY SIMILAR YOUNG PEOPLE ELSEWHERE IN THE WORLD.

BUT THE TRENDS ARE DISTURBING.

'Walk along any street in Addis Ababa and you will discover an overwhelming number of street children. Today in Ethiopia there are well over half a million young people living or working on the streets. Reviled and written-off by large sections of their community, street children survive by doing odd jobs, begging and seeking out food and shelter as best they can. In a land of chronic unemployment and badly overcrowded schools these neglected young people face a bleak future.'

Alemayehu Yifru/Andrew Coggins; Street Symphony 1996

Street Symphony is a project which began in 1995, initiated by Ethiopian and UK film-makers and a design-educator. Street Symphony's overall aim was to tell the world about the potential of these children in particular, and of street children in general.

Street Symphony puts the means of communicating their message into the hands of the children themselves mainly through training in video and film-making and production; life story-telling through dance, drama, art and design and psycho-drama; dance-drama training and performing.

The British Embassy in Addis Ababa is one of the organisations which supported the Street Symphony project from its earliest stages. This led the Embassy staff to involve the Ethiopian and UK-based Street Symphony project management team in their plans – both for the performing element and as the management team of the whole event. Also, the expertise needed to design and manage the production of the large-scale set required had to be sought outside of the country, as nothing at all like this had happened in Addis Ababa for a very long time.

Frank Walsh had worked with the Project Co-director, many times, so the Embassy staff asked Frank to come to Addis Ababa to see what he thought about the situation and to make some preliminary designs and suggestions. The Embassy staff, together with Street Symphony, had generated an outline of what might be needed.

Design limitations and opportunities

Frank had already been briefed by Street Symphony project workers and the choreographer in the UK and had a broad idea of the conditions he was likely to encounter; event-management team members were already in Ethiopia.

Some of the things Frank would encounter were:

◆ limited materials – probably he would have to use mainly wood, or re-usable materials
◆ limited expertise in construction – but there were local builders who would help
◆ a central power-supply that regularly failed
◆ a water-supply that was equally erratic
◆ limited electrical expertise – but some basic stage lighting available from the theatre
◆ overpowering heat when the sun is high, cooler evenings and early mornings
◆ red dust over everything thrown-up from the roads
◆ lots of very friendly and inquisitive street children.

This presented something of a challenge!

During his few days in Addis, Frank had discussions with the Embassy staff and members of the local community. This enabled him to get his own picture of the limitations, but also the opportunities for design and construction that were available.

His designs had to encompass the needs and wants of:

◆ the British Embassy (the client)
◆ the Circus Jari performers
◆ the Street Symphony performers, their project staff and choreographic team
◆ the Massed Band of the Royal Marines

◆ the fireworks team
◆ the Police and street children ushers
◆ the community
◆ businesses within the community who would sponsor or otherwise support the event
◆ the lighting designer from the UK
◆ the sound team from UK and Ethiopia
◆ the likely audience – over 200 000, including Ethiopian and UK Government officials, dignitaries and business people.

He had to think about, not only the sequence of activities that were to take place on or around the set and what the set would look like, but how well it would perform. He had to work out how it could be constructed, what from and by whom, and how safety could be ensured. Local labour, skills and materials had to be used for the design and found. He also had to work out a schedule for the construction.

Designing in Addis Ababa

The brief Frank set himself was based on the following criteria:

1 The solution had to ensure that the differing elements of the show must flow seamlessly together so the evening would have a professional, cohesive quality.
2 The concept should be a simple solution, with a good chance of success in the form presented; potential sponsors' expectations had to be addressed based on the proposal put before them.
3 The show had to be realised within a fixed budget.
4 Every opportunity to maximise the scale of the concept must be exploited, because of the benefits from promoting the Embassy and the children involved.
5 The client should not economise on the budget for the fireworks, due to the nature of the event and scale of the venue – the finale would need to be the crowning moment for the evening so the design should ensure the audience could appreciate the full impact of the display.
6 There was only a short time scale to realise the concept.
7 Much of the concept had to be realised locally, because the budget would make it difficult to import many of the usual technical elements from conventional sources in Europe (such as lighting, sound, special finishes etc.).
8 UK people's skills should be integrated with those in the local community, exploiting these local skills and relevant cultural references.
9 A space needed to be created for the performance.

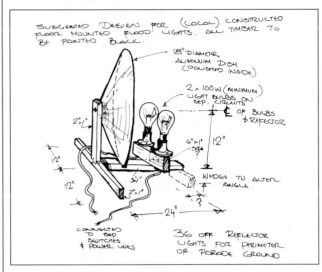

Developing the designs.

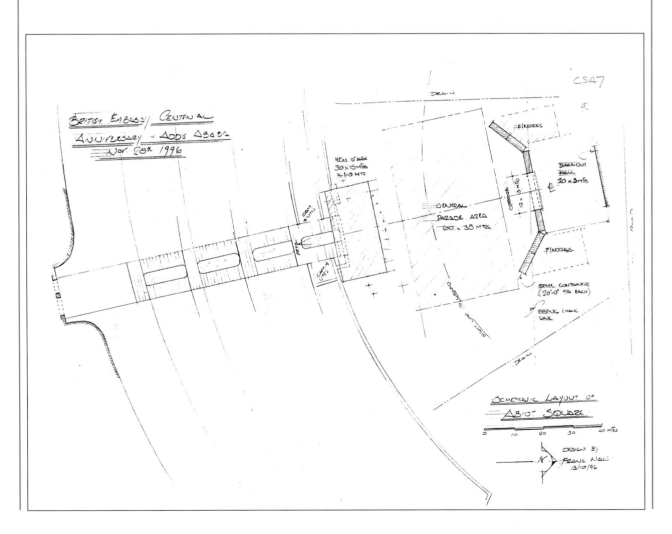

Description
The proposal is to create a new stage area at the base of the flight of steps to the south east corner of Meskal Square, a dedicated seated area for VIP's south of this, a walled enclosure to the north (incorporating a curtained arch) which forms a natural containment to an open 'parade ground' between. At the back of the stage hang seven plain white fabric banners.

The performance is enhanced by the use of coloured back light falling onto the fabric banners, interspersed with shadows of dancers etc., to increase the spectacle. At the end of the performance, the stage would be clear, the lights dimming, allowing quiet removal of the platforms, banners and flag poles, the re-positioning of the low back lights and the lifting of the curtain on the far wall revealing a blacked out void. On cue, lights positioned beyond the opening, and facing directly at the audience would illuminate, silhouetting the Royal Marines Band.

1 The Stage
A new stage is to be constructed with legs to be sleeved to allow for fitting into the frames on site. On assembly, each individual unit will be bolted to each adjoining unit to ensure the entire stage retains a structural integrity. Fixing holes for the bolts to be pre-drilled to allow for speed of assembly on site. Thin packing pieces to be inserted below legs to ensure the tops are flush with adjoining units and accommodating slight site irregularities.

2 The Stage Set
Along the back face of the stage, and resting directly on the ground in a shallow semicircle, stand eight 6.5 m flag poles 3.0 m apart, painted in a matt black finish. These are to be securely fixed into weighted bases that will allow their easy removal from this position during the show. Strung between the posts will be selected cotton banners 2.0 m × 6.0 m long.

3 The Back Wall
To be constructed from either loaned steel box containers or timber panels to make a wall with two side wings 7.0 m × 4.8 m high with a centre section running parallel with the stage 24.0 m wide with a central opening 12.0 × 3.0 m high. The opening to have a white cotton curtain fixed to a simple bottom rail attached to ropes and pulleys to allow for the whole to be lifted clear on cue. The face of the wall and the curtain to be painted with designed mural.

Rehearsals in progress.

Constructing the stage.

The mural in place.

Frank Walsh: Celebrating the centenary of the British Embassy in Ethiopia *continued*

Teamwork in the UK

Frank flew back to the UK on 16 October. During the following few weeks he met with the choreographer, the lighting director and the Project Co-ordinator, who had been out in Addis with him.

Frank produced a design for the reflector lights for the perimeter of the parade ground. This was faxed to Addis so that work could start on the construction. However, this plan changed.

Local supplies of conventional lighting equipment were virtually non-existent and there was a difficult lighting problem. This was the need to light the stage area for a complex dance performance and to light a very large parade ground for the drill-sequence of the Marine Band. Therefore a local solution had to be found. Those that were considered included:

1 Using fire to light the stage

◆ Polished reflectors over oil drums filled with combustible materials (abandoned due to inability to control the light output and problems with drifting smoke etc.).
◆ Gas-fed burners which would create exciting visual possibilities (abandoned because of the cost of the gas in Ethiopia).

2 Manufacturing new lamps locally

◆ All available theatre lights were to be employed lighting the stage, supplemented with purchased industrial lighting.
◆ Parade ground lighting could be constructed from sheet aluminium dishes made locally. These were based on the traditional metal dishes made to serve the national dish of endura. These acted as simple reflectors to side-light the band, and utilised local labour to construct the units. (Abandoned idea, as the cost of cabling up the units was prohibitive and local sponsors were unable to supply this one element to make the design work).

3 The parade ground

This would be lit by vehicles parked along the sides. Ultimately these were the local Police Land Rovers. The drivers were coached to follow simple cues which allowed the parade ground to be flooded with light in a sequential manner as the band marched on.

Frank also generated a spreadsheet of items and details (size, material, source) together with an outline schedule of build (12 days). He included in this schedule other matters not included before such as:

◆ steel clad 'container' wall with opening (for fireworks)
◆ infill panels for storm drains etc.
◆ security passes
◆ floral decorations

◆ special programmes/gifts/refreshments for VIPs
◆ sanitation facilities for crew
◆ torches.

Teamwork in Ethiopia

Frank effectively had less than five days before the Spectacular day. On the rehearsal day – the day before the event – there was no power in the Square. The choreographer reported that they sang completely through the music five times!

However, construction and rehearsals were all completed in time for the show. The task had been greatly helped by the enthusiasm of the street children. For example, when a local building firm were constructing the staging, some of the children decided to help and out-performed the adults in the time they took to complete the tasks, by a very long way, although the adults had tools and they did not.

Things that ultimately were not realised

The stage builder made the stipulation that the timber boarding for the top deck must not be damaged in any way. Fortunately, the spin-off from this loss offset the poor lighting available, as the light colour of the ply deck reflected and maximised the light available.

Frank Walsh: Celebrating the centenary of the British Embassy in Ethiopia *continued*

The fabric hangings (derived from traditional costume) and silhouettes of the dancers were designed to integrate traditional Ethiopian motifs and to expand the scale of the performers. This was eventually abandoned because the choreographer felt unable to coach the inexperienced dancers in the time available to perform in a situation akin to an extended solo. So the fabric was adapted to create a small backstage areas for costume changes.

The entry of the Marines was conceived to be from a position with an intense backlight to throw long shadows across the parade ground towards the audience. Early discussions with the fireworks team suggested they could cheaply source a powerful light from the UK. Unfortunately, at the last moment it was discovered that the bulb had broken and, as there was no replacement, the team had to source industrial halogen lamps.

These were nailed to tea chests behind the band, and hot-wired to a spare road-side junction box. The lights were operated mainly by an audio cue (the presenter's introduction coming faintly over the PA system) and by Frank pushing the plugs into the unearthed socket!

Things that nearly spoilt everything

- The local power supplier's inability to get a live feed until the last minute.
- The lighting director having to resort to buying sheets of corrugated iron so that he could cut out simple flaps to shape the light coming from the spotlights.
- The Government security men operating on the same waveband as the team's walkie talkies and confusing the whole situation on the night.

Students working with industry

ASDA supermarkets — with students from Bosworth College in Leicestershire

The first project: Multi-decks

Our local shopping mall has many outlets with ASDA as the largest. Supermarkets, it seemed, could provide situations for exciting and creative designing. We made contact with ASDA corporate headquarters in Leeds and found out who the Head of Design was. We wrote to her and asked if we could meet to discuss a project. An initial meeting was scheduled in Leeds and to our delight we found support and a willingness to work on a joint venture. We emphasise **joint**, as it was important to see the project as a two way process – a partnership. We talked about possibilities, while looking at the latest ideas in the world of supermarket interiors.

The brief from ASDA

We received our brief from ASDA which was extremely open-ended to begin with. We were asked to design multi-deck freezers and delicatessen cabinets for the millennium.

We decided to visit our local ASDA branch to examine both the context in which multi-decks are used and the products themselves. At this stage we were already starting to learn about the right ways to go about working with industry, how to make contacts, how to present ourselves, the need for forward planning etc. ASDA people were extremely co-operative. The manager introduced us to the store and we

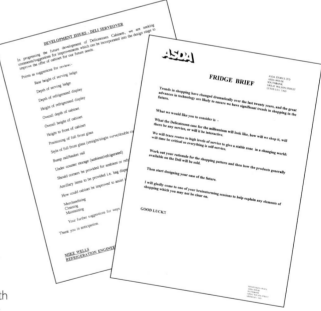

were left to talk to the staff who worked on the shop floor. We conducted our primary research and documented all aspects as thoroughly as possible. Once back at college the information had to be collated and used to examine both the context and the products. Our initial preparation paid off – we had used a range of audio-visual equipment to record our visit. By using a range of media we found that we could examine areas at a later date and pick out problems, as it was impossible to understand all the issues on a first encounter. Some of the detailed photographs of multi-decks showed how their display potential was reduced because of cardboard boxes which were stacked at either end in the battle for space, which is a constant problem in supermarkets.

We then used brainstorming techniques to identify areas for further investigation – merchandising, maintenance, styling, airflow, loading to unloading, ergonomics and hygiene/cleaning.

We had established further contacts with ASDA technical division who suggested a visit to a factory to see the present multi-decks being manufactured and to understand the problems of airflow within the units.

Establishing a design theme

We decided to use two themes — 50s 'retro' marketplace and high-tech as the bases for our designs. Initial drawings were presented to ASDA's technical staff to see if there were any obvious conflicts between styling and function with special reference to airflow. Some of our students made a visit to NRC Ltd. who are one of the few manufacturers of multi-decks in the country. We were given a tour of the factory and gained a valuable insight into industrial practices – methods of construction, assembly, design constraints, costing, buying in of existing components. Technical constraints and various features of multi-decks were carefully explained to us.

Back at college, two designs were chosen to develop into scale models. The first would use existing methods of constructing multi-decks, being cheap and easy to produce but would combine textiles into the design. The second was a far more innovative stand-alone, which would have to be built from scratch, but would have the benefit of working anywhere on the supermarket floor and could be refilled or cleaned out of the customers' sight. The modelling went ahead, building-in features such as bump rails, slanted shelves (better visibility), which were features we had recognised in earlier work. A deadline was set for the final presentation to the ASDA team.

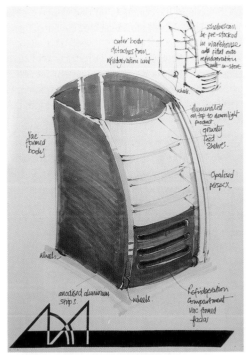

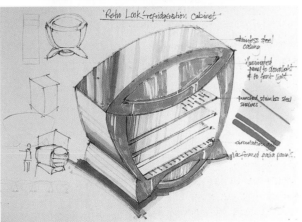

Students' design drawings.

Working as a team

We found that as the deadline approached it was much better to work as a group: discussing problems, sharing decisions, co-operating in a way which was totally different from our normal way of working – on our own, on individual projects. As time slipped away chaos reigned, brains were disengaged, models were glued and cramped on painted surfaces and fell apart. Hairdryers were being used to cure glue five minutes before our guests were due to arrive. We learnt the hard way that time management was not one of our strong points but we made the deadline – just!

Presentation time

What a difference it made having to present to unfamiliar external clients! We had to organise a demonstration area, obtain and arrange all of the resources we needed, present our designs well, and justify them in the face of some searching questions. ASDA's design department quickly understood some of the concepts (in one design we had tried to reduce visually the bulk of the cabinet by lifting it on dynamic leg sections at either end). "I see," said one designer, "you have tried to float it. I like the introduction of textiles into this design; it really does give it a marketplace feel. Will airflow work with this material?" The presentation went well – a debrief helped us to clarify what further changes could be made to the models and to the presentation.

When we thought it was over, ASDA came back to us and said they would like to go further and build the models to full size working prototypes. A year later we were to visit the factory to view the two designs!

The students' final design models.

Production prototypes.

A second ASDA project: Cafeteria furniture

The success of the first project led to a second project with ASDA. This time we centred on a store that was due for refurbishment. The brief was to re-design furniture for their in-store cafeterias that would:

◆ maximise the number of customers
◆ have somewhere to store trays at the tables
◆ cater for people with disabilities
◆ create a children's area
◆ be easy to clean underneath
◆ not be too comfortable – to encourage customers into the store!
◆ be flexible for both indoor and outdoor use.

We used the same format as the previous project, working in teams and benefited from the previous experience – organisation improved and everyone (students and teacher) were calmer with time to reflect on and modify initial designs.

Communication with the client involved being provided with the brief, on-site research, discussing design ideas and models with the client and making a presentation. A broad range of ideas were presented, including interactive furniture for children, electronic environments and use of themes with different levels of sophistication for children and adults. Designs were no longer finite, instead we presented options: design options, options for material, manufacture and cost.

These designs would not be made into full size prototypes but the working drawings were sent to the Sloane Group (designers and manufacturers of retail display and merchandising equipment) for costing. We then spent a day with their designers who talked us through how products are costed in industry, what modifications would have to be made to our designs in order to manufacture at different volumes of production. We learnt a lot from working with professionals.

The factory itself was alive and exciting, with young designers working on CAD-stations. Point-of-sale displays for clients like Virgin Megastore and Children's World were being worked on. Examples of all kinds of manufacturing processes were seen: including injection moulding, spark erosion, anti-corrosion treatments and vacuum forming. We were familiar with many of these processes but the scale of the machines was totally different. It's impressive to see a 2440 × 1830 mm moulding coming off a vacuum former. This ability to design, develop and manufacture retail merchandising on one site really showed us 'state of the art' design and technology. The visit proved to be so much more effective in aiding us to understand some aspects of D&T than a classroom lesson ever could.

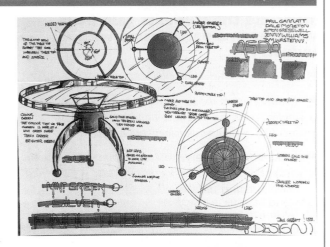
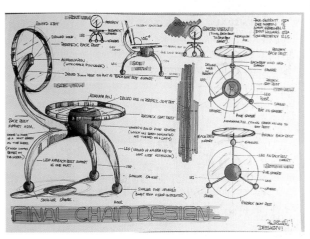

Students' design drawings.

Students' final models.

ASDA supermarkets — with students from Bosworth College in Leicestershire *continued*

What did the students gain from working in a partnership with industry?

Here are some things they said.

❝ *I really enjoyed the experience of working with professionals, learning first-hand 'state of the art' practice, current terminology and technology.*❞

❝ *It was different because you were working for someone else and you had to consider their needs. We also had to work to their deadlines.*❞

❝ *Because we were working to the standard set by our industrial client we had to work to a higher standard than we might normally.*❞

❝ *In industry you have to work in teams to unite individuals' skills and use them to the best advantage. We soon found that we had to work in a team, sorting out roles within the team and learning to share*

decisions. We had to accept changes in our personal ideas in order to move forward the overall design. We had to develop personal skills within the team and work out how we could work to specific strengths. We found out how a team can generate ideas and respond more quickly to solve problems.❞

❝ *Communication did not always work because people were used to working on separate tasks and did not work as a team. We tried to solve this by putting in place a regular meeting slot to brainstorm and modify ideas and organise the week ahead's tasks.*❞

❝ *We soon found out that we needed to improve our skills of communication, managing time and meeting deadlines.*'

❝ *Modifying the design to standard section materials changed the visual qualities and the proportions of the original design were lost.*'

A new collection box for the PDSA – students from Thomas Telford CTC

This case study illustrates how a group of students in Thomas Telford CTC met the challenge of a real design brief working for a real client, identifying and clarifying the specification and developing proposals to meet the specification and wider aspects of the brief. An interesting feature is how the students refined and developed their ideas to enable high volume production to take place.

The client and the brief

The PDSA (Peoples Dispensary for Sick Animals) is a charitable organisation dispensing treatment to animals through a large number of veterinary practices. It relies solely on donations to maintain its service including the use of 'countertop' collection boxes. The existing collection box was purchased as a standard box with custom artwork applied. It was very expensive to buy in this way and was yielding less than 40 pence per box in 'profit'. The box was clearly not proving very effective in attracting donations and the charity was looking to revitalise collection by re-designing and producing its own custom box. With this background information the students were given a brief to re-design the collection box to make it more cost-effective.

The existing collection box was not attracting donations, was customised only through the applied artwork and was very expensive to purchase.

Developing a specification

The students first discussed at length what was needed from the box and from this they developed a specification with clearly identified priorities. This was discussed at length with the client who confirmed that they felt it was appropriate to their needs.

Specification for the new collection box

In the final specification it was required that the collection box would:

◆ have a clear identity as a PDSA box and be in the corporate Pantone-blue colour
◆ hold in excess of £5 in assorted change
◆ survive being dropped from counter level
◆ offer the facility to display graphics and text
◆ cost less than £4.50 per box
◆ occupy the minimum surface area on a counter, yet be stable
◆ possibly be 'dynamic' in its collection of the coin
◆ have access to remove money and utilise the standard seal for the 'hole'
◆ be durable and robust
◆ offer some means of fixing to a surface for security.

Investigating production methods

A plastics box was anticipated from an early stage and the next step was to investigate production methods for manufacturing a plastic box in quantity. The anticipated first batch was 4000 and the total overall production run may be as many as 100 000. The students felt that manufacturing the box in plastics would be the best method for this quantity at an acceptable cost and for it to conform to other aspects of the specification. They approached the British Polymer Training Association (BPTA) who specialise in training operatives in the plastics industry and have extensive facilities in all processes involving the forming of plastics. They were an invaluable source of information about production requirements and gave the students the principal requirements for the forming of a container in plastics and the relative costs of producing the special tooling necessary. This was done prior to producing designs as, clearly, weighing different production considerations was a priority. The students felt that they needed to know what could be made before offering suggestions on the product itself.

Generating and developing proposals

The next phase saw extensive proposals produced in the form of sketches and drawings. These were presented to the client who identified six that they wished to see worked up. Ideas were then refined and card models produced which were presented to a potential manufacturer to ensure that the forms intended could be achieved in production, before

the designers spent more time working on the proposals. The advice received on production implications and production times and costs led to further modifications. Cutlines and joints were planned for and incorporated by cutting up the card models to simulate production items. Further models were then produced to incorporate the lessons learned. These refined models were then re-presented to the client. A further selection was then made to reduce the number of 'live' proposals to two. These were then worked up in the form of very high quality models which were dimensionally accurate and emulated the colour scheme and art work possible.

3D models were a vital method of communicating with both the client and the potential manufacturers.

The proposals were diverse and flexible, one relied on the ability to add a coin cascade to attract younger children through the 'dynamic' nature of the box. The other represented a challenge, again a dynamic approach. The PDSA selected this design as it represented the logo of the charity clearly and offered flexibility to add the dynamic coin cascade or string that would enable it to be used on flag-day street collections.

The final design was selected for its flexibility and because it met most closely the specification requirements.

 Design considerations   **108**

Working with manufacturers

From these models detailed drawings were produced and sent to thirteen potential manufacturers. Some were companies specialising in the production of tooling for blow- and injection-moulding, others had the capability to produce both tooling and the product. The companies were invited to quote for the manufacture of the boxes at various volumes of production to establish the economies of scale in the production process. The tooling represented a cost of about £10 000 and this had to be spread over the production run. However, a lower cost tool was also proposed as it would be unlikely that very large batches would need to be produced. This injection moulding 'die' would require an overhaul after 100 000 mouldings.

Assembly time was also a consideration. Injection-moulding would make it necessary to produce the box in two halves resulting in an extra gluing process and a joint line. Some companies required further details based on the specification and the production quantity. Some responded by suggesting further refinements or modifications. Others failed to respond to the request for quotations at all, so lost the business!

The students visited the two manufacturers who were showing the greatest interest in the project and in discussion developed production prototypes and a tooling schedule for the injection mould required. One manufacturer, Link Plastics, a local firm, was most helpful in their advice and produced by far the lowest quote for the box. Their tool design division offered a few further refinements. They incorporated the text, PDSA, into the injection of the box, and placed a snap-out section in the base to enable a chain to be added to secure the box if desired, or to remain in place unseen if not. These modifications were made in consultation with the students and the tooling was ordered. This was made in the production factory and remained the property of the commissioning client, the PDSA, to allow the production of further batches as and when required.

The first order was placed with Link Plastics for 6000 boxes, and provisional orders for a further 96 000 over the next three years were also put in place. The cost of the original box that the PDSA had been using was three times the price of the custom-designed box that resulted from this project. This has saved the charity hundreds of thousands of pounds over a three year period!

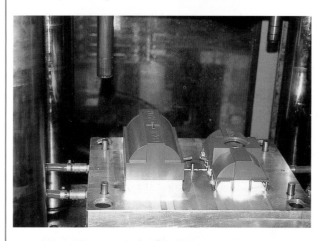

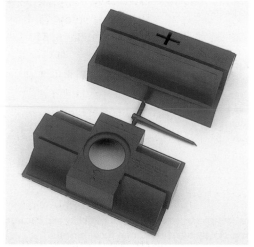

The tooling design was based on a low-cost process using an aluminium die, capable of producing about 100 000 mouldings before needing a major overhaul.

The Telford CTC/PDSA collection box project

Brief

Initial specification
| | | | | | | | | | | |
Numerous sketched initial ideas

Client presentation

6 selected
| | | | | |
Sketched developments
| | | | | |
3D models
| | | | | |
Manufacturer check
| | | | | |
Revisions to sketches and 3D models
| | | | | | |
New 3D models
| | | | | |
Client presentation

2 selected
| |
Developed and re-modelled
|
Final design

Design specification to manufacturers

Changes suggested

Manufacturing specification

Production prototype and tooling schedule

Production

The Telford PDSA product development process.

INDEX

Acknowledgements

The illustrations were drawn by: James Cross of Tom Cross Illustration; Bill Donohoe; Richard Dusczack; Hardlines Illustration and Design and Design and Tony Wilkins Illustration.

The cover illustration was prepared by fab 4 studio

The publishers would like to thank the following individuals, institutions and companies for permission to reproduce photographs in this book. Every effort has been made to trace ownership of copyright. The publishers will be happy to make arrangements with any copyright holder whom it has not been possible to contact.

Addis Tribune/Tamber international Publications 219; J. Allen Cash 94 (top), 172, 214; Andrew Yeardon/Haymarket Publishing 198 (top right); Austin Smith: Lord 105 (both); Ron Bagley 46; Ben and Jerry/Beer Davies 63; John Birdsall 129; Gareth Boden 167, 168 (all), 169; British Aerospace Ltd 147, 148, 154, 156 (right), 171, 179 (bottom); Britvic Soft Drinks 155 (bottom left); Casio Electronics 59 (middle); Chris Roe/ASDA 221 (all), 222 (all), 223 (all); Anne Constable/IFR 56 (all); Courtaulds Fibres 102 (bottom); Denfords Ltd 90 (both); Design Management Institute 209, 210 (all), 211; Design Museum 57 (bottom 3), 58 (both); Dixons Mastercare 71 (both); Dualit/Grant Butler Coomber 74 (top); Andrew Elley 28 (top); Ford Motors Ltd 149; Gerber Garment Technology 87 (both), 98; Johnny Grey/Richard Trevor 191 (bottom), Johnny Grey 191 (top left, top right); Heinz Co Ltd 165, 166; Hoggie 70; HomePac Ltd 194 (both); Jenny Holt 192 (all); Husqvarna 67, 158: IDEO 57 (top 2); Jonathan Ive, Apple Computer Inc. 12 (both); Jaguar 201, 202 (all), 203 (all), 204, 206 (all), 207 (all); Jim Lowe/P&S Photography 155 (top, bottom right); Joe Bloggs 104 (top); Kenwood Ltd 150 (left); Kinnier Dufort 212 (all), 213; Land Rover/Paul O'Conner 86 (right), 141; Link Picture Library/David Ramkalawon 94 (bottom); Littlewoods/Roger Quale 88 (bottom); Littlewoods 88 (top); Living and Learning 59 (bottom); London College of Fashion 9 (middle); MFI Ltd 62 (both); McLaren 198 (middle right), 199 (right); Malcolm Couzens 69 (both), 120 (bottom 2), 224, 225 (both), 226 (bottom); Marks and Spencer Ltd 84 (top); Philip Marshall 126, 127; Monsanto/Biopol 112; Nick Davies Photography 9 (right); Parametric Technology 76; PI Castings 180 (both); Psion Ltd 77; Quorn 122; RCA 64 bottom, 131 (both), 132 (all); Robert Harding 191 (bottom right); Rolls Royce Ltd 86 (left); Sarah Welch 11; School of Engineering and Built Environment, University of Wolverhampton 9 (left); Shapemasters Systems 179 (top); Shima Seiki 183 (all), 184 (top 2, bottom left); Simon Turner 197 (centre, right); Sinclair C5 owners Club 64 (top right); Street Symphony 215 (top right); Teknit 184 (bottom right); Thomas Telford 226 (top); Trevlyn Tanner Architects 27 (top); UK Ecolabelling Board 100; John Urling Clark 102, 120 (top); Morley von Sternberg 197 (top); John Walmsley 53 (both), 64 (top left), 111, 115 (both), 143, 144, 145, 150 (top right, bottom), 198 (left, bottom), 199 (left, top and bottom), 200 (all); Frank Walsh 215 (left 3), 217, 218; John Wender/British Steel/PPL 156 (left); Copyright © Yahoo! Inc. 38; Yoplait 68.

The publishers would also like to thank the following for permission to reproduce material in this book: Gavin Hadland for extracts from his article *Supercar goes on the server*; Rachelle Thackray for extracts from her article *It's only rack 'n' roll*. The publishers would be happy to make arrangements with any copyright holder whom it has not been possible to contact.